Wingfield College and its Patrons

Wingfield College and its Patrons

Piety and Patronage in Medieval Suffolk

Edited by

Peter Bloore and Edward Martin

THE BOYDELL PRESS

First published 2015
The Boydell Press, Woodbridge

ISBN 978 1 84383 832 6

The Boydell Press is an imprint of Boydell & Brewer Ltd
PO Box 9, Woodbridge, Suffolk IP12 3DF, UK
and of Boydell & Brewer Inc.
668 Mt Hope Avenue, Rochester, NY 14620–2731, USA
website: www.boydellandbrewer.com

A catalogue record for this book is available
from the British Library

The publisher has no responsibility for the continued existence or accuracy
of URLs for external or third-party internet websites referred to in
this book, and does not guarantee that any content on such websites is,
or will remain, accurate or appropriate.

This publication is printed on acid-free paper
Printed and bound in Great Britain by
TJ International Ltd, Padstow, Cornwall

Contents

Illustrations

Contributors

Dr Rowena E. Archer, lecturer in medieval history at Christ Church and fellow of Brasenose College, Oxford

Sally Badham, MBE, vice-president of the Church Monuments Society

Professor Mark Bailey, professor of late medieval history at the University of East Anglia and high master at St Paul's School, London

Dr Peter Bloore, senior lecturer in creativity at the University of East Anglia

Professor Eamon Duffy, emeritus professor of the history of Christianity and fellow of Magdalene College, Cambridge

Dr John Goodall, architectural editor of *Country Life* magazine

Professor Robert Liddiard, professor of history at the University of East Anglia

Professor Diarmaid MacCulloch, Kt., professor of the history of the Church at Oxford University and president of the Suffolk Institute of Archaeology and History

Edward Martin, retired archaeological officer with Suffolk County Council and a vice-president of the Suffolk Institute of Archaeology and History

Abbreviations

BL	British Library, London
Bod	Bodleian Library, Oxford
CAD, vol. IV	*Descriptive Catalogue of Ancient Deeds*, vol. IV (London 1902)
CAD, vol. V	*Descriptive Catalogue of Ancient Deeds*, vol. V (London 1906)
Canterbury	Canterbury Cathedral Archives
CChR 1226–57	*Calendar of the Charter Rolls*, vol. I, Henry III, 1226–1257 (London 1908)
CChR 1300–26	*Calendar of the Charter Rolls*, vol. III, Edward I and II, 1300–1326 (London 1908)
CChR 1327–41	*Calendar of the Charter Rolls*, vol. IV, Edward III, 1327–1341 (London 1912)
CCR 1288–96	*Calendar of the Close Rolls, Edward I*, vol. III, 1288–1296 (London 1904)
CCR 1307–13	*Calendar of the Close Rolls, Edward II*, vol. I, 1307–1313 (London 1892)
CCR 1354–60	*Calendar of the Close Rolls, Edward III*, vol. X, 1354–60 (London 1908)
CCR 1413–19	*Calendar of the Close Rolls, Henry V*, vol. I, 1413–1419 (London 1929)
CCR, 1447–54	*Calendar of the Close Rolls, Henry VI*, vol. V, 1447–1454 (London 1937)
CCR 1476–8	*Calendar of the Close Rolls, Edward IV, Edward V, Richard III, 1476–85* (London 1954)
CFR 1272–1307	*Calendar of the Fine Rolls, Edward I*, vol. I, 1272–1307 (London 1911)
CFR 1445–52	*Calendar of the Fine Rolls*, vol. XVIII, Henry VI, 1445–52 (London 1939)
CIM 1348–77	*Calendar of the Inquisitions Miscellaneous, 1348–77*
CIPM, vol. I	*Calendar of Inquisitions Post Mortem*, vol. I, Henry III (London 1904)
CIPM, vol. XXII	*Calendar of Inquisitions Post Mortem*, vol. XXII, Henry VI (Woodbridge 2003)
CIPM, vol. XXV	*Calendar of the Inquisitions Post Mortem*, vol. XXV, 1437–42 (Woodbridge 2009)
CIPME	*Calendarium Inquisitionum Post Mortem sive Escaetarum*, vol. II (London 1808)

CoA	College of Arms, London
CPapR 1447–55	*Calendar of the Papal Registers, vol. X, 1447–55* (London 1915)
CPR 1272–81	*Calendar of the Patent Rolls, Edward I, vol. I, 1272–1281* (London 1901)
CPR 1301–7	*Calendar of the Patent Rolls, Edward I, vol. IV, 1301–7* (London 1898)
CPR 1307–13	*Calendar of the Patent Rolls, Edward II, vol. I, 1307–1313* (London 1894)
CPR 1313–17	*Calendar of the Patent Rolls, Edward II, vol. II, 1313–1317* (London 1898)
CPR 1317–21	*Calendar of the Patent Rolls, Edward I, vol. III, 1317–1321* (London 1903)
CPR 1324–7	*Calendar of the Patent Rolls, Edward II, vol. V, 1324–1327* (London 1904)
CPR 1343–5	*Calendar of the Patent Rolls, Edward III, vol. VI, 1343–1345* (London 1902)
CPR 1345–8	*Calendar of the Patent Rolls, Edward III, vol. VII, 1345–48* (London 1903)
CPR 1350–4	*Calendar of the Patent Rolls, Edward III, vol. IX, 1350–54* (London 1907)
CPR 1354–8	*Calendar of the Patent Rolls, Edward III, vol. X, 1354–58* (London 1909)
CPR 1358–61	*Calendar of the Patent Rolls, Edward III, vol. XI, 1358–61* (London 1911)
CPR 1361–4	*Calendar of the Patent Rolls, Edward III, vol. XII, 1361–1364* (London 1912
CPR 1374–7	*Calendar of the Patent Rolls, Edward III, vol. XVI, 1374–1377* (London 1916)
CPR 1377–81	*Calendar of the Patent Rolls, Richard II, vol. I, 1377–1381* (London 1907)
CPR 1381–5	*Calendar of the Patent Rolls, Richard II, vol. II, 1381–1385* (London 1897)
CPR 1385–9	*Calendar of the Patent Rolls, Richard II, vol. III, 1385–1389* (London 1900)
CPR 1405–8	*Calendar of the Patent Rolls, Henry IV, vol. III, 1405–1408* (London 1895)
CPR 1429–36	*Calendar of the Patent Rolls, Henry VI, vol. II, 1429–1436* (London 1907)
CPR 1436–41	*Calendar of the Patent Rolls, Henry VI, vol. III, 1436–1441* (London 1907)
CPR 1441–6	*Calendar of the Patent Rolls, Henry VI, vol. IV, 1441–1446* (London 1908)

CPR 1446–52	*Calendar of the Patent Rolls, Henry VI, vol. V, 1446–1452* (London 1909)
CPR 1467–77	*Calendar of the Patent Rolls, Edward IV & Henry VI, 1467–1477* (London 1900)
Davy MS	David Elisha Davy (1769–1851), papers and collections relating to the history of Suffolk, BL Add. MS. 19092.
FA, vol. III	*Inquisitions and Assessments Relating to Feudal Aids*, vol. III (London 1904)
FA, vol. V	*Inquisitions and Assessments relating to Feudal Aids*, vol. V (London 1908)
LP	Lambeth Palace, London
Northants RO	Northamptonshire County Record Office
NRO	Norfolk Record Office, Norwich
PR	*Pipe Roll for 31 Henry II*, Pipe Roll Society vol. XXXIV (London 1913)
PROME	Given-Wilson, C., et al. (eds), 2005. *Parliamentary Rolls of Medieval England*, London
RBP pt I	*The Register of the Black Prince, part I, 1346–48* (London 1930)
RBP pt II	*The Register of the Black Prince, part II, Duchy of Cornwall 1351–1365* (London 1931)
RBP pt III	*The Register of the Black Prince, part III, Palatinate of Chester 1351–1365* (London 1932)
RBP pt IV	*The Register of the Black Prince, part IV, England 1351–1365* (London 1933)
RHundred	*Rotuli Hundredorum*, vol. II, London 1818
SROI	Suffolk Record Office, Ipswich
SROL	Suffolk Record Office, Lowestoft
TNA	The National Archives, Kew
VCH Chester	*Victoria County History of Chester*, vol. II, ed. B.E. Harris (Oxford 1979)
VCH Hants	*Victoria County History of Hampshire*, vol. IV, ed. W. Page (London 1911)
VCH Suffolk	*Victoria County History of Suffolk*, vol. II, ed. W. Page (London 1911)
VCH Yorks ER I	*Victoria County History of Yorkshire, East Riding*, vol. I, ed. K.J. Allison (Oxford 1969)
VCH Yorks ER I	*Victoria County History of Yorkshire, East Riding*, vol. II, ed. K.J. Allison (Oxford 1974)

Manuscript Sources

Bod: Gough Maps 223c.
Bod: Gough Maps 227.
Bod: Mss DD Ewelme
Bod: MS Suffolk 7, fol. 48.
Bod: Ewelme MS A40.
BL: Add. MS 19092. David Elisha Davy (1769–1851), papers and collections
relating to the history of Suffolk
BL: Egerton Roll, 8779
BL: Harleian Mss
BL: Additional Mss
BL: MS Add. 19092.
CoA: MS L8.
Canterbury: CCA-DCc-Register/F 118–119
LP: Register Stafford
LP: Register Chichele
Northants RO: Fitzwilliam (Milton), MS 2046
SROI: CG17–775
SROI: HD2418–51
TNA: PROB 11/2b, 245r–245v
TNA: PROB 11/2B/203

Introduction

PETER BLOORE AND EDWARD MARTIN

Wingfield may now be a quiet and rather small rural village in north Suffolk, but in medieval times it was the seat of the de la Pole family, who used it as a springboard for their meteoric rise from lowly Hull merchants to the upper levels of the aristocracy – first as earls and later as dukes of Suffolk – and even to the brink of taking the English Crown from the Tudors. The foundations at Wingfield were put in place by Sir John de Wingfield, the father-in-law of Michael de la Pole, the 1st earl of Suffolk. As well as being a veteran of the battles of Crécy and Poitiers, Sir John was also a very able administrator who rose to become the 'business manager' of Edward the Black Prince. Sir John died around 1361 whilst in the process of setting up a chantry college at Wingfield, a plan that was brought to fruition by his executors in June 1362. A substantial rebuilding of the parish church followed the establishment of the college, and this was soon after followed by the conversion of his moated manor house into a castle by his soon to be ennobled son-in-law. Together, these buildings presented a coherent and growing statement of the family's status and prestige.

The 650th anniversary of the foundation of Wingfield College was the occasion for a special two-day history symposium on the weekend of 9 and 10 June 2012 in the atmospheric setting of Wingfield Barns, the Tudor barn complex in the grounds of the former college. The symposium was organised by the editors, in association with the Suffolk Institute of Archaeology and History and the Centre of East Anglian Studies at the University of East Anglia (UEA). The programme for the symposium is shown below. This event was also the culmination of a three-year UEA-funded research project into the college and castle, including new building surveys, geophysics, and expert architectural advice. A highlight of the symposium was the first full public screening of the two digital reconstructions of the medieval appearance of Wingfield Castle and Wingfield College, created by the Virtual Past team at UEA.

1362: A history symposium to mark the 650th anniversary of the foundation of Wingfield College and Church

The programme

Day One: *Purgatory and the Dukes of Suffolk: The History of Wingfield and the de la Poles.*

- Professor Mark Bailey, professor of late medieval history at UEA: 'The Black Death in England c.1348–c.1381, and the Death (and Life) of Sir John Wingfield'.
- Professor Eamon Duffy, fellow of Magdalene College Cambridge: 'Wingfield College and Purgatory'.
- Screenings of two digital reconstructions of the medieval appearance of Wingfield College and Castle, created by the Virtual Past team at UEA.
- Dr Rowena E. Archer, fellow of Brasenose College, Oxford: 'Ruling East Anglia in the Fifteenth Century: The role of Alice Chaucer, Duchess of Suffolk'.
- Professor Diarmaid MacCulloch, professor of the history of the Church at Oxford University and president of the Suffolk Institute of Archaeology and History: 'The Wars of the Roses and the Downfall of the de la Poles'.
- Evening commemoration concert in Wingfield Church: 'Sacred Music from the Wingfield Tudor Organ and the Amici Choir'. The Wingfield Organ is a twentieth-century reconstruction of a Tudor organ, based on the genuine Tudor organ soundboard that was found at Wingfield.

Day Two: *Wingfield: Landscape and Architecture (Church, College, and Castle).*

- Latin requiem mass for Sir John Wingfield and the de la Poles celebrated in Wingfield Church by Father David Standley and Professor Duffy.
- Edward Martin, archaeological officer with Suffolk County Council and chairman of the Suffolk Institute of Archaeology and History: 'From Hall-and-Church Complex to Castle Green – A Landscape History of Wingfield'.
- Dr Robert Liddiard, senior lecturer in history at UEA, and Peter Bloore, senior lecturer in creativity at UEA: 'The Digital Reconstructions of the Medieval Appearance of the College, Castle and Deer Park, and the Research and Creative Processes that Went into Them'.
- Sally Badham, president of the Church Monuments Society: 'Medieval Monuments to the de la Pole and Wingfield Families'.
- Dr John Goodall, architectural editor of *Country Life*: 'Castle, College and Church: The Architectural Context of Wingfield'.
- Andrew McCrea, director of academic development at the Royal College of Organists: 'Tudor Organs and the Way they Were Used'.
- Evensong in the church, accompanied by the Wingfield Organ.

Prestige, piety and patronage in the fourteenth and fifteenth centuries

The building projects of the late medieval aristocracy largely focused on their homes (both their rural castles and their urban palaces) and the particular religious or charitable institutions over which they exercised patronage, particularly the monasteries, churches or chantry foundations where they and their family were buried and, importantly, commemorated. The scale, structure and decoration of chantry colleges indicates that the wish to display status and power was as powerful as the wish to save souls in purgatory through the extravagant yet diligent worship of God and charitable activities. The commemoration of the dead allowed a celebration of their achievements, status and lineage, and the scale and prestige of this commemoration reflected on the fortunes of the family as a whole. In recent years the academic study of chantry colleges has been boosted by the addition of Clive Burgess and Martin Heale's fine anthology of essays *The Late Medieval English College and its Context* and Burgess's and Nigel Saul's papers on St George's College, Windsor. We hope that this book will be a worthwhile addition to those studies.[1]

Like their colleges, the aristocracy's castles were also multi-faceted social constructs, designed to be symbolically read in a variety of ways. From the beginning they were more than just defensive military structures.[2] They were intrinsic statements of status, closely bound up with martial reputation, local administration and justice, and the reflection of ideals of chivalry and courtly love. There are also similarities between the symbolic roles of the castle and the chantry college, since both reflected power and wealth through the employment of the latest fashions in architecture and the arts to demonstrate aristocratic status, displays which carried with them an implicit domination of the surrounding landscape and population.

This book explores these themes through the fortunes and patronage of one family in one place – the knightly Wingfields and their de la Pole descendants. The latter were probably the most successful aristocratic upstarts of the late mediaeval period. Within just two generations the head of the family went from being a merchant in Hull to being earl of Suffolk and chancellor of England. Within another three generations the de la Poles were making viable bids for the throne of England. No other family of that period rose so fast and became so powerful, even arranging the marriages of kings and queens. To legitimise themselves they fought for the English king in France and tried to marry into the aristocratic elite, with weddings and bloodlines linking them to the Staffords, the Mowbrays, the Beauforts, the FitzAlans of Arundel, the Scropes and even the Plantagenets. This last royal marriage was perhaps a marriage too far and was to prove their undoing, as we shall see.

But this was also a story of old money versus new money. Their 'true blue-blood'

---

[1] Burgess and Heale 2008; Burgess 2005; Saul 2005.
[2] Pounds 1990; Creighton 2002; Liddiard 2005.

aristocratic competitors never let the de la Poles forget their humble origins as wool and wine merchants of Hull, with jokes about fish being made in parliament to embarrass Sir Michael de la Pole when he was lord chancellor (his grandmother's second husband had the unfortunate surname of Rotenheryng). The de la Poles could never really become 'one of them'. So these mercantile upstarts had to invest their hard-earned cash in building projects at their castle and college to reflect their new aristocratic status and silence their local and national critics. They were not just vanity projects but serious bids for power and reputation in a society that placed a lot of emphasis on public display, bloodlines and personal loyalty and piety. The political consolidation and authentication of the de la Poles is a major theme in the interpretation of the landscape and architecture of Wingfield.

The history of the landscape that underlies the siting of the castle and college is introduced through Edward Martin's chapter 'From Hall-and-Church Complex to Castle Green and College – A Landscape History of Wingfield'. It is followed by Professor Mark Bailey's examination of the life of the founder of the college in his chapter entitled 'Sir John de Wingfield and the Foundation of Wingfield College'. The details of the foundation are covered in a chapter on the foundation document, and its dissolution is analysed by Professor Diarmaid MacCulloch. The context of chantry colleges more widely is discussed in Professor Eamon Duffy's chapter 'Wingfield College and the Late Medieval Cult of Purgatory'.

When the University of East Anglia began its research project in 2009, Wingfield was academically under-researched and not well known to the general public. Wingfield Castle had never been excavated or even subjected to a detailed architectural survey. An important part of the project involved negotiating access for academic research, geophysical surveys and archaeological analysis. This is potentially of regional and national academic importance, and the digital reconstructions on the DVD enclosed with this book represent a form of public and academic access. Professor Robert Liddiard's chapter 'Reconstructing Wingfield Castle' provides the context and background for this important work, and helps to explain the recent research findings, including the landscape context of the deer park and artificial water features.

Wingfield College is a fine survival of a fourteenth-century timber-framed accommodation unit for the college priests, with a substantially intact great hall and the remains of a medieval cloister. It is now a private house, but originally it accommodated ten priests, a school with boarding pupils and probably servants and estate workers. The college was founded by the will of Sir John de Wingfield in 1362, whose heiress daughter married into the de la Pole family and took with her the fortunes and manorial properties of the Wingfield family. Wingfield is a good case study of a relatively typical small medieval chantry college of that period, and its study is a useful addition to the literature of chantry colleges that typically focuses on the larger and much wealthier foundations, such as Windsor, Westminster, Eton, Warwick and Winchester.

This takes us on to the physical structure of the college. There was an archaeological and architectural survey of the college in 1997, funded by Suffolk County Council and English Heritage, which included some dendro-dating and geophysical surveys. The 2009 UEA research project added further geophysical surveys and architectural surveys, resulting in enough data to be able to extrapolate a digital reconstruction of what may have formerly been on the site. This work is described in Dr Peter Bloore's chapter 'Historical Digital Reconstruction: The Role of Creativity and Known Unknowns – A Case Study of Wingfield College'. This describes the new research findings about the college and its structure, and discusses wider issues around the role of academic judgement and creativity in digital reconstruction.

Alongside the college is the parish church (previously the collegiate church) which contains fine monuments of some of the de la Pole earls and dukes of Suffolk, and is of major importance as a representation of medieval piety. The 2009 research project undertook the first detailed assessment of these monuments and their place in the context of other monuments of the period. The result can be seen in Sally Badham's chapter 'Medieval Monuments to the de la Pole and Wingfield Families'. Another area of controversy over the years has been the original role of the current vestry of the church, which may previously have been a chantry chapel, a sacristan's watching chamber or a private parclose chapel for the de la Poles. These options are discussed in both Dr John Goodall's chapter, entitled 'Chancel or Closet? The Question of the Vestry at Wingfield Church', and in Dr Bloore's chapter on the college.

One of the results of the downfall of the de la Poles in Tudor times is that they became the 'also-rans' of history. If the battle of Stoke in 1487 had turned out differently there would have been a de la Pole sitting on the throne of England, and the house of Tudor would have been a brief and minor intermission. No Henry VIII and no Virgin Queen. Instead, the de la Pole's candidate for king, the earl of Lincoln, was defeated and allegedly buried at the battlefield with a greenwood stake through his heart. Henry VII's position on the throne of England was made secure, and the de la Poles became one of history's failures. As Winston Churchill is supposed to have said 'history is written by the victors', and the de la Pole earls and dukes of Suffolk have tended to appear scattered as brief references and footnotes through histories of the fourteenth and fifteenth centuries: mere bit players in the endless wars against France and the tumultuous dynastic wrangling of the Wars of the Roses and the early Tudors. However, scholarship over the last ten years has cast more light on their vacillating fortunes, and is placing them far more centre stage, as one of the most influential families of the late fourteenth and fifteenth centuries.

In terms of modern scholarship, the first earl, Michael de la Pole (chancellor of England 1383–6), remains under-researched, but his influential grandson William de la Pole has emerged from historical footnotes into the light through Susan Curran's accessible and evocative account of his life; and through Juliet Barker's account of the last forty years of the Hundred Years War, which reflects on William's leadership of the English army in 1428–9, before his capture at Jargeau; and his crucial involvement in the peace treaties of 1443–4.[3] John Goodall's doctorate and subsequent book on Ewelme has identified William and his wife Alice's patronage and building work, drawing clear comparisons between Wingfield and the school and palace at Ewelme.[4] The life in East Angiia of Alice de la Pole (born Alice Chaucer, granddaughter of the poet Geoffrey) is explored in Dr Rowena Archer's chapter 'Alice Chaucer, Duchess of Suffolk (d.1475), and her East Anglian Estates'.

In academic circles there has recently been an important rediscovery of the claims to the throne of the later de la Poles, earls of Lincoln: John and Edmund, through the bloodline of their Plantagenet mother, and their serious threat to the stability of the Tudor monarchy.[5] Professor Diarmaid MacCulloch's chapter, 'The Wars of the Roses, the Downfall of the de la Poles and the Dissolution of Wingfield College', provides an overview of the context of these claims to the throne, and the politics behind Charles Brandon's arrival as the new duke of Suffolk and the eventual dissolution of the college.

The last book on Wingfield was the Revd Aldwell's *Wingfield: Its Church, Castle and College* (1925). Samuel William Hemphill Aldwell (1866–1938) was vicar of Wingfield from 1910 to 1935 and was also an enthusiastic and thorough local historian. He was the first to propose that some of the medieval structure of the college survived within the apparently Georgian and Victorian building, especially the crownpost in one of the upstairs bedrooms; a hunch that was to be proved correct when the then owner, Ian Chance, restored the college in the 1970s and rediscovered most of the medieval hall and west wing surviving behind the later plaster. We hope that this new book is a worthy and timely successor to Aldwell's book, adding the latest research and thinking into castles, medieval landscapes, church monuments, chantry colleges and the role of creativity in historical reconstruction. The new technology contained in the DVD in the back of the book includes geophysics surveys of the landscape and digital reconstruction films that may have been beyond the imagination of Aldwell, but he would surely have been fascinated and excited by the possibilities that these techniques have opened up our understanding of the past and our relationship to it.

Taken as a whole, we hope that this book successfully draws together and expands on the presentations given at the 1362 symposium; and during the writing process it has given the individual academics a chance to clarify their thinking and continue their research. Wingfield is a special place with a unique history, and this latest research helps us to understand and appreciate it all the more, as well as expanding our wider understanding of the patronage and displayed piety of the late medieval aristocracy. And if the book captures and shares some of the spirit of insight and exploration that was generated on those two days in June 2012, then it will have succeeded in its aim.

---

3 Curran 2011; Barker 2010.
4 Goodall 2001.
5 Wroe 2003; Arthurson 2009; Penn 2011; Gristwood 2013.

THE FOUNDING OF THE COLLEGE

1

From Hall-and-Church Complex to Castle Green and College – A Landscape History of Wingfield

Edward Martin

Landscape character, like human character, may not be fully apparent on first introduction – it often reveals itself slowly as our acquaintance deepens and as we meet their friends and relatives. So to understand a particular landscape we usually need to place it in its wider context, acknowledging that many of its aspects will be governed by what happens generally in its region. Wingfield shares, in ever greater concentration, aspects of the landscape history of lowland Britain, eastern England, Suffolk and then, and most particularly, the clayland plateau of High Suffolk.

In the 1930s Sir Cyril Fox introduced us to the concept of a 'Lowland Zone' where the physiographical conditions of low hills and plateaux, subject to the 'controlling factor' of 'soil character', made it suitable for early and dense settlement, in contrast to the rocky and higher hills of the 'Highland Zone'; to him a diagonal line drawn from Teesmouth (Durham) to Torquay (Devon) roughly indicated the boundary between the two areas (see Figure 1.1).[1] In the 1980s, Oliver Rackham saw a 'remarkable contrast' in this Lowland Zone between the landscapes with hamlets, medieval farms and thick hedges, and those with big villages, brick farmsteads and thin hawthorn hedges – the first he saw as being the 'product of at least a thousand years of continuity' and was labelled 'Ancient Countryside'; the second was seen as a 'drawing-board landscape' arising from the enclosure acts of the eighteenth and nineteenth centuries and was labelled 'Planned Countryside'.[2] His zone of Planned Countryside runs through the centre of England, with areas of Ancient Countryside both to the east and west, and in its mapped bounds there is quite a resemblance, unsurprisingly, to the maps produced by Gilbert Slater (1907) and Edward Gonner (1912; see Figure 1.2) showing the areas with common fields that were enclosed by acts of parliament.[3] But the perception that there were two contrasting agrarian

---

[1] Fox 1932, pp. 77–8.
[2] Rackham 1986, pp. 4–5 and Figure 1.3.
[3] Slater 1907, map facing p. 73; Gonner 1912, Map A.

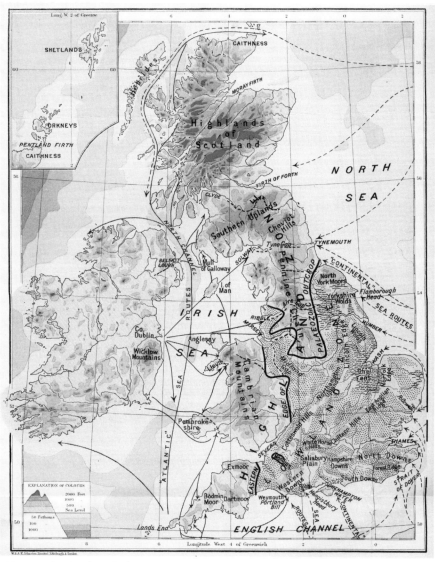

Fig. 1.1. Sir Cyril Fox's division of Britain into a Lowland Zone and a Highland Zone, as published in his book, *The Personality of Britain* (1932).

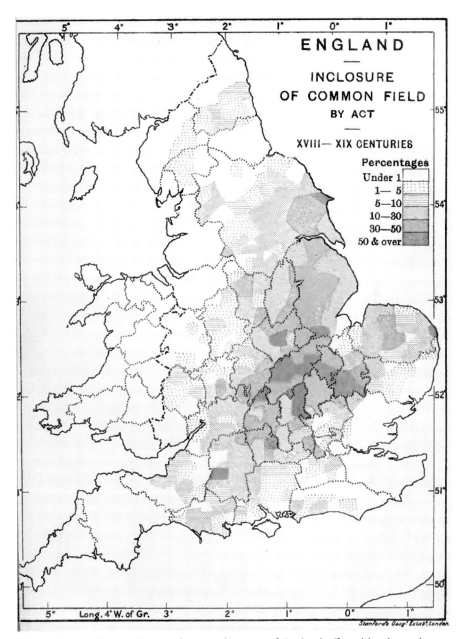

Fig. 1.2. Edward Gonner's map showing the areas of England affected by the enclosure of common fields by parliamentary acts, and the percentages of land involved, from his book *Common Land and Inclosure* (1912).

landscapes in England was much older. In 1587 William Harrison (1535–93), the rector of Radwinter in north-west Essex, noted that:

> It is so that, our soil being divided into champaign ground[4] and woodland, the houses of the first lie uniformly builded in every town together, with streets and lanes, whereas in the woodland countries (except here and there in great market towns) they stand scattered abroad, each one dwelling in the midst of his own occupying.[5]

He not only recognised two different farming systems, one of common fields and the other of enclosed lands, but had also linked them with settlement patterns, one linked to nucleated villages and the other to dispersed farmsteads. Similarly, the great Victorian historian, F.W. Maitland, contrasted the nucleated village with its 'spacious common fields' with the 'vill of scattered steads' or clusters of houses where 'we see no traces of very large fields'.[6] His last comment is particularly significant because only a few years before another influential historian, Paul Vinogradoff, had confidently stated that 'the chief features of the field system which was in operation in England during the middle ages have been sufficiently cleared up by modern scholars … everybody knows that the arable of an English village was commonly cultivated under a three years' rotation of crops; a two-field system is also found very often; there are some instances of more complex arrangements, but they are very rare and appear late'.[7] H.L. Gray was, however, a mite more open-minded, and his detailed researches, published in 1915, even led him to question, perhaps rather despairingly, whether 'common arable fields ever existed' in parts (at least) of counties like Kent and Essex (see Figure 1.3).[8] To many modern agrarian historians, however, it is still an article of faith that all medieval agriculture in lowland England involved common fields!

In the late twentieth century, interest in the evolution of the English landscape changed from being a purely academic pursuit to a more urgent need to understand it for the purpose of developing more effective conservation strategies in the face of extensive landscape changes due to ever more mechanised forms of farming. The issue was raised in the government's White Paper entitled 'This Common Inheritance' in 1990.[9] In response, English Heritage commissioned two strands of research, one a national, 'top-down' Terrain and Rural Settlement Mapping Project and the other a series of mainly county-based and 'bottom-up' Historic Landscape Characterisation (HLC) projects. The first centred on the mapping of nineteenth-century settlement patterns, as recorded in early Ordnance Survey mapping, and this demon-

---

4 The term *champaign* or *champion*, from Old French *champagne* 'open country', was used by many early writers to describe open common fields.
5 Harrison 1587, p. 217.
6 Maitland 1897, p. 15.
7 Vinogradoff 1892, pp. 224–5.
8 Gray 1917, pp. 272, 388.
9 Department of the Environment 1990.

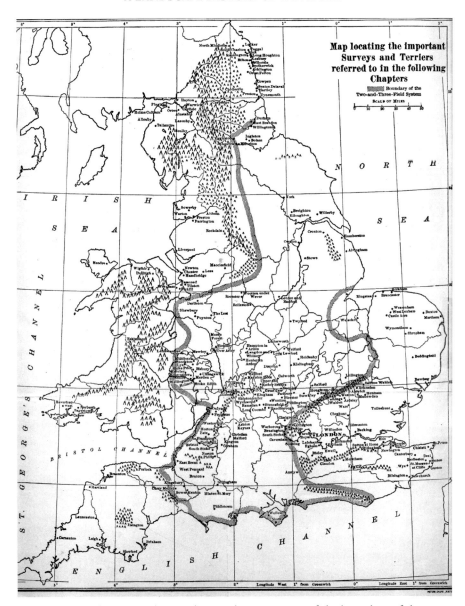

Fig. 1.3. Howard Levi Gray's map showing his estimation of the boundary of the area with classic Midlands-type two- and three-field common fields, from his book *English Field Systems* (1915).

strated that England could be divided into three broad 'provinces' of distinctive settlement and landscape – a Central Province where nucleated settlements (villages and market towns) predominated, and a Northern and Western Province and a South-Eastern Province (including East Anglia) where dispersed settlement was the norm.[10] Broadly, this mirrored Rackham's three zones, but using settlement patterns rather than field systems as the defining factors. In most of East Anglia (particularly in Essex, Suffolk and southern Norfolk) there were about 55 nucleations per 25 × 25 square kilometres, which contrasts with figures of 70–80 in the Central Province, where the nucleated settlements were not only more numerous but larger. It is only in north-western Essex, the western fringes of Suffolk, western Norfolk, together with smaller areas in the Broads of north-east Norfolk, the Sandlings of south-east Suffolk and the Tendring peninsula of north-east Essex, that the settlement pattern is significantly more nucleated.[11] These are also the areas of East Anglia where the evidence for the former existence of common fields is strongest.[12] The occurrence of common fields and nucleated settlements is clearly linked.

The Suffolk HLC project used computerised mapping to build up a detailed county-wide map by interpreting individual components of the landscape – the current version has 11,993 separate polygons of interpretation.[13] The methodology was easily able to distinguish between 'pre-eighteenth-century enclosure' and 'eighteenth-century and later enclosure' – the distribution of the latter being comparable to known areas of parliamentary or other forms of late enclosure.[14] 'Eighteenth-century and later enclosure' also showed a strong correlation with the areas of lighter, sandy soils in the north-west (Breckland) and the south-east (the Sandlings) of the county; 'pre-eighteenth-century enclosure' being the dominant characteristic of the central clayland zone (see Figure 1.4).

The HLC mapping, however, distinguished two types of 'ancient countryside': a northern area with field systems that had layouts that were co-axial (i.e. with one prevailing axis of orientation) to a greater or lesser degree, and a southern area with field systems that were mainly 'random' in their arrangement, having no dominant axes. The boundary between the two approximated to the line of the Gipping valley through the centre of Suffolk, leading it to be termed 'the Gipping Divide' (see Plate II).[15] This 'divide' is partially explicable on topographic grounds – the northern area is predominantly a flat area with inherent drainage problems, the southern area is one of gentle slopes that help with drainage.[16] The result is a southern area with

---

[10] Roberts and Wrathmell 2002, 5, figure 1.1
[11] Roberts and Wrathmell 2000, 8, pp. 41–2.
[12] Martin and Satchell 2008, p. 210.
[13] See www.suffolk.gov.uk/libraries-and-culture/culture-and-heritage/archaeology/historic-environment-record/
[14] Dymond and Martin 1999, p. 105.
[15] Martin and Satchell 2008, pp. 202–7.
[16] Hoppitt 1989; Martin 2008, pp. 351–2.

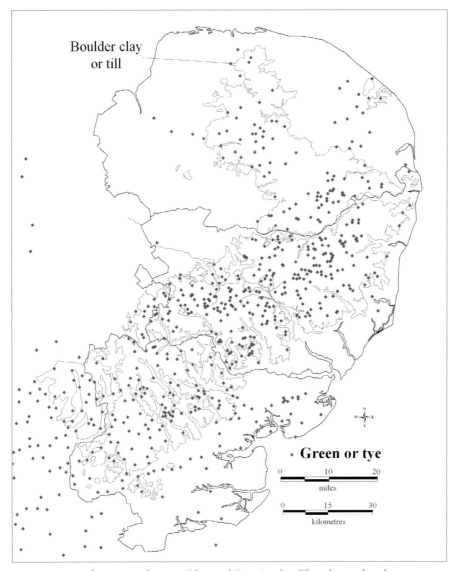

Fig. 1.4. Map of greens and tyes in 'Greater' East Anglia. This shows the place-name evidence for existing or former greens and tyes and their strong relationship with the areas with clay soils.

a much higher potential for arable farming (reflected by a reasonable amount of Grade 2 agricultural land by today's standards) and a northern area that was used mainly for animal pasture until the introduction of effective under-field drainage in the nineteenth century (and still has only limited amounts of Grade 2 agricultural land).[17] But this 'divide' was also found to re-occur in datasets that related to human culture rather than to the physical word – for instance, in place-names (e.g. the term 'tye' for a green is only found in the southern area); in medieval dialect (a differential pronunciation of 'f' and 'v'); in vernacular carpentry traditions (notably the frequency of queenpost roofs in the northern area and their scarcity in the south); and probably in inheritance customs.[18]

Wingfield lies on the north side of the 'Gipping Divide', towards the northern edge of the clay plateau in north Suffolk – the expectation therefore is a predominantly flat landscape with little natural drainage, a 'fieldscape' of pre-eighteenth-century enclosure with a tendency towards a co-axial layout, and a dispersed settlement pattern (see Plate III). And this is exactly what is there. The soil is mainly classi-fied as belonging to the Beccles 1 and 3 associations – seasonally waterlogged clay soils – with only a small amount of better-drained Hanslope soil on the sides of a small eastward and then northward-draining tributary of the River Waveney (see Plate IV).[19] *White's Directory* for 1844 describes Wingfield as 'a widely scattered village' and the earliest map of the parish, the tithe map of 1841, shows an enclosed landscape with few signs of ever having had extensive common fields.[20] There are two adjacent fields, both named Partible Piece, to the east of Earsham Street that were all in the same ownership in 1841,[21] but whose names suggest that they were once in divided ownership and may have formed part of an area of common fields, a suggestion that finds reinforcement by this being an area with an irregular co-axial field pattern on the edge of the area with Hanslope association soil. In many north Suffolk parishes there is evidence for small areas of common fields on the locally best soil for arable farming – in effect a sharing of a limited resource. These disap-peared very early, usually by 1700, but often earlier.[22] The largest share of the best soil was usually reserved for the demesne of the manorial lord. At Wingfield there is, however, an apparent oddity because its medieval castle, ostensibly a marker for the location of the main manorial demesne, is sited away from the Hanslope soils on the less good Beccles 3 soil.

The castle is in fact located next to Wingfield Green and at nearly 40 acres this large green is one of many similar greens that are a key characteristic of the land-

[17] East of England Regional Assembly 2004, Map 9.3 (Defra 2003 data).
[18] Martin and Satchell 2008; Martin 2012, p. 236.
[19] Soil Survey of England and Wales 1983.
[20] *White's Directory of Suffolk*, Sheffield 1844, p. 475; SROI FDA 292/A1/1a and b.
[21] SROI FDA 292/A1/1a and b: fields 63 and 64, 4a 3r 38p and 5a or 22p respectively, both owned by Alice Cotton and both arable.
[22] Martin and Satchell 2008.

scape of the north Suffolk clayland (see Plate V). These large communal pastures are usually sited on flat or even concave plateaux that have drainage problems, a topographical location that they share with woodland. Just to the north of Wingfield Green and on the same plateau there was another large green – Syleham Great Green – and close to the eastern side of these two greens there was a sizeable wooded area called Wingfield Park, from which four hundred oaks and fourteen elms were sold in 1597.[23] There is evidence to suggest that the greens are the product of medieval woodland clearance, as is perhaps illustrated by a tale associated with the parish of Fressingfield, Wingfield's eastern neighbour. Preserved in the List of Benefactors of Bury Abbey is a story about Ulf son of Manning, who lived just before the Norman Conquest. He revoked his father's gift of land to the abbey and was promptly bitten by a snake; in fear of his life, he offered the monks a choice of his estates in either Syleham or Chippenhall in Fressingfield. The monks chose Chippenhall because 'it abounded in woods'.[24] In 1066 there was wood for 160 pigs at Chippenhall, which had been reduced to one hundred by 1086; by the eighteenth century there was virtually no woodland at Chippenhall, but there was, and still is, a fine large green, with the partial ghost of another green close by. The ghost was called 'Hussey Green' in the eighteenth century and 'Hushaye' in the mid thirteenth century, and the suffix of the name is a term used for woodland in East Anglia.[25]

Domesday Book records woodland for four hundred pigs in Stradbroke and Wingfield, which could equate to some 750 acres of woodland.[26] However, there are early thirteenth-century references to assarts (woodland clearances) in places called Northagh, Hunteswyk, Bircholt and Bradeleye in Stradbroke, and in 1240 some of the tenants of the manor of Stradbroke were in dispute with their lord, William le Rus, over their obligation to pay pannage – a payment for the right to feed pigs in woodland – for, as they declared, 'the wood is entirely devastated so that the land is arable and no pig food is able to exist there'.[27] By the eighteenth century, woods were rare but there was a string of greens on Wingfield's border with Stradbroke – Battlesea Green, Rattlerow Green and Pixey Green. Archaeological evidence from elsewhere in north Suffolk suggests that these greens, together with Wingfield Green itself and another small green in Wingfield called Bleach Green, were starting to take shape around the twelfth century when farmsteads began to appear on their margins. These greenside settlements are, however, clearly later and secondary to the Domesday-period settlements in those parishes. By both its location and its associa-

---

[23] Staffordshire Record Office D641/3/A/3/1/1.

[24] Hervey 1925, vol. II, p. 291.

[25] For *Hushaye* see Brown 1992, no. 304, pp. 222–3; for -*haye* names see Martin and Satchell 2008, pp. 102, 108, 188 and 206.

[26] Using the methodology in Rackham 1980, pp. 120–1 and Figure 9.4.

[27] Brown 1994, p. 109, no. 370; Brown 1992, pp. 77–8, no. 72, pp. 68–9, no. 64; Gallagher 2009, no. 1118, pp. 233–4.

tion with a green, Wingfield Castle does not appear to be the primary settlement in Wingfield.

Wingfield is first recorded around 1035 as Wingefeld, when Thurketel of Palgrave gave it to his brother's sons, Ulfketel and Thurketel.[28] Thurketel is described as a 'noble hero' in the list of benefactors to the Abbey of Bury St Edmunds, but very little else is known about him other than he was a landowner with estates in and around Palgrave, including Whittingham in Fressingfield.[29] The Domesday record is confusing because two of the entries name Wingfield as 'Wineberga', whilst a third names it as 'Wighefelda', leaving it unclear whether these are two different aspects of the same place or scribal errors; in the first the suffix *berg* means a hill, in the second the suffix *feld* means an open place, but usually in the context of a generally wooded landscape.[30] The occurrence of the name as 'Wihingefeld' in 1184–5[31] lends credence to the suggested interpretation of the first element as *Wiginga* 'the people of Wiga', though it is still possible that it is a derivative of Old English *weoh* 'a pagan temple'.

The Domesday Book also reveals a complexity in the land holdings in Wingfield in 1086, with Robert Malet, the bishop of Thetford and the abbot of Ely all being recorded as holding land there, with further holdings being recorded for Malet, the bishop and for Roger of Poitou in Chickering. Chickering is now just a farmstead bisected by the Wingfield/Hoxne boundary, but a settlement there was in existence by the mid tenth century and it had a church of its own in 1086 that probably became the medieval chapel of Our Lady.[32] Robert Malet, the lord of the Honour of Eye and the dominant landowner in east Suffolk, is recorded as holding five and a half carucates (660 acres) in Stradbroke and 'its berewick [i.e. subsidiary settlement] Wingfield', with a further carucate (120 acres) held by seventeen of his sokemen and 95 acres by his various Norman subtenants (Walter of Caen 40 acres, Robert of Glanville 20 acres, Walter son of Grip 15 acres and Loernic 20 acres); this holding also included two churches – presumably those at Stradbroke and Wingfield – with a further 40 acres. The bishop of Thetford only held 10 acres in Wingfield, but the abbot of Ely held two carucates (240 acres) plus another church with 24 acres – but his holding was disputed by Roger Bigod. This additional church might be the medieval chapel of the Holy Trinity at a place recorded as 'Esham' in the mid thirteenth century, which is now a hamlet called Earsham Street in northern Wingfield, the modern form of the name being influenced by Earsham in Norfolk.[33]

---

[28] Whitelock 1930, p. 68, no. XXIV: will of Thurketel of Palgrave, dated before 1038.

[29] Hervey 1925, vol. II, p. 287.

[30] Rumble 1986, sections 6.308, 21.45 and 19.8; Martin 1999.

[31] *PR* vol. XXXIV, p. 36.

[32] Hart 1966, p. 53, no. 49

[33] Not far from Earsham Street, the Ordnance Survey first-edition map of 1886 confusingly marks 'Abbey (Site of)' at Abbey Farm, but there never was an abbey in Wingfield. In the fourteenth century the priories of Eye and Butley both owned land in Wingfield (TNA E135/1/14 – assessment for tax of temporalities of religious houses in Suffolk, c.1327–50) and the farm name is probably

This confusion gets a bit clearer in the early twelfth century when one of Robert Malet's successors as lord of the Honour of Eye, Stephen of Blois (later to be King Stephen) granted Stradbroke with Wingfield, with the advowson of the two churches, in fee farm to Ernald Ruffus son of Roger in 1113 x 1125.[34] The Ruffus or le Rus family were also manorial lords in nearby Whittingham in Fressingfield, at Salle and Heydon in Norfolk, and in Akenham, Clopton and Hasketon in south-east Suffolk.[35] Ernald's grandson, another Ernald, founded Woodbridge Priory around 1193 and had a grant of a market in his manor of Whittingham in 1199,[36] and his son Hugh had grants of markets in Stradbroke and Woodbridge (for the benefit of the priory there) in 1227. Hugh's granddaughter, Alice le Rus, was the eventual heir of the family. She was still a child at her father William's death around 1253 and her custody was granted to Giles le Ruffus, who was probably the same as Giles le Rus, parson of Wingfield. Whilst only about fourteen or fifteen she was married to Richard Lungespeye, but he died shortly afterwards in 1261.[37] Her second husband, who she married around 1270, was Sir Richard de Brewse, a younger son of John de Brewse, the lord of Bramber in Sussex and of Gower in South Wales.[38] Sir Richard seated himself at one of his wife's Norfolk properties – Stinton Hall in Salle – but he and his wife are recorded as having a park at Wingfield in 1285.[39] Shortly after Sir Richard's death in 1296/7, Alice settled Stradbroke and Wingfield on her younger son, another Richard, the remainder going to her eldest son Giles.[40] At about the same time, the young Richard married Eleanor, the wealthy widow of Sir John de Verdon of Brixworth in Northamptonshire and Bressingham in Norfolk, and the daughter of Sir Thomas de Furnivall of Sheffield Castle in Yorkshire. She brought with her a dowry of manors in Bressingham, Saxlingham and Great Moulton in Norfolk and in Martlesham and Stanstead in Suffolk, as well as lands elsewhere in Essex, Northamptonshire, Norfolk and Suffolk.[41] John and Eleanor de Verdon were married by 1276,[42] which implies that Eleanor was considerably older than her second husband, but as discussed more fully below, Richard had one son, but

just a commemoration of land formerly owned by a monastery, as is the case with the majority of 'Abbey Farm' names.

34 CChR 1226–57, p. 47; Brown 1994, p. 78.
35 For details of this family see: Brown 1994, pp. 77–81.
36 Farrer 1925, p. 439.
37 CIPM, vol. I, p. 143, no. 505: writ 27 December 1261.
38 This family took its surname from Briouze-Saint-Gervais in Normandy and the surname is spelt in many different ways: Braose, Breouse, Breuse, Breux, Brewose, Brewse, Briouze etc. They were powerful Marcher lords in Wales until they fell foul of King John.
39 Brown 1992, no. 324, p. 234.
40 Rye 1900, 101: 25 Edw. I [1296–7], no. 42. Richard de Brewosa v. Alice who was wife of Richard de Brewosa, of the manor of Stradebrok and advowson of church of Wyngefeld.
41 CCR 1288–96, pp. 447–9.
42 Farrer 1923, pp. 116–7.

necessarily by this marriage, as he appears to have married a second wife, Joan, by 1332–3.[43]

In 1302–3 Richard was returned as holding a quarter of a knight's fee in Wingfield of Robert fitz Roger, and he of the Honour of Eye – this feudal sequence indicating that the manor of Wingfield was reckoned to be a part of the barony of Horsford (Norfolk) which was then in the hands of Robert fitz Roger of Clavering in Essex (d.1310).[44] Robert was the descendant and heir of Walter of Caen, an important subtenant of Robert Malet in Wingfield and elsewhere in Suffolk and Norfolk at the time of Domesday; his extensive lands were later known as the barony of Horsford, so-called after the family's small castle there. However, Richard held a great deal more in the wife's right – one fee and an eighth of a fee in Bressingham, half a fee in Great Moulton, one fee in Saxlingham, and a quarter and an eighth of a fee in Martlesham.[45]

In 1306, Richard, his older brother Giles, and his stepson Thomas de Verdon, were among the 267 young men knighted with Prince Edward in London, prior to the prince's departure with an army to Scotland.[46] It is to be presumed that they all accompanied that army to Scotland. Sir Thomas de Verdon later disgraced himself by being among the twenty-two knights, including the prince's favourite, Piers Gaveston, who deserted the campaign to attend tournaments in foreign parts.[47] Whether this episode unsettled Sir Richard is not known, but there are few other records of him being involved in national or county affairs. He was summoned as a knight of Suffolk to the Great Council at Westminster in 1324, but in 1343 secured an exemption for life from being put on assizes or juries, or from appointment as sheriff or to any other office against his will.[48] More locally, he was granted, in 1309, the right of free warren in his demesne lands in Stradbroke and Wingfield, and the right to have a yearly four-day fair in Stradbroke.[49] In 1316 he was recorded as the lord of Stradbroke and Wingfield, and also, in his wife's right, of Great Moulton, Saxlingham, Bressingham, Martlesham, Newbourn and Waldringfield.[50] His not inconsiderable wealth is shown by him being taxed 26s 9d in Stradbroke and Wingfield and 8s 6d in Fornham All Saints in the Lay Subsidy of 1327.[51] In 1346 he still held a quarter of a knight's fee in Wingfield, but now of Eva de Ufford (the daughter and heiress of Robert fitz Roger and the widow of Sir Thomas de Ufford), and she

---

[43] Rye 1900, p. 173, 6 Edw. III [1332–3], no. 9; Richard de Brewosa and Johanna his wife *v.* Richard Skyn parson of Saxlyngham church, in Fornham All Saints, Westle, Hanegrave, and Flempton.
[44] Munday 1973, p. 13: Ricardus de Breuse et tenentes sui tenent in Wyngefeld unum quarterium de Roberto filio Rogeri, et idem Robertus de Eye.
[45] Munday 1973, p. 31; *FA*, vol. III, 393, 412 and 430.
[46] Shaw, vol. I, pp. 112, 116.
[47] *CFR 1272–1307*, pp. 543–4.
[48] Moor 1929, vol. I, pp. 143–4; *CPR 1343–45*, p. 132.
[49] *CChR 1300–26*, p. 132.
[50] *FA*, vol. III, pp. 476, 477, and vol. V, pp. 37, 41.
[51] Hervey 1906, pp. 48, 168.

of the earl of Suffolk (as lord of Eye).[52] The other lands in Norfolk and Suffolk had, however, passed on Sir Richard's wife's death to Sir John de Verdon, her grandson and heir by her first husband. The exact date of the transfer is not known, but by 1346 Verdon was a middle-aged and battle-hardened veteran of many campaigns, including the battle of Crécy.

One of Sir Richard de Brewse's last but very important acts was to transfer his manor of Wingfield, with its appurtenances, by means of the 'feet of fines' procedure, in 1357, to John de Wynewyk, David de Wollore, Sir John de Wingfield, his brother Sir Thomas de Wingfield and Gilbert de Debenham, acting as trustees for the heirs of Sir John de Wingfield.[53] The first two were influential king's clerks – John was a chaplain to King Edward III, Clerk of the Privy Seal, Treasurer of York Minster and a Prebendary of Lichfield, Lincoln, Salisbury, Wells and Chichester, while David was Master of the Rolls, Keeper of the Seal, Principal Clerk of the Chancery and a Prebendary of London and Lincoln; while the last-named, Gilbert de Debenham of Little Wenham in Suffolk, was a lawyer who counted the Black Prince, the earl of Suffolk and Sir John de Wingfield amongst his clients. The transfer to Sir John's heirs was to take place after the death of Katherine, who was the wife of Richard, son of Sir Richard de Brewse. This younger Richard is otherwise unknown, as is the identity of his wife, but the implication is that she was a childless widow by 1357. This property transfer was followed soon after, in November 1359, by another, whereby the manors of Stradbroke and Wingfield (but not the advowsons of their churches) were settled on Sir John de Wingfield and Eleanor his wife by David de Wollore and Gilbert de Debenham (John de Winwyk having died in the winter of that year).[54] This deed rehearses the life tenure of the manors by Richard de Brewse junior and his wife Katherine, with remainder to Sir John and Eleanor, and then adds remainders to their only daughter Katherine, the wife of Sir Michael de la Pole (later earl of Suffolk) and their heirs, to Sir John's brother Sir Thomas and his heirs and finally to his cousin William de Wingfield.[55] The fact that the wives of both Richard de Brewse and Michael de la Pole were named Katherine may just be

[52] *FA*, vol. V, p. 63: Ricardus de Breuse et tenentes sui tenent in Wyngefeld quart. f. m. de Eva de Ufford, et illa de comite Suffolkie, et comes de rege, quod Ricardus de Breuse nuper tenuit in eadem de Roberto filio Rogero.

[53] TNA: CP 25/1/221/90; Rye 1900, p. 220: 31 and 32 Edw. III [1357–8 and 1358–9], no. 40. John de Wynewyk, clerk, David de Wollore, clerk, John de Wengefeld, chevalier, Thomas de Wengefeld and Gilbert de Debenham *v*. Richard Breouse, chevalier, of the manor of *Wengefeld* with appurtenances.

[54] TNA: CP 25/1/221/91; Rye 1900, p. 223: 33 Edw. III [1359–60], no. 27. John de Wingfield, knight and Alianora his wife *v*. David de Wollore, clerk and Gilbert de Debenham, of the manors of *Stradebroke* and *Wyngefeld* (except the advowson of the churches).

[55] It is highly unlikely that Katherine was a child bride, as would be implied by her apparent age of '26 and more' at her mother's death in 1375 (i.e. born c.1349 and only ten at her marriage) (Cokayne 1953, p. 440). Her parents were married by 1330 (see below) and Katherine's son Michael was knighted in 1377 (Shaw 1906, p. 126) – even if she was just sixteen at his birth, he would then only have been twelve. It is much more likely that Katherine was born in the 1330s and that Michael was born c.1360–1, making him sixteen or seventeen when knighted.

a coincidence, but it is possible that Sir John's daughter had a short-lived marriage to Richard before her marriage to Sir Michael. If this was the case, the property transfer effectively converted her life interest in the estate to a permanent one for her children.

In November 1361 it was noted that King Edward III had 'lately granted licence for the alienation in mortmain by John de Wyngefeld, now deceased, and Eleanor his wife, or their heirs or executors, of £30 yearly of land or rent and advowsons of churches to the value of £100 yearly, to the chaplains of a chantry to be founded by them at Wingfield'. In furtherance of this the king now granted licence for Eleanor to assign to the 'chantry founded by her in Wingfield church, a messuage, 170 acres of land, 5 acres of meadow, 24 acres of pasture, 2 acres of wood and 12s of rent, in Wingfield, Earsham Street, Fressingfield and Weybread, as well as the advowsons of the churches of Wingfield, Stradbroke and Sylham with *Esham* chapel annexed thereto'.[56] Finally, the foundation charter of Wingfield College, dated 8 June 1362, states that Sir John de Wingefeld 'whilst he lived ... for his own salvation and that of his parents, kinsfolk, benefactors and all those for whom he, or his parents and progenitors, were in any way bound ... proposed to establish a college of certain secular priests in the parish church of Wingfield ... and to provide an endowment for such [a] college'.[57] This was now being done by the executors of his will – his widow Eleanor and his brother Sir Thomas. Prominent among the souls to be prayed for, named immediately after Sir John and his unnamed father and mother, ancestors, children, kinsmen and benefactors, was Sir Richard de Brewse. Intriguingly, Sir Thomas Wingfield, in his will dated 1378, gave to his son John, among other family heirlooms, 'six pieces of silver with the arms of Brews [on them]', suggesting that more than just land had been transferred from the de Brewses to the de Wingfields.[58]

From the above it is clear that, prior to 1357, the family of Sir John de Wingfield was not in possession of the main manor of Wingfield and their acquisition of it was connected with their establishment of Wingfield College, making it likely that the college was built on the site of the original manor house of the de Brewse family. This enables one to view the close siting of the college and church as an example of the hall-and-church complexes that are a strong and recurrent feature of the East Anglian landscape. These hall-and-church complexes, of Middle to Late Saxon origin, often consist of a roughly square area that contains a church in one quarter, as can be seen in Suffolk at Brockley and Wattisham, and very clearly here at Wingfield (see Figure 1.5; Plate I). As I have argued elsewhere, these complexes can probably be identified as being the *burhs* of Saxon thegns, bringing together their domestic buildings and private chapel within a weakly fortified perimeter that might

[56] CPR 1361–64, p. 104.
[57] Aldwell 1925, pp. 102–7.
[58] NRO: will of Thomas de Wyngfeld of Letheringham, proved 1378 Norwich Consistory Court (154 Heydon).

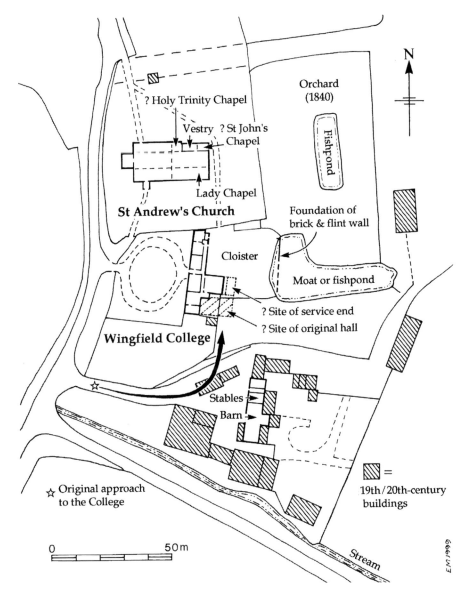

Fig. 1.5. Plan of the Wingfield College complex.

be enhanced by a more imposing gateway.[59] In the case of Wingfield, the college site is likely to have formed the core of the *burh* of Thurketel of Palgrave and his family in the eleventh century. Very significantly, the land associated with the college adjoined the stream that is the main watercourse in the parish, and included some of the adjacent meadows and a part of the area of better Hanslope soils – land that could be regarded as the best available in the parish and what one would expect for the manorial demesne.[60]

The origins of the de Wingfield family are therefore not as the ancient Saxon lords of Wingfield – as is suggested by the title of a nineteenth-century history of the family – and needs more explanation.[61] The first mention of the family seems to be in 1279, when a John de Wyngefeld was appointed, together with Richard de Brewse, as an attorney to act for William de Brewse who was 'going with the king beyond seas'.[62] William can be identified as the lord of Bramber and Gower and Richard as his younger brother, who, as we have seen above, had acquired the manor of Wingfield though his marriage to Alice le Rus. This immediately suggests that the de Wingfields arose through service to the more powerful de Brewse family. John de Wyngefeld appears to have marked the family's rise through the acquisition of 69 acres in Wingfield that were held in chief from the Crown.

In 1326 Sir John de Wingfield was granted a pardon because his grandfather John had acquired those 69 acres without royal licence from Fromund le Flemyng.[63] At about the same time a William Frombald, parson of Grundisburgh, petitioned for the restitution of rents and services in Wingfield that his grandfather Frombald Flemyng had purchased, which should have come to him after the death of his father Roger, but which had been granted by the king to John de Wingfield.[64] The original grantee's name seems to have caused some difficulties, but other documents do seem to substantiate the story: a Roger Thrumbald was living in Wingfield in 1240 and in 1274–5 'it was said' that King John had enfeoffed Frimbald with 60 acres in Wingfield for an annual rent of two white doves and that that land was now held

---

[59] Rippon 1996, p. 124; Dymond and Martin 1999, p. 88; Martin and Satchell 2008, *passim*; Martin 2012, pp. 230–4, 242.

[60] The lands of the College Farm, belonging to Robert Butcher of Upland Grove in Bungay, are shown on the Wingfield tithe apportionment of 1840–1 (SROI: FDA 292/A1/1a and 1b). See also the map in Aldwell 1925.

[61] Powerscourt 1894.

[62] CPR 1272–81, p. 308: 25 April 1279: Letters for Edmund, the king's brother, going with the king beyond seas, nominating Richard de Fukeram and Hugh de Vienna, his attorneys for one year. The like for Richard de Breus and John [unfinished entry]; William de Breus, going with the king beyond seas, nominating Richard de Breus and John de Wyngefeld until Michaelmas.

[63] CPR 1324–27, p. 242: 13 February 1326. The like [pardon] to John de Wynkefeld, with respect to 69 acres of land in *Wynkefeld*, held in chief of Edward I, which were acquired in fee by his grandfather, John de Wynkefeld, from Fromund le Flemyng and entered into by both grandfather and grandson without licence.

[64] TNA: SC 8/14/680; Record Commission 1783, p. 382, no. 25.

by tenants of Richard de Brewse and the prior of Thetford.[65] In 1362–3, Eleanor, the widow of Sir John de Wingfield, enfeoffed Richard Damondevill (as a trustee) with 69 acres in Wingfield called Fromondeland.[66] On Eleanor's death in 1375, her daughter Katherine and her husband, Sir Michael de la Pole took seisin of 69 acres in Wingfield, held in chief from the king.[67] This land reappears in 1419 in the inquisition post-mortem of Katherine, countess of Suffolk, as Frumbaldes and was still 69 acres. In 1422–3 it was the Frumbaldy fee (69 acres) and in 1856 it was deemed to be the manor of Wingfield Frumbalds.[68] This and Old Wingfield Hall were the two manors in Wingfield held by Lord Berners at the sale of his estate there in 1856.[69] The sale also included his three farms in the parish: the Castle Farm (366 acres, including 'unlimited commonage on Wingfield Green'), the adjoining Farrow's Farm (66 acres) and the separate Wingfield Hall Farm (176 acres), Wingfield.[70] The manor of Old Wingfield Hall and the farm surrounding Wingfield Hall (at TL 240758) are likely to be linked, which suggests that Wingfield Frumbalds covered the Castle Farm and the adjoining Farrow's Farm (now called St Martin's, at TL 226764). The sources sometimes imply the presence of a third manor, called Wingfield Castle, but it is very difficult to separate it from Wingfield Frumbalds.[71] Wingfield Hall (sometimes called Old Wingfield Hall) may have been the original home of the de Wingfield family, but it was probably eclipsed by their acquisition, in the later thirteenth century, of Frumbalds with its superior cachet of being held in chief from the king, it was probably on that land that they built their main house – a moated house that was later transformed into Wingfield Castle. Interestingly, nineteenth-century field boundaries suggest that there was a parcel of land that included the castle site and was bounded on the west by Wingfield Green, on the north by the former deer park and on the south by the road, which contained 69 acres.

The first member of note of the de Wingfield family was not, however, a knight but a cleric – Roger de Wingfield, a royal official or king's clerk who appears as a Clerk or Receiver of the Chamber from 1309 until his death in 1314.[72] Roger rapidly became a pluralist, holding church livings in the dioceses of York, Lincoln, Norwich,

---

[65] Gallagher 2009, no. 1118, p. 249; *RHundred*, vol. II, 186.

[66] *CIPME*, vol. II, p. 257: 36 Edw. III, 2nd nos., no. 24.

[67] Copinger 1904, vol. V, p. 393: Order to take fealty and deliver seisin to Sir Michael atte Pole and Katherine his wife daughter and heir of Alianora who was wife of Sir John de Wyngefeld decd., of 69a of pasture in Wingfield, held of the king in chief.

[68] *CIPM*, vol XXII, p. 28: 1 Hen. VI. [1422–3] Elizabeth one of daughters and heirs of Michael, son of Michael de la Pole, Earl of Suffolk and one of kin and heirs of Katherine late wife of said Earl: 69 acres of land called Frumbaldy Fee in Wingfield; SROI: FC 84/N1/1.

[69] SROI: FC 84/N1/1: sale catalogue of 1856.

[70] The exact location of the farms and the fields can be confirmed from the Wingfield tithe apportionment of 1840–1 (SROI: FDA 292/A1/1a and 1b). *Farrow's Farm* was named after the then tenant, Mrs Bilby Farrow; her husband held it in 1840, when it was called *Buntings*.

[71] NRO: KNY 18 369 x3.

[72] Tout 1933, vol. VI, 54.

Exeter, Worcester and Lismore in Ireland, including the post of prebendary and precentor of St Patrick's in Dublin.[73] He also undertook more secular duties, being appointed, in 1311, the keeper of the lands of the Knights Templar that were in the king's hands, and in 1312 he was given custody of the town and castle of Orford.[74] His duties also took him overseas, as in 1313 he was granted protection 'going beyond seas on the king's service'.[75] He even appears as the owner of half a ship called *la Mariole* which he had 'laden with divers wares'.[76] Perhaps significantly, the grant in 1309 to Sir Richard de Brewse of free warren in his demesne lands in Stradbroke and Wingfield, and a fair in Stradbroke, was granted 'at the instance of Roger de Wyngefeld, king's clerk'.[77] This suggests that the connection between the de Brewse and the de Wingfield families that was seen in 1279 was being continued.

A magnificent late sixteenth-century roll pedigree of the Wingfield family begins with a John de Wingefeld and ascribes to him four sons: Richard, Roger, Gyles and William.[78] The last-named is an error, but the other three seem to be correct as likely sons of the John who was serving the de Brewes family in 1279. Richard also appears to have entered a form of royal service, being granted the custody of the parks of Framlingham, Kelsale and Earl Soham in 1310, then in the hands of the king following the death of Roger Bigod, earl of Norfolk, in 1306.[79] The actual grantor was John de Uffeton, Bigod's chamberlain, who had been given a life grant by the earl. By 1314 Richard had managed to obtain the reversion of the manor of Dennington and he established a short-lived branch of the family there.[80] Giles was the rector of Kelsale and, intriguingly, has the same first name as Sir Richard de Brewse's older brother, Sir Giles de Brewse, who was one of the manorial lords in Fressingfield where Giles de Wingfield was taxed in 1327. The roll pedigree, unfortunately, confuses Richard's son, Sir William de Wingfield of Dennington, with his uncle, John de Wingfield, who continued the family in Wingfield. Very little is known of this John, but he heads the pedigree of the family as recorded at the Heralds' Visitation in 1561.[81] On this, his wife is stated to be the daughter of a man with the surname Honypott, who in latter pedigrees is said to be Elisabeth, the daughter and heir of John Honeypot of Wingfield.[82] The father is probably to be identified as the John Honipot of Wingfield who, with his wife Juliana, acquired property in

73   *CPR 1307–13*, pp. 198, 199, 210, 213, 415, 575; *1313–17*, pp. 47, 94 and 175.
74   *CCR 1307–13*; *CPR 1307–13*, p. 506
75   *CPR 1307–13*, p. 583
76   *CPR 1317–21*, pp. 360–1, 365.
77   *CChR 1300–26*, p. 132.
78   SROI: HD2418/86.
79   *CPR 1307–13*, p. 275.
80   *CPR 1313–17*, p. 44.
81   Corder 1984, pp. 211–22.
82   BL: Add. MS 33247: R. Hawes, MS *History of Framlingham and Loes Hundred*, c.1712–24, fols 490–1.

Hoxne, Stradbroke and Horham in 1295–6.[83] What property he had in Wingfield is, unfortunately, unknown, but it doubtless added to the wealth of his son-in-law John de Wingfield. It is this John's son, Sir John de Wingfield, who greatly increased the wealth and status of the family through both royal service, like his uncles, and by an advantageous marriage.

Sir John de Wingfield's wife is described in the 1561 pedigree as 'Elenor daughter of … Glanvyll erll of Suffolk' – on the face of it this is nonsense, as no member of the Glanville family was ever earl of Suffolk.[84] There is, however, good reason to think that there was some sort of a link with the Glanville family that may have involved Eleanor. This is in connection with the manors of Saxmundham and Sternfield in south-east Suffolk. The feudal aid roll for 1346 lists Sir John de Wingfield as holding half a knight's fee in Sternfield (held of Eleanor Ferre, and she of Robert, earl of Suffolk, and he of the king) that Robert de Glaunville formerly held of Guy Ferre.[85] And in Saxmundham, Sir John held a quarter of a fee (of Mary, countess of Norfolk, and she of the king) that was part of a full fee that Robert de Grennlie had formerly held of Roger Bigod.[86] An earlier roll, that for 1302–3, reveals that 'the heirs of Robert de Glanvyle' held half a fee in Sternfield of Guy Ferre, and 'the heirs of Robert de Grymyle' held a fee in Saxmundham of Roger Bigod.[87] The connection between these two holdings is revealed by a record in the Patent Rolls. In 1302, Roger Bigod, earl of Norfolk, had granted to John de Uffeton 'his yeoman, in consideration of his service, all the lands sometime of John de Glaunvill and Joan de Grymeleys his wife, of the inheritance of the said Joan in the towns of Saxmundham, Kelsale, Rendham and Sternfield'.[88] This John de Uffeton, elsewhere described as Bigod's chamberlain, is the same man who, in 1310, granted Sir John's uncle, Richard de Wingfield, his life interest in the custody of the former Bigod deer parks of Framlingham, Kelsale and Earl Soham.

The sequence of ownership for Saxmundham and Sternfield is not totally clear, but in 1310 Thomas de Verlay, king's yeoman, was granted the right to hold a

---

[83] Rye 1900, p. 100: 24 Edw. I [1295–6] no. 28 John Honipot of Wyngefeld and Juliana his wife v. William de Stubbecroft of Hoxene in Hoxene, Stradebrok and Horham.

[84] The seventeenth-century pedigree in the Norfolk Visitations has her as 'Elizabeth, daughter of Randall Glanvile, Earl of Suffolk' – Rye 1891, p. 312. For a detailed examination of the very complex early history of this family see Mortimer 1981.

[85] Guy Ferre the younger (d.1323) was a Gascon who was a household knight of Queen Eleanor 1277–90 and household steward to her 1288–90, Seneschal of Gascony 1298–9 and 1308–9. He acquired the manor of Benhall in Suffolk, with the patronage of Butley and Leiston priories, in 1290.

[86] FA, vol. V, p. 86.

[87] Munday 1973, p. 34. Robert can probably be identified with the Robert de Grimilies who was a frequent member of juries of the Suffolk eyre in 1240 and was himself a defendant in a case where he entered the rabbit warren of William the Breton in Sternfield by force and beat his serjeant – see Gallagher 2009, p. 46, no. 264.

[88] CPR 1301–7, pp. 125–6.

weekly market at his manor of Saxmundham.[89] In the same year he was pardoned for acquiring 7 acres of land in Saxmundham from William de Biskeleye without licence.[90] In 1316 he and his wife Joan were defendants in a feet of fines suit concerning Sternfield and Saxmundham that was probably intended to put their property there into the hands of a trustee, the plaintiff, Henry de Wetheryngsete, chaplain;[91] and in 1317 they were defendants in another suit concerning land in Saxmundham and Kelsale, with Henry le Warner of Saxmundham this time as the plaintiff.[92] In 1316 Thomas de Verlay was returned as the lord of Saxmundham, and in 1327 he was taxed 4s 6d in Sternfield.[93] In the meantime, described as a serjeant with responsibility for the hall, he had accompanied the royal household overseas in 1320.[94] In 1323–4, he and his wife Joan acquired land in Iken, Sudbourne and Orford.[95] Then, in 1330, Thomas and Joan made a larger settlement of lands in Sternfield, Saxmundham, Benhall, Farnham and Holton and the advowson of Saxmundham church to Oliver Ermeger and Thomas de Wingfield (presumably, the younger brother of Sir John) as trustees to resettle the lands on Thomas and Joan for life, with remainder to John de Wingfield and Eleanor his wife and their heirs, and, if they had no heirs, a final remainder to John, son of Robert de Glannvyle.[96] Although it is not explicitly stated, this suggests that Eleanor was the daughter of Thomas and Joan and this settlement was made to secure Eleanor's inheritance on her marriage to John de Wingfield. The final remainder was presumably to a more distant kinsman, and suggests that Joan de Verlay was a Glanville, probably the daughter of John de Glanville and Joan de Grymeleys.

The next record of Thomas de Verlay and his wife Joan is in the foundation charter of Wingfield College, where they are listed immediately after Sir Richard de Brewse as souls to be prayed for.[97] This confirms that they were important people in the eyes of the founders, and supports the idea that they were the parents of Eleanor, Sir John's wife. She certainly brought to the Wingfield family lands that had

---

[89] CChR 1300–26, p. 165.

[90] CPR 1307–13, p. 319.

[91] Probably a relative of Robert de Wetheringsete, parson of Sternfield in 1301.

[92] TNA: CP25/1/217/57, Rye 1900, p. 134: 9 Edw. II [1315–6] no. 7. Henry de Wetheryngsete, chaplain v. Thomas de Verlay and Johanna his wife in Sternefeld and Saxmundham; TNA: CP25/1/217/58, Rye 1900, p. 138: 10 Edw. II [1316–17] no. 35. Henry le Warner of Saxmundham v. Thomas de Verlay and Johanna his wife in Saxmundham and Keleshale.

[93] FA, vol. V, p. 41; Hervey 1906, p. 105.

[94] CPR 1317–21, p. 420.

[95] Rye 1900, p. 153: 17 Edw. II [1323–4] no. 20. Thomas de Verlay and Johanna his wife v. Nicholas de Storteford and Elizabeth his wife, Roger Blome and Margaret his wife in Iken, Southbourne and Orford.

[96] TNA: CP25/1/219/70; Rye 1900, p. 167: 4 Edw. III [1330–1] no. 6. Thomas de Verlay and Johanna his wife v. Oliver Ermeger and Thomas de Wyngfeld concerning lands Sternefeld, Saxmundham, Benhall, Farnham and Holton and the advowson of Saxmundham church. Ermeger was probably the man of this name who was parson of Sutton in 1314.

[97] Aldwell 1925, pp. 102–7.

been held by the Glanvilles, but it seems that it was her maternal not her paternal inheritance.

The landscape history of Wingfield encapsulates many things that are not only true for the claylands of 'High Suffolk' but also more generally for Suffolk and East Anglia as a whole. Yet, as with all landscapes, it is also unique – its individual physical features and history give it a character that separates it from all other places. Understanding a landscape enables one to see a place more fully – as East Anglia's greatest landscape painter, John Constable, once remarked 'we see nothing truly till we understand it'.[90] Hopefully this study has helped to make Wingfield more truly visible.

[98] Leslie 1845, p. 350.

2

Sir John de Wingfield and the Foundation of Wingfield College

Mark Bailey

The foundation of Wingfield College was confirmed on 8 June 1362, thus fulfilling one of the key terms of the will of its founder, Sir John de Wingfield.[1] Unfortunately, only a few sketchy details are readily recoverable about John himself. He was married by 1330, fought with distinction in the royal army during a golden era of English military action and rose to become the director of the business affairs of Edward of Woodstock, the Black Prince. His effigy in Wingfield church depicts a splendid armoured knight, 5 feet 9 inches tall. Beyond this, the published record about him is frustratingly thin. We do not know exactly when, how or where he died, although it was sometime in the autumn of 1361. No copy of his will is known to have survived. Little has been written about him: how did he acquire the wealth to found the college, what motivated him and why did he choose to locate it in the sleepy Suffolk backwater of Wingfield?

Despite the sketchiness of the life of John de Wingfield, it is possible to piece together enough details of his career to reveal a fascinating story of a remarkable man. De Wingfield confounded the immense challenges posed by the Black Death of 1348–9 – which killed round 40 per cent of the population of England within twelve months – to marshal enough money, men and material to enable the Black Prince to prosecute the Poitiers campaign in the mid-1350s. The campaign is regarded as one of the most dazzling feats of arms in English military history, but, coming so soon after the catastrophic loss of so many people to a single epidemic, it could also be regarded as one of the most dazzling feats of mobilisation and organisation in English military history. Sir John is an exceptional example of the new rank of 'senior knight' accommodated within the upper ranks of English society in Edward III's reign, who had proved himself first on the field of battle and then as an administrator.[2] Indeed, it would not be inappropriate to go much further and to claim for him a place among that small group of brilliant administrators – including Sir

---

[1] *VCH Suffolk*, vol. 2, p. 152. For a more detailed history, see Aldwell 1925, pp. 77–95.
[2] Coss 2003, pp. 241, 248–9.

William Shareshull, Bishop William Edington and John Thoresby – who in the 1350s played a major role in 'restoring public confidence in the Crown and rebuilding the reputation and prestige of the English monarchy'.[3]

Basic biographical details

The origins of the de Wingfield family are obscure. During the 1270s John's grandfather – also called John – was in the service of the de Brewse family, themselves middling gentry lords from the same corner of Suffolk who at that time held the main manor of Wingfield.[4] The patriarch acquired the small manor of Wingfield Frumbalds at some point during the late thirteenth century, and one of his sons, Roger, subsequently rose through royal service to become a senior financial officer in the household of Edward II.[5] We do not know when or where John was born. However, it is probable that, even though uncle Roger died in 1314, his contacts and name provided the initial openings in our John's career during the 1320s.[6]

John appears in the historical record for the first time in the mid-1320s. In 1326 he saw off a challenge to the family's ownership of Wingfield Frumbalds, whose manor house must have served as his principal residence at this date and was located on the site of the later Wingfield Castle.[7] Around the same time he was running errands in France for Edward II.[8] We might guess that he was no more than twenty years of age, seeking to establish himself in royal service. His success in pursuing that career provided a backdrop to his marriage by 1330 to Eleanor de Verlay, whose mother was a member of the prominent de Glanville family.[9] She was an excellent match for a promising young newcomer to royal service, and he was to prove a very good match for Eleanor, too.

John's main early successes were achieved as a soldier in the armies of the young Edward III. He was involved in the successful siege of Berwick in 1333, where he might have been knighted: certainly, from the mid-1330s he is usually described as Sir John. In the 1340s he was firmly established in the retinue of Sir Bartholomew de Burghersh, a notable diplomat and soldier, and he had also become close enough to William de Montacute, first earl of Salisbury, to be appointed as an executor to his will. After William's death in a tournament in 1344, John became a member of his

---

[3] Ormrod 1990, pp. 86–90, 94.
[4] Dewing 1889, p. 57; Blomefield, vol. V, p. 488.
[5] Tout 1920, pp. 317–19, 324.
[6] For a comprehensive assessment of the evidence for the origins of the de Wingfield family, see Martin, this volume, pp. 25–29.
[7] CPR, 1324–27, p. 242.
[8] Wrottesley 1897, p. 192.
[9] Martin, this volume, pp. 27–29.

son's (also William) retinue.[10] Both Burghersh and the elder Montacute were highly trusted by Edward III, so John's own standing and experience must have risen in their service. William de Montacute II was closely associated with the adolescent Black Prince, the king's eldest son. In 1346 Edward III appointed Sir John to the retinue and council of war of the sixteen-year-old prince, with whom he fought against the French at the battle of Crecy, followed by the successful siege of Calais in 1347.[11] Robert Reyce records that John earned this prestigious appointment because he was regarded as 'a man of great wisdom and experience of counsel, and a most valiant captain for resolution and action':[12] the ideal person to guide the inexperienced, but highly promising, heir to the throne through his first major military campaign.

The stunning success at Crecy, followed by the siege and capture of Calais, must have forged a powerful bond of trust and respect between Sir John and the Black Prince. Given the generation gap between the two men, and John's relatively humble background, the relationship was unlikely to have been especially close: John seems to have been a valued mentor than a close friend.[13] The esteem in which the prince held him is reflected in John's role as his chief financial and operating officer from 1350 until his death in late 1361; the title of his office is rarely mentioned, but he dominated the prince's business affairs and 'his name was of itself authoritative'.[14] Thus did the aging soldier reinvent himself as one of the leading estate administrators in England. However, his campaigning days were not yet over, because he served actively with his lord on the southern French campaigns of the mid-1350s, including fighting at the battle of Poitiers. Indeed, two of his letters from the front provide some of the most colourful testimony of warfare in the 1350s.[15] He did not initially accompany the prince on the Rheims campaign of the later 1350s, remaining in England instead to organise additional cash and resources, before eventually joining him for a short period between the autumn of 1359 and the early spring of 1360.[16] One active participant throughout the whole campaign was Michael de la Pole, son of the wealthy Hull wool merchant who had bankrolled much of Edward III's military activity, who around this time became betrothed to Katherine, John and Eleanor's only surviving child (born in the late 1340s). Michael later rose to prominence under Richard II, being created earl of Suffolk in 1385.[17]

Sir John Wingfield was clearly a very loyal and able man, upon whom some of the most important people in England relied to get things done. In the late 1350s he made

[10] Wrottesley 1897, pp. 127, 132, 161, 259. I am grateful to Edward Martin for these references.
[11] Barber 1978, p. 114.
[12] Reyce 1902, p. 144.
[13] Barber 1978, p. 114.
[14] Tout 1930, pp. 386–7.
[15] Barber 1979, pp. 50–2, 55–6.
[16] *RBP*, pt III, p. 367; RBP pt IV, pp. 11, 304, 326; Barber 1979, pp. 157–9; Booth 1981, p. 84, n. 153.
[17] Fryde 1988, p. 228.

the final preparations for two key events in his own life. First, and in the absence of a surviving male heir, he arranged an excellent match for his daughter, one which also benefited the de la Poles who thereby cemented their contacts in royal circles. Second, he arranged for Wingfield College to be founded after his death. Now that his affairs were in order, the elderly John was duly prepared for his death. He did not have to wait long, for he died sometime between June and November 1361.[18] It is probable that he succumbed to the second outbreak of the Black Death, which struck the eastern counties in the late summer and autumn of 1361.[19] If this was indeed the cause of his death, then it is imbued with irony, because the first epidemic in 1348–9 had created the platform for John to reinvent himself as an administrator and royal enforcer, and to accumulate the wealth necessary to fund his college. A mournful but grateful prince paid the princely sum of £57 13 s 4 d to cover the funeral expenses of his devoted servant.[20]

Administrative Career

The Black Death of 1348–9 presented all English landlords with immense challenges. The deaths of nearly half of the population of England between August 1348 and the autumn of 1349 resulted in acute shortages of tenants and labourers. Landlords therefore faced administrative dislocation and serious financial losses, as vacant landholdings caused rental income to fall and higher wages increased costs.[21] Yet the problems created by the Black Death also provided a great opportunity for anyone with the energy and resourcefulness to solve them. Sir John de Wingfield was appointed as steward of all the lands of the Black Prince in 1350, an office which had been newly created in the 1340s and conferred authority far beyond the conventional job of a steward of estates: according to Booth, it 'had no real parallel on other large English estates at the time, and is an indication of the large measures of both centralisation and professionalism in the prince's administration.'[22] In 1351 he was described as 'chief of the prince's council', and at other times thereafter as 'the prince's bachelor' and even as 'governor of the prince's affairs': his title varied, but there is no doubt that he ran

[18] John was alive, directing the Black Prince's business, in June 1361, see *RBP*, pt II, p. 183. A sheet of the prince's expenses, appended to an order issued on 5 November 1361, includes payment for John's funeral expenses, *RBP*, pt IV, p. 402. Thus he probably died in September or early October 1361. See also Aldwell 1925, p. 6.
[19] Bailey 2007, p. 183.
[20] *RBP*, pt IV, p. 402. This was a substantial sum of money. For comparison, in the 1350s a skilled labourer might earn around £3 per annum, and a typical gentry lord in East Anglia might receive income of around £20 per annum.
[21] For the general problems, see Horrox 1994, pp. 234–41; and for a survey of the initial problems on the prince's own estate, see Green 2007, pp. 59–60.
[22] Tout 1930, pp. 387, 440; Booth 1981, p. 65; Booth 1971, p. 19.

the prince's business affairs between 1350 and 1361.[23] This meant overall control of all the prince's lands, which comprised the vast landed estates of the Duchy of Cornwall, the earldom of Chester, extensive lands in (especially) North Wales and Aquitaine, and also all of his administrative departments.[24]

John was greatly occupied, but not fully employed, by his work for the Black Prince. In the 1340s he had served on the councils of successive earls of Salisbury, the earl of Surrey (who died in 1347) and Thomas Holland; in 1353 he was attorney general of the council of the earl of Surrey's widow, Joan de Bar, who had lived in France for most of her life, but who had returned to London in that year, and in 1357 she promoted him to the head of her council.[25] He also undertook duties as a royal justice, hearing cases and making judgements on behalf of Edward III. In 1351 John was labelled as a King's Justice, and in 1354 he served as one in Cornwall, hearing a case at Lostwithiel with Sir William Shareshull.[26] John was not a trained lawyer, as far as we can tell, but his practical legal knowledge and understanding were strong. His letters from southern France were written in French, the language of the court, and he used Latin for estate administration, the language of the law. He was highly literate, and savvy with figures.

De Wingfield's work for the Black Prince in the 1350s is well documented thanks to the survival of the remarkable *Register of the Black Prince*, which is a log book of his business affairs between 1346 and 1365.[27] In particular, it contains copies of hundreds of letters, orders and instructions on a wide range of both important and relatively trivial matters, most of which include a note of warrant indicating who had authorised them: whether the prince himself, or the prince's council, or one of his leading officials. A detailed analysis of these relating to Cheshire between 1351 and 1361 reveals that decision-making was centralised to an uncommon degree, which resulted in unusually consistent and direct management of the affairs of the estate. It also reveals that John de Wingfield dominated the issue of warrants, delegating very little business to other officials, and acting decisively upon his own initiative. The concentration of power in John's hands, and the influence he wielded, was unusually high, even for this highly professional and centralised estate: 'it is no exaggeration to say that Wingfield was the principal policymaker for the prince's estates at this time … Wingfield ruled alone.'[28] On occasions he even over-rode personal instructions from the Black Prince himself, wherever he regarded them as contradictory or damaging to estate administration.[29] His value to the prince was immense, which

---

[23] *RBP*, pt IV, pp. 31, 234, 263.
[24] Tout 1930, p. 391.
[25] *CPR 1345–48*, pp. 139, 145; *CPR 1354–58*, p. 15; *RBP*, pt II, p. 128; *RBP*, pt III, pp. 249, 254; *RBP*, pt IV, pp. 96, 249, 254.
[26] *RBP*, pt II, p. 64.
[27] *RBP*, pts I–IV.
[28] Booth 1981, pp. 71–4.
[29] Ibid., p. 85 n. 150.

is partially reflected in his handsome salary: he received 10 s per day when on the prince's business, twice the rate of his predecessor, Peter de Gildesburgh.[30]

The Black Prince clearly regarded John as exceptionally competent, trustworthy and loyal. Furthermore, John's management of the prince's estates in the 1350s reveals his brilliance as a businessman. Upon his appointment in 1350 John immediately set about addressing the issues of reduced revenues and disrupted administration on the Cheshire and Cornwall lands, which together generated around 40 per cent of the prince's total revenues.[31] In Cheshire he changed the system of accounting, introducing new controls and placing a greater emphasis on the collection of fines and rents, both of which improved cash generation and flow. Greater use was made of a financial management tool known as 'assigned annuities', which was a device to incentivise the collection of the prince's rents and perquisites in the localities.[32] New policies were introduced to increase revenues from the Cheshire lands: manors were leased to generate a more predictable flow of cash; capital assets – such as wood-lands – were assessed and liquidated as required; and the potential for stock rearing was realised through, for example, the ingenious creation of a large, and eventually lucrative, cattle herd in Macclesfield.[33] John proved tenacious in the defence and the exploitation of the prince's rights in Cheshire, yet also combined this toughness with flexibility and pragmatism when necessary.[34]

The Duchy of Cornwall was also managed with impressive flexibility and atten-tion to detail in the immediate aftermath of the Black Death. Payments of rent were remitted where genuine hardship could be proved, new forms of tenancy were intro-duced to encourage the occupation of land and careful consideration was given to local conditions and circumstances.[35] John was especially active in directing solutions to knotty financial, and complicated legal, issues, the resolution of which was some-times delayed until it could receive his personal attention.[36] John Hatcher comments admiringly upon the 'wisdom and the foresight' of these policies, which constituted 'a plan of action which showed a comprehensive understanding of the economic and social factors involved in the problems it faced'.[37]

[30] *RBP*, pt IV, p. 263; Booth 1981, p. 65.
[31] Green 2007, p. 63.
[32] *VCH Chester*, vol. 2, pp. 19, 25; Booth 1981, pp. 17–29, 76–7, 79, 121–4, 135–6.
[33] *VCH Chester*, vol. 2, p. 23; Booth 1981, pp. 70–4, 79, 94–6, 122–31, 139. Mature timber in woodland attached to a newly acquired estate at Peckforton was hastily sold for £533, Booth 1981, pp. 131–2.
[34] Booth 1981, pp. 98–9, 128.
[35] Hatcher 1970, pp. 104–16.
[36] See, for example, his domination of warrants relating to Cornwall in 1359, which are signed off in various ways, such as 'by command of Sir John de Wingfield ... by advice of Wingfield ... by Wingfield ... by advice and ordinance of Wingfield ... by command of the prince on the information of Sir John Wingfield ... by command of the prince and by Wingfield ... by advice and command of John de Wingfield', *RBP*, pt II, pp. 152–66. His intervention in financial and legal affairs is demonstrated in *RBP*, pt II, pp. 38–9, 56, 66–9, 72–3. See also Tout 1930, p. 388 n. 2.
[37] Hatcher 1970, p. 116.

The principle of active reform of financial administration on these distant estates was also applied to the heart of the Black Prince's household, because in 1352 its central financial system was changed. Payments from the earldom of Chester were made direct to the prince's wardrobe rather than via the exchequer at Westminster, and tighter controls were introduced over expenditure within the prince's own household.[38] These adjustments increased the speed at which cash reached the prince, while reducing the scope for leakage. De Wingfield was a key figure in these changes, which are similar to William Edington's successful reforms of Edward III's private finances.[39] Indeed, his imprint on the prince's business is especially apparent in financial affairs. He visited estates when necessary, whether in Cheshire in 1351 and 1353, or Cornwall in 1354, but he was relentless in his pursuit and chivvying of local officials through written orders and correspondence.[40] Sometimes he even wrote his orders from his bed or 'the chimney corner' of his house.[41]

The scale of John's achievement can be demonstrated through the crude financial out-turns from the Cheshire estate. In the 1290s, when local hereditary office-holders ran the earldom of Chester on the Crown's behalf, the estate had yielded around £500 per annum. In 1353, under the personal direction of Wingfield, the same estate yielded nearly £3,000. This was an exceptional sum, which was only achieved by resorting to exceptional methods. It was boosted by the levying of a common fine on the county and by conducting a one-off judicial inquiry: Cheshire was being squeezed. Yields in other years during the 1350s were not as high as 1353, but still usually exceeded £2,000.[42] As Booth observes, these impressive 'sums have no parallel in Cheshire's medieval history'.[43] To achieve them in the immediate aftermath of the Black Death was a stunning feat of financial management.

The major objective of these financial and administrative reforms was the creation of a war chest to enable the prince to support the pursuit of his father's dynastic and territorial claims in France. One of the most astonishing aspects of the Poitiers campaign of the mid-1350s, and the Rheims campaign of the late 1350s, is the manner in which Edward III and the Black Prince were able to fund and wage war as if the Black Death had never happened. Wars were costly at any time, but especially in a decade when demographic collapse severely compromised landed incomes and caused wage-bills to rise. The Poitiers campaign of 1355–6 cost £110,000, much of which was funded by governmental sources.[44] However, the prince still had to meet

---

[38] Tout 1930, pp. 345–6, 357–8; Booth 1981, pp. 75, 136–7.

[39] Ormrod 1990, pp. 88–9.

[40] See, for example, the order issued on 11 December 1351, when all local officials were summoned to London to report on 'the state of the prince's affairs and lordship in [their] bailiwick', RBP, pt III, pp. 54, 64, 70: Hatcher 1970, p. 117; Booth 1971, pp. 18–22.

[41] Tout 1930, pp. 395–6.

[42] VCH Chester, vol. 2, p. 23; Booth 1981, pp. 67, 121, 133; Booth 1971, pp. 18–22, 25.

[43] Booth 1981, p. 122.

[44] Ormrod 1990, p. 89; Booth 1981, p. 135.

the running costs of his own household, which on a wartime footing numbered around 250 people and cost around £10,000 per annum, demands which placed extreme pressures on his financial resources.[45] Throughout the 1350s John de Wingfield exploited the prince's lands with the primary objective of maximising income, squeezing assets for cash and freezing non-essential expenditure.[46] He also arranged loans from the London mercantile community to bridge any shortfalls in funding.[47] His understanding of the financial realities underpinning the successful waging of war is revealed through the content of his letter to William Edington from southern France in December 1355, in which he assessed, meticulously and approvingly, the impact of the scorched-earth policy of the English army around Carcassonne and Limoux in terms of the loss of fiscal revenue to the French Crown: he even sought out documentary evidence to verify the figures, citing them directly to Edington.[48] John's focus upon finance and war-making capacity reveals much about his mentality.

The hard-driving, cash-generating, policies adopted on the estates of the Black Prince in the first half of the 1350s were not sustainable beyond the short-term. The imposition of a common fine, and the holding of trailbaston proceedings, in 1353 created disquiet among the population of Cheshire; some of the sharp practices used to acquire new lands caused resentment locally; and the asset stripping of woodland, and the freezing of capital investment on the estate, could not continue indefinitely and would eventually need to be addressed. Hence the policies stored up problems, some of which provoked unrest in the 1360s and 1370s in Cheshire, Wales and Aquitaine.[49] Booth's candid assessment is that the policies of the 1350s 'had a deleterious effect on good government' in Cheshire.[50] Sir John did not live long enough to have to deal with the medium-term consequences of his policies on the prince's English estates in the 1350s. However, it is unlikely he would have been repentant, because his management policies, no less than his reform of the prince's private finances, was entirely fit for its specific – and immediate – purpose of creating a secure financial foundation from which to resume war in France. Building up financial reserves and providing logistical support for an overseas army were challenging tasks in the wake of the Black Death, yet they were as important to the prince's military success as his ability and luck on the battlefield. Sir John de Wingfield achieved these goals triumphantly.

De Wingfield was a highly reliable fixer, and an energetic and industrious administrator. Getting things done in mid-fourteenth-century England, even on behalf of the heir to the throne, required many attributes, one of which was knowing the

---

[45] Green 2007, pp. 129–30. By the end of the 1350s, after the Poitiers campaign and the onset of the Rheims campaign, the Black Prince was running out of cash, Booth 1981, p. 136.
[46] Booth 1981, pp. 136–7.
[47] Green 2007, p. 131.
[48] Barber 1979, p. 52.
[49] Booth 1981, pp. 139–40; Green 2007, p. 62.
[50] Booth 1981, p. 137.

right people. The Black Prince's retinue drew extensively upon members of the East Anglian gentry, and John enjoyed a web of links and associations with many of these people, which he would have deployed when errands had to be run and influence brought to bear.[51] When in 1358 the prince demanded that a legal inquiry of oyer and terminer be held in Norfolk to resolve a dispute in which he himself had an interest, John was appointed as one of the commissioners charged with hearing and judging the case: John was there to look after the prince's interests, a responsibility which was aided by his East Anglian connections.[52] He appears to have commanded loyalty himself. For example, a series of chance references reveal that John was served by the same clerk, known simply as Edmund, between 1355 and 1358, and one suspects that if the surviving historical record was more complete we would discover that Edmund was with his lord for much longer.[53]

De Wingfield's remarkable accomplishments throughout the 1350s could not have been achieved without exhibiting ruthlessness when necessary. As Booth observes wryly, John 'could [not] have been accused of being soft towards the prince's tenants' in Cheshire during the early 1350s.[54] Ruthlessness is also implied in John's handling of certain events in April 1351, when he sold 160 quarters of wheat and 300 quarters of malt to Edward III, which was collected in Ipswich and then shipped directly to supply the garrison at Calais.[55] The brief details of this transaction skate over the scale and difficulty of the task and, by extension, the harsh methods John must have employed in order to complete it. The harvest of 1350 had been very poor, hampered by a sustained period of cold, wet weather and the disruption to the labour force caused by the Black Death. In addition, grain was always least plentiful in the months immediately preceding the next harvest. Thus it is likely that the newly acquired garrison at Calais had run dangerously short of food in the spring of 1351, and Edward III turned urgently to a dependable fixer to stem the mounting crisis. John would not have had such large quantities of surplus grain readily available on his own estates, not least because his largest manors were concentrated on the heavy clays of north-east Suffolk, where malting barley was seldom grown.[56] Despite the shortages, John delivered. He could only have done so by drawing upon other East Anglian suppliers at a time of general scarcity, which required considerable initiative, and, most likely, a resort to requisitioning and compulsory purchase.

There are other glimpses of ruthlessness and sharp practice as John built up his own landed estate in the 1350s. For example, when in 1347 one John Charles was convicted of a felony and thrown into Norwich prison, his lands in north-west Suffolk – 80 acres of arable, 6 acres of pasture and 6 acres of woodland – were

[51] Green 2004, pp. 86–90.
[52] CPR 1358–61, p. 159; Green 2004, p. 93.
[53] RBP, pt III, p. 282; RBP, pt IV, pp. 132, 245.
[54] Booth 1981, p. 98.
[55] CPR 1350–54, p. 60.
[56] Bailey 2007, pp. 75–7.

temporarily granted to John through an act of royal favour until Charles had made his peace with the Crown. However, Charles died in Norwich prison in March 1349 without having done so, at which point the land should have reverted to his son, Thomas. Yet John proved reluctant to return the land, forcing Thomas to seek legal recourse in 1353 to try and recover it.[57] In 1351 John obtained another manor, that of Lee (Cheshire), but in April 1354 the Black Prince ordered that the manor be returned to its rightful heir, while simultaneously confirming 'a pardon granted to the said Sir John of all trespasses arising from past alienations of the said manor without licence of the prince'.[58] The brevity of this reference, and the absence of any further detail about the case, is frustrating, but it would appear that John had used his position of responsibility to profit personally from the deployment of the manor: a flagrant abuse of trust and power by modern standards, but, by medieval standards, merely an inappropriate perk of office.[59]

Estates and Income

Sir John de Wingfield also possessed a landed estate of his own, which he augmented during the course of his lifetime. Unfortunately, the exact extent, location and value of these lands are impossible to recover, and all we have are a few partial insights derived from snippets of evidence. There are no household accounts to reveal the level and sources of his personal wealth, and hardly any manorial records to illustrate how he managed his own estate. However, it is improbable that such an able and innovative manager of the Black Prince's estates did not exhibit the same shrewdness and canniness on his own.

The core of the estate was established by the early 1330s, located in north-east Suffolk and founded upon his own inheritance and that of Eleanor after their marriage. Its extent in 1335 is fortuitously revealed by John's acquisition of a licence for the right of free warren over each of his main manorial holdings at that time: Wingfield, Syleham, Earsham, Fressingfield, Sternfield, Weybread and Saxmundham.[60] Thereafter, John was active in developing and augmenting his estates. In 1347 he bought a second manor in Saxmundham, known as Murkets, and applied successfully for a fair to be added to the commercial franchises already there.[61] In the 1340s he obtained another two manors in Syleham, and a second manor in Sternfield to supplement the one which had been part of Eleanor's original inheritance.[62] The great mortality in 1348–9 and the associated failure of heirs also created some oppor-

---

[57] CIM 1348–77, p. 196.
[58] RBP, pt III, p. 155.
[59] RBP, pt III, pp. 54, 155.
[60] CChR, vol. IV, p. 342.
[61] Copinger 1905–11, vol. V, pp. 161–3; CPR, 1345–58, p. 530.
[62] Copinger 1905–11, vol. IV, p. 90, 93; Copinger 1905–11, vol. V, pp. 171–2.

tunities for a well-connected man to acquire either temporary control or permanent ownership of manors further afield. In 1349 he acquired the small manor of Caldwell hall in Hollesley (Suffolk), and the lease of the sizeable manor of Crondall (Hampshire); he obtained the leases of four manors in Cheshire; and in 1352 he obtained Snape Hall (Suffolk).[63] In 1357 he finally acquired the main manor in Wingfield for his family, and the next year obtained a lifetime interest for him and Eleanor in a second manor in Syleham and other lands in Norfolk.[64] In 1359 he bought the main manor in Stradbroke from another branch of the de Brewse family, and he also acquired Shelton Hall manor in Stradbroke around the same time.[65] Finally, he bought a house, known as 'Wingfield's Inn', somewhere in London.[66]

Thus the estate came to comprise seven main manors around Wingfield itself; a number of smaller manors, both in the vicinity and elsewhere in East Anglia; and half a dozen manors acquired either permanently or at lease scattered around Hampshire, Cheshire and the north. These represent the bare minimum of his properties, for there must have been others which extant sources do not record. We do not know the annual yield of these properties, because the evidence has simply not survived, although in 1388 six of the seven largest Suffolk manors in John's original estate were leased for £108 net.[67] We might estimate that the larger manors each generated around £20 (net) per annum, and the smaller manors anything from £5 to £10.[68] Thus in the late 1350s the landed estate would have generated comfortably in excess of £200 per annum. To this must be added the stipends from his work in the service of the Black Prince and other lords. John must have served the prince for at least a hundred days per annum at 10 s per day, and, with other stipends (such as from the Countess Warenne), he could have earned in excess of £100 per annum from this source.

There were other sources of income. At some stage, probably in the 1330s, Edward III had granted John the lease of the judicial profits of Blything and Wangford Hundreds in Suffolk. It was common practice in the fourteenth century for the king to grant the profits of such legal franchises to family and friends in return for an annual fee, although the practice was increasingly unpopular with ordinary people because of concerns about a decline in the quality of justice provided at these hundred courts. John held these particular privileges for the rest of his life, which, together with other similar but unrecorded perquisites, might well have generated £20 per

---

[63] Copinger 1905–11, vol. VII, p. 254; *VCH Hampshire*, vol. 4, p. 7; *RBP*, pt III, p. 363; Copinger 1905–11, vol. V, p. 169.

[64] Martin, this volume, pp. 21–22; Copinger's description of the early history of the two main manors in Wingfield is obscure and unreliable, Copinger 1905–11, vol. IV, pp. 108, 114–15. The Syleham reference is from *CCR 1354–60*, p. 510.

[65] Copinger 1905–11, vol. IV, pp. 85–6.

[66] In May 1358 John issued an order 'from his inn at London', *RBP*, pt IV, p. 249.

[67] Roskell 1984, p. 124.

[68] Bailey 2007, p. 32.

annum.[69] Certainly, his occupation of high public office would have presented many opportunities for personal profit, as his occupation of the manor of Lee demonstrates. On top of this regular income should be added windfalls from various sources. The greatest single windfall followed his capture of the Sire d'Aubigny during the battle of Poitiers in 1356, after which Edward III paid John £1,750 for the ransom rights.[70] John also received periodic 'gifts' from a grateful Black Prince, which were partly intended to recompense John for expenses incurred on royal business, but they also appear to have partly represented some form of bonus 'for his great labours': for example, he received £150 in 1355, and nearly £300 in 1359.[71]

The mixture of a few reliable figures and much informed guesswork is hardly ideal, but, in the absence of any extant household accounts, it represents the only method of estimating John's annual income in the 1350s. On the eve of his death, John's annual revenues easily exceeded £300, and, in some bumper years, may have reached as high as £600. This level of income was equivalent to that associated with the lower levels of the nobility at that time, so John was a very wealthy member of the knightly class.[72] The day-to-day running costs of his household had to be deducted from this income. Again, without John's household accounts we can never know how much he spent each year, but the sums were likely to be significant. Food, fuel, furnishings and horses were the major items of expenditure in every gentry house-hold, and, in addition, John had homes and domestic staff to maintain in London, Wingfield and probably elsewhere.[73] There were other large areas of cost: he was an intrepid traveller, his lifestyle had to be commensurate with his status as one of England's highest-ranking royal officials and he still had some active soldiering to fund. His running expenses were therefore high. Perhaps he made a surplus of up to £100 in most years.

The founding of Wingfield College

We can only guess at John's motivation for creating his college at Wingfield: he did not record his thoughts, and personal faith is difficult to capture. Our only clue is the documented provision for his death, which can be deployed as a window into his religious beliefs. His choice of a perpetual chantry was certainly conventional: as Christopher Harper-Bill observes, this 'became the common aspiration of men

---

[69] Ormrod 1990, p. 118. In the mid-1350s John fell behind in his payments to the Crown for this franchise, CPR 1354–58, p. 514.

[70] Cammidge 1943, p. 213; Keen 2003, p. 119.

[71] RBP, pt IV, pp. 162, 169, 318; also pp. 53, 90.

[72] The level of income expected to support a barony, the lowest tier of the nobility, was c.£600 per annum, Ormrod 1990, p. 58.

[73] These observations about the cost structure of households like John's are based upon Dyer 1989, pp. 55–75.

and women of wealth and status' in the fourteenth century.[74] By providing masses in perpetuity for the souls of the benefactor(s) and their immediate relatives, the institution of a chantry was both a powerful demonstration of piety and a means of speeding those souls through purgatory and into heaven. It is probable that the Black Death of 1348–9 served as a chilling reminder to John – no less than all survivors of the catastrophe – of the extent of divine anger, the unpredictability of death and the need to prepare for that death, all of which could be suitably addressed through the foundation of a chantry.

Another motive could well have been John's desire to express his gratitude for the divine favour behind his extraordinarily successful military and administrative career. After all, was it not God's will that John had succeeded so gloriously in his military adventures, and in the service of the Black Prince? In which case, it would be entirely appropriate to glorify God through a splendid chantry. The foundation charter of the college states that 'John, whilst he lived, pondered deeply and meditated upon the truth' that 'God recompenses with fitting reward the merits of those who increase the resources of His house':[75] this had been 'true' for John's relationship with the Black Prince, so why not for God Himself? The fact that this pious act also served to commemorate John's life, and to perpetuate his memory, must have been a further attraction. If so, then the choice of Wingfield for the location of the college was both apt and carefully considered. In this way, the college served to perpetuate the name of the Wingfield family in his home village in the absence of any male heir. By allocating the main manor of Wingfield to the endowment of the college, and by locating the college on the site of the main manor house and right next to the parish church, John was cannily ensuring that, in future, no other family could colonise either and thus diminish *his* memorial.

Most fourteenth-century chantries were founded in the aisles or side chapels of existing churches, principally because it was much less expensive than constructing new accommodation to house them: endowing a perpetual institution to generate sufficient annual income to maintain an altar and to pay the wages of priests was expensive, but it was still cheaper than founding a perpetual institution *and* constructing a new chantry chapel.[76] John's provision was therefore grander than most, because he had to fund the construction of a new collegiate building with domestic ranges and outhouses, together with an appropriate collegiate church in which to house the chantry, and he also had to provide an endowment generous enough to maintain those buildings, and sustain the college brethren, in perpetuity. Nor was the provision of such large financial resources sufficient in itself, because after the 1290s a royal licence had to be obtained for permission to divert land into ecclesiastical foundations. The king's permission could not be taken for granted,

[74] Harper-Bill 1996, p. 111.
[75] Aldwell 1925, p. 102.
[76] Harper-Bill 1996, pp. 111–13.

although, in John's case, it is likely that Edward III would view an application from such a loyal and devoted royal servant approvingly.

In 1357 John and Eleanor acquired the main manor in Wingfield, which was to be the site of the new college. In 1358 John obtained a licence from Edward III to assign in mortmain land and rents to the value of £30 per annum, and advowsons to the taxable value of £100 yearly, to establish a chantry.[77] By this date he had acquired sufficient lands to create a solid endowment for his college *and* to ensure a lucrative dowry for his daughter. He endowed the college with land in Wingfield, Earsham, Fressingfield and Weybread, together with rectorial income from the parish churches of Wingfield, Stradbroke and Syleham, and the chapel of Earsham. It is certain that the de la Poles added to the endowment subsequently, enabling the college to expand to the nine chaplains and three choristers envisaged in John's will, and also enlarging the chancel of the church.[78] It seems unlikely that he was able to conceive of such an expensive memorial until the mid 1350s. The windfall ransom from Poitiers in 1356 might well have made the difference.

From 1358 the foundation of Wingfield College was as inevitable as John's mortality. We cannot know when construction work first began, but there is no reason why it should not have commenced immediately. Indeed, it seems highly doubtful that such an assiduous, energetic and determined administrator would have taken no active role before his death in the detailed planning of his grand commemorative project. We know that in May 1359 the busy and itinerant John attended to business in Beccles, and, by extension, he must have spent some time at Wingfield.[79] It is tempting to speculate that he used this opportunity to oversee his plans for the college, and possibly view some of the early construction work.

The main priority was the work on the church. The existing parish church of Wingfield was to be adapted to serve as the collegiate church, and the second-ranked chaplain of the college was also required to serve as the parish priest, which strengthened the link between the parochial and collegiate functions of Wingfield Church.[80] In fact, the parish church was rebuilt anew. The foundation charter of the college states that 'in order to make it more suitable for such a college [the church] must in great part be built anew … on a larger scale than before … at a very great expense'.[81] Modern opinion of the architecture of the existing church confirms that this stated intention was indeed converted into action: 'the architectural details of the nave, the nave aisles … the tower and the chancel arch would all be consistent with the 1360s, and their regularity of layout suggests that they were executed as part of a

---

[77] CPR 1358–61, p. 112.
[78] Aldwell 1925, pp. 37, 81.
[79] CIM 1348–1377, p. 116. John was also at Wingfield around Christmas 1357, RBP, pt IV, p. 234.
[80] Aldwell 1925, pp. 102–3.
[81] Ibid., p. 103.

single plan'.[82] Furthermore, the foundation charter of 1362 confirms that the family 'have had, and propose to have' (my italics) the church reconstructed, which provides the clearest possible hint that John started and directed the initial works.[83] Many building projects across England ceased in the 1350s in the aftermath of the Black Death, with the result that the wage rates paid to master builders were sticky during that decade: it would have been characteristic of John to recognise the advantage of pushing ahead with his programme while the costs of hiring masons were relatively favourable.[84] Work on the domestic buildings for the college was less urgent, as the priests could initially be accommodated in the existing de Brewse manor house. In the early 1360s a two-storey cross-wing was added to the western end of the original hall, probably to provide separate lodgings for the master: the ground floor was built with bricks from the de la Poles' brickworks in Hull. The main work on the college buildings followed in the 1380s.[85]

The considerable construction costs of the church and the collegiate buildings had to be funded in hard cash, and mainly separate from the endowment. If work began on the church in the late 1350s, and the domestic range was finished in the 1380s, then the requirements for cash were spread over a manageable period of time. It is impossible to know the total construction cost of the whole project, because no building accounts have survived. From other late medieval construction projects, we know that it cost £6,000 to build the castle and college at Tattershall, £113 to rebuild the body of Catterick (Yorkshire) Church, £75 to extend the chancel and Lady Chapel of Wingfield Church and £13 to erect a large timber framed house in Bury St Edmunds.[86] On the basis of these crude comparators, John's outlay must have run into several hundreds of pounds.

Wingfield College was thus established with three chaplains, one of whom was the master, with the prospect of increasing its size to nine chaplains and three choristers as and when an enhanced endowment could support it. They were to pray for the souls of John, 'his parents, kinsfolk, benefactors and all those for whom he, or his parents and progenitors, were in any way bound'.[87] The college was dedicated to the Holy Trinity. The cult of the Trinity dates back to the twelfth century, although it was not established as a general festival within the Church calendar until 1333. It then grew in popularity rapidly, largely due to the Black Prince's example and to his devotion to the Trinity, whose powers of intercession were held to have contributed to the

---

[82] Goodall 2001, p. 56. Aldwell's argument that the nave and aisles were the later work of the de la Poles is now discredited, Aldwell 1925, p. 37: they extended the chancel and perhaps remodelled the northern aisle.
[83] Aldwell 1925, p. 103.
[84] Munro 2012, p. 317.
[85] Aitkens et al. 1999, pp. 392–4.
[86] Dyer 1989, pp. 80–1; Aitkens et al. 1999, pp. 395–6; Dymond 1998, pp. 276–7.
[87] Aldwell 1925, pp. 102–3.

victory at Poitiers in 1356.[88] 'Many examples can be found of [his] retinue members founding institutions and giving patronage to those with links to the Trinity.'[89] Even in death, Sir John de Wingfield remained loyal to the life and influence of Edward of Woodstock.

Conclusion

One of life's perennial ironies is that a catastrophe affecting many people creates new and lucrative opportunities for some. It is especially ironic that the greatest recorded catastrophe in human history, the Black Death of 1348–9, created the opening for Sir John de Wingfield to make his fortune in the 1350s, but then the wheel of fortune turned again and, when the disease returned in 1361, it took his life. As the veteran of the two most significant English battles of the fourteenth century, and two prominent sieges, John must have been a formidable fighting machine of great courage and skill: even as an aging man, he purportedly 'did grievous execution' at Poitiers.[90] In addition, his personal demeanour and keen intelligence were impressive enough for some of the highest-ranking nobility of the age, including the king himself, to seek his counsel and expertise. He was therefore able to reinvent himself in his twilight years as a brilliant organiser of royal business affairs at a time of immense economic upheaval and uncertainty. He grasped the reality of the post-Black Death world with alacrity and shrewd understanding. As a consequence, he contributed nobly and materially to the stunning military successes, and to the reputation, of his lord, the Black Prince.

As a consequence of his varied and successful career, John acquired the considerable wealth necessary to finance the foundation of Wingfield College. A chantry was a conventional outlet for piety, although the nature and scale of his collegiate chantry was exceptional. In his career, and through his charity, John attracted attention and admiration, then and now. He was unquestionably a man who achieved great things: perhaps he was even a great man. Yet the towering scale of his achievements in the most testing of conditions, whether on the battlefield or in business, must also reveal something else about his character. Successful enforcers draw variously upon reserves of determination, single-mindedness of purpose, loyal – probably fanatical – devotion, and ruthlessness. One suspects that Sir John evoked respect but also, for those under him, fear in equal measures. He was astute and pragmatic enough to maintain the accommodating yet rewarding policies initiated before his appointment on the Duchy of Cornwall, but the cash-squeezing policies he initiated in Cheshire and (almost certainly) North Wales caused much resentment. Sir

---

[88] Barber 1979, pp. 240–1.
[89] Green 2001, p. 121.
[90] Cammidge 1943, p. 199.

John probably contended that the fulfilment of his master's goals justified whatever means, even though his means of getting things done involved conduct which caused severe hardship to others. Wingfield College is an impressive and lasting memorial to one of Suffolk's brightest boys made good. It might also have been a memorial that helped, just a little, to ease his conscience about the conduct necessary to become so conspicuously good.

3

Wingfield College and the Late Medieval Cult of Purgatory

Eamon Duffy

Wingfield College was the product of an age of crisis: the foundation of Wingfield in 1362 is poised between the Black Death and the Peasants' Revolt. Between the summer of 1348 and Christmas 1349, the Black Death wiped out about half the population of England and probably more than half the clergy. A generation on, the Peasants' Revolt of 1381 had its own bloody East Anglian climax in the battle of North Walsham, when the local bishop, Henry Despenser, famously led his own troops in the slaughter of the rebellious peasantry of his diocese. Hence it would be perfectly plausible to conclude that the later fourteenth century in England in general, and in East Anglia in particular, was very much an age of anxiety. It used to be thought obvious that an event as devastating as the Black Death must have caused profound cultural upheavals and transformations – Millard Meiss's famous and influential 1951 study, *Painting in Florence and Siena after the Black Death*, for instance, argued that the plague had caused a profound shift and darkening of the themes and iconography of Italian painting in the later fourteenth century. According to the French religious historian Jean Delumeau 'No civilization had ever attached so much importance to guilt and shame as did the Western world from the thirteenth to the eighteenth centuries.'[1] Delumeau thought that most late medieval people's minds were preoccupied with the fear of sin and its consequences, and he saw the Church as pursuing 'an Evangelism of Fear', which reinforced panic and pessimism about the human condition, a 'vast enterprise of guiltification' which originated in medieval monasteries and spread to the laity through theological writings, sermons, devotional literature, confessors' handbooks and iconography.[2] Delumeau believed that one reason for all this was the pessimism provoked by the disasters like the Black Death.

In this chapter I want to consider the religious context of the foundation of institutions like Wingfield and to ask whether or not we should think of Wingfield

[1] Delumeau 1990, p. 3.
[2] Ibid., p. 495.

and its glorious church rather differently, as a monument not to established power and status but an institution born out of the uncertainty and fear which Delumeau thought characterised late medieval culture.

Readers might certainly be forgiven for seeing fear as one of the major motives for the creation of Wingfield, because of course death lay at the bottom of it all: this was a perpetual chantry foundation, and the main business of the nine priests and their master or provost provided for in the foundation charter was to say and sing prayers for the dead in the church which the Wingfields and then the de la Poles rebuilt, as a suitably glorious setting for the celebration of elaborate commemorative liturgies: architecture, glass and wall painting, carving and music, not to mention the services of educated clergy and musically talented boys, were all directed here to the service of the dead. The urban historian Clive Burgess has described late medieval parish churches as ante-rooms of purgatory because so many of them were built and furnished and staffed with money given so that the donors might avoid or at any rate shorten the torments they believed awaited all but the very holy after death before they could be admitted to the presence of God. And that of course was doubly true of a church like the one at Wingfield, which was rebuilt, staffed and furnished specifically as a chantry, a building devoted to the liturgy of the dead, and a very lavish and expensive witness to the late medieval aristocratic belief in the reality of purgatory.

So how far should we think of Wingfield as haunted by death, and the fear of what might come after death?

Chantry colleges were one of the more elaborate forms of perpetual chantry, and the fourteenth century in East Anglia was the great age for the foundation of perpetual chantries – we know of 130 of them founded between 1300 and 1399, compared with just thirteen in the thirteenth century, and eighty-one in the fifteenth century. Historians used to link this fourteenth-century surge in the provision of permanent institutions to pray for the dead to the traumatic effect of the Black Death. In theory this seems plausible enough, as it is hardly unreasonable to suppose that an epidemic that wiped out half the population in a matter of months would leave a permanent scar on the national psyche, as the famine did in nineteenth-century Ireland, and would focus people's thoughts on the reality of death and give added urgency to beliefs about the afterlife. But that does not seem to be the case. In Suffolk as elsewhere in England, there was as much or slightly more provision for the dead in the fifty years before the Black Death as in the fifty years after it, and there was in fact a steep decline in the creation of permanent chantry institutions in the first half of the fifteenth century, exactly the opposite of what might be expected if the Black Death really had traumatised people and left a heightened fear of death and what came after death. Permanent chantry provision begins to climb again in the second half of the fifteenth century, but so did every other kind of religious expenditure. There was more money about, and people were taking a more active interest in religion, and hence it would appear that intercession for the dead was just one of the many ways in which fifteenth-century people chose to display their piety and their prosperity: lay people were into devotional retail therapy in a big way in the later fifteenth century.

So, counter-intuitively, in terms of chantry provision, the Black Death does not seem to have been any kind of landmark. More than half of the 130 fourteenth-century perpetual chantry foundations in the Norwich diocese were created before 1350, and the foundation of chantry colleges in particular was well under way even before the plague arrived in England. On a superficial level, the establishment of Wingfield in 1362 might look like a reaction to the great mortality, but it takes its place in a sequence of East Anglian foundations which straddles the arrival of the Black Death –Rushworth College near Thetford in 1342, Campsey Ash in 1346, Thompson College and Raveningham College in 1349 and 1350, then Wingfield in 1362. The sequence would continue with the establishment of St Gregory's College at Sudbury in 1375, and the relocation of Raveningham College to Mettingham in the early 1390s, and then on into the fifteenth century with the establishment of Mortimer College at Stoke by Clare in 1415 – and there is a broadly similar pattern in the creation of colleges with chantry obligations at Cambridge, where the fourteenth-century sequence begins with Michaelhouse in 1324, Clare in 1326, Pembroke in 1347, Gonville Hall in 1348 and Trinity Hall in 1350.

Chantry colleges were a lavish way of providing the kind of mortuary liturgy once available only in monasteries. The Black Death may not have traumatised the national psyche, but it had shown people that an isolated chantry foundation – typically a single priest serving a side altar or chapel in a parish church – was very vulnerable to acts of God, and specifically to large-scale mortality. A lot of single-priest chantry foundations must have disappeared without trace as both their incumbents and the current generation of the families paying for them perished in the plague. Thus after 1350 many of the new chantry foundations were placed by their founders in local monasteries rather than parish churches to improve their chances of survival in any future epidemic, and clergy were supplied to serve them (though even monastic chantries were more often than not staffed by secular priests). The staffing of chantry colleges in fact deliberately replicated the resources and in theory at least the religious and moral standards of a small monastery – Wingfield was to have up to nine priests living under the surveillance of a master, plus at least three choral scholars, presumably with a pool of other singers available from the other boys who were to be educated here. Music was central to Wingfield, as it was in all these colleges. These intentions were of course not always realised: the college at the priory at Campsea Ash established by the Ufford family in 1346 was moved to Bruisyard after ten years because it was felt it interfered with the nuns' choir. Eight years after that its patron, Lionel duke of Clarence, suppressed it altogether, because the priests were misbehaving themselves, living dissolute lives and neglecting their duties. He instead diverted the resources to founding a house of Poor Clares, women being more reliable in the morals department even if they could not celebrate mass.

The statutes of Mortimer College at Stoke are fairly representative of the staffing and regime such establishments provided.

There were to be eight vicars-choral and two senior clerks sworn to continual residence, and instructed in plain song and part-song (*in plano cantu et discantu*); five choristers of good life to help in singing and to serve in quire; clergy or choristers absent from matins, mass or evensong were fined. There were to be, in addition, two under-clerks to act as keepers of the vestments, bellringers, lamp-trimmers, doorkeepers, clock-winders and so on. The matins bell was to be rung at five, high mass to be finished at 11 a.m. and evensong at 5 p.m. The mass of Our Lady was to be sung daily as well as the mass of the day, except when the mass of the day was of the Blessed Virgin, and then the second mass was to be of requiem. Matins and evensong were to be sung daily immediately after the ringing of the bell, save in Lent when evensong of Our Lady was to follow evensong of the day. The dress of the canons and vicars was regulated, and there was to be a schoolmaster to teach the boys reading, plain song and polyphony.

Every evening at eight the curfew bell was to be rung for a sufficient time to admit of walking from the church to the college, and when the bell finished every outer door was to be fastened, and no-one of the household of the college, from canon to chorister, was to be outside the house. None of the personnel was to frequent taverns, and they were not to hunt; nor were greyhounds or any kind of hunting dogs to be kept within the college, save by the dean, whose dogs were not to exceed four. No canon or minister of the college was to carry arms of any kind within the college. As I have said, there was an elaborate musical regime at all these foundations, so the Wingfield organ is probably a typical part of musical provision in colleges: there are references to the singing of elaborate polyphony at both Rushworth and Mortimer Colleges, and Mettingham not only had polyphonic music at its liturgy but the canons also copied and sold musical manuscripts, and bought themselves an organ in 1414.

This liturgy was paid for and intended to benefit the founders and the founder's kin, but it was of course also an amenity for the parish within which it was located. Chantry colleges offered a range of additional benefits and amenities to the communities in which they were established, and these cumulatively constituted the incentive to allow a parish church to be high-jacked by a private patron, as Wingfield was. The parishioners gained from enhanced architecture, more elaborate and better-celebrated liturgy, from the charitable provisions and doles which were part of the intercessory regimes in the colleges, from the guarantee of competent pastoral provision which a clerical community could offer, and from the schools and expert preaching and catechesis the colleges provided.

And it was the guarantee of a supply of well-qualified clergy which Bishop Percy of Norwich emphasised when he granted the licence for the establishment of the college at Wingfield – too many parishes, he said, were in the hands of ignorant and mercenary curates, 'hirelings rather than shepherds', and hence God would greatly reward anyone who 'so increases the resources of his House that the necessities of Christ's family may be better provided for, and their numbers augmented', and therefore, considering 'that in this place the number of minsters of God's worship will be increased' by the college, the bishop granted permission to turn the parish church into a collegiate foundation, with the sacrist of the college as *ex officio* parish priest.

Still, the declared purpose of a chantry college was intercession for the souls of the dead. Medieval Catholics believed that most ordinary Christians might be saved, but that few would die in a sufficient state of sanctity to be admitted at once to the beatific vision. All would have to undergo a process of painful purgation. Medieval people imagined purgatory in a variety of ways, with purgatory variously conceived as punishment or as therapy. In the most famous of all medieval evocations of purgatory in Dante's *Commedia*, therapy is emphatically the central theme – purgatory is a mountain rising by terraces towards paradise: it is guarded by angels and no demons can enter it, and the souls who suffer there are eager participants in their own cleansing. The souls to whom Dante talks often end the conversation by saying they must return to their sufferings because by means of them they are on their way to God; thus Dante's purgatory is a place of hope and renewal, its theme colour is green. But that by and large was not how medieval English people imagined it. In almost all the English literature on purgatory, it is portrayed as a torture-house, a dungeon of ice or fire, or a kind of infernal concentration camp where the guards and torturers are gleeful demons, let loose to do whatever they please to the suffering souls. A fair example here is the early fifteenth-century vision attributed to an anonymous holy woman, which she is supposed to have had on 10 August 1422 and the days immediately following. As in all purgatory visions, the woman talked with one of the suffering souls in purgatory, a former nun named Margaret. In this vision, purgatory was a pit filled with three great fires, one leading out of the other, the central fire 'so horrible and stynkande that all the creatures in the world might never tell the wicked smellynge thereof: for there was pykke and tarre, ledde and brymstone and oyle and alle manere of thynge that myghte brynne, and alle manere of paynes that mane couthe thynke, and alle manere of crystene mene and womene that hath lefed here in this werlde of what degree thay were'. Those in the horrible fire 'had so grete paynes that for drede I might not describe them', but they included having their hearts and bowels torn out by demons and raked with sharp irons, or being nailed up in barrels full of poisonous snakes: the nun Margaret was covered with bleeding wounds, and out of the wounds poured fire, and when the visionary first encounters her, the suffering soul of Margaret herself seems like a malevolent demon, and the visionary reports that 'me thought sche wolde have casten fyre upon me, and styrte to me to hafe slayen me'. Margaret cries out to the visionary 'Cursed mote thou be and wo worth thee bot if thou haste thee to be my helpe'. In the end, it turns out that the point of the vision is to reveal an elaborate regime of masses and prayers absolutely guaranteed to release a soul from even the deepest torments of purgatory – this regime included a hundred masses of the Trinity, a hundred of

Our Lady, fifty of St Peter and fifty of requiem, together with three hundred recitations of the *Miserere mei Deus* psalm, and the *Veni Creator Spiritus* hymn. If these prayers and masses are procured for a soul in purgatory 'what manere of synne that he had done in his life, there shall no manner of pain in purgatory hold him that ne hastily he shall be delivered frae thayme, and many other saules be delivered for his sake'. But for those who cannot afford such lavish provision, the same result will be achieved by thirteen masses, three of the Trinity, two of St Peter, two of the Holy Ghost, three of Our Lady and three of All Saints.

Texts like the Revelation indicate a widespread belief that certain kinds of sustained devotional regimes – particular sequences of masses, particular numbers or kinds of prayers – were especially effective in getting souls out of purgatory, and the visions often provide expert guidance, as it were from the horse's mouth, because they were provided by a purgatory soul. They also present a ferocious and terrifying picture of the fate which awaited, in the words of the Revelation, 'alle manere of crystene mene and womene that hath lefed here in this werlde of what degree thay were'.

Hence it would be surprising if late medieval men and women had not taken the prospect of purgatory seriously. It was a preacher's commonplace that the agonies of purgatory were so intense that a few minutes there felt like years to those enduring them. In *The Stripping of the Altars*, I collected extracts from wills from all over England which suggested that some late medieval people were deeply affected by this kind of visionary horror, and so wanted intercession and good works done on their behalf to begin at the very moment of their death or even sooner to minimise the torment they would have to suffer once they entered the other world. People making wills might ask for diriges, masses and doles to begin 'as hastily as possible after my departing from this world', or 'as soon as I am dead without any tarrying', or at the earliest moment 'as by mon erthly it may be perceived that my soule shuld be from my body separate', or 'when ye see me in the panges if death'. One Bedfordshire gentleman even asked for two friars to begin saying trentals or sets of thirty masses for him 'if tyme and season may be, when I lye in the article and point of death labouring towards the everlasting lyfe'.[3]

On the face of it, these sorts of requests lend some support to Delumeau's idea that the religion of fourteenth- and fifteenth-century men and women was driven by fear, and might seem to suggest that we should see a foundation like Wingfield as a reflection of a panic-stricken Christianity, a worldview blighted by savage imaginings and terror of what awaited every soul after death. Although I do not hold this view, I thought it would be interesting to test it statistically, and two substantial volumes of fifteenth-century wills edited for the Suffolk Record Society by the late Peter Northeast seemed to offer a way of doing just that.[4] Northeast edited 2,342 wills from the archdeaconry of Sudbury proved between 1439 and 1474. Every single one

3 Duffy 1992, p. 346.
4 Northeast 2001; Northeast and Falvey 2010.

of them makes some kind of provision for post-mortem intercession, and some of that provision is very elaborate indeed, with some testators commissioning hundreds of masses from all the houses of friars in the region, sending pilgrims near and far to famous and not so famous shrines – Walsingham and Woolpit, Canterbury and Bury St Edmunds, Rome and Compostella – securing indulgences and arranging for doles to the poor and for elaborate funeral display. The wills demonstrate unequivocally the universal acceptance of belief in purgatory and the attitudes towards death and the afterlife which make the huge outlay involved in an institution like Wingfield intelligible. Indeed, it is only in the context of that kind of universally accepted belief in the value of intercession that the vast proportion of family resources involved in creating and maintaining a college of priests and singing boys can be seen as a sensible investment.

But I wanted to use the wills specifically to explore whether or not the men and women of fifteenth-century Suffolk seemed driven by *fear* in making these elaborate arrangements. What indications were there in these intimate death-bed documents that belief in purgatory really was a source of anxiety or panic, or that might suggest that the driving force behind all these elaborate funeral and post-mortem arrangements, and so behind Wingfield, might be naked fear?

And sure enough, one can find in some of the wills definite hints that the prospect of purgatory was viewed in at least some cases with something approaching panic. Several dozen of these fifteenth-century Suffolk testators specifically emphasised the need for hurry in providing the masses, prayers and works of charity which would speed them out of the pains of purgatory. As I have already mentioned, all the wills make provision for intercession and good works in some form or other, but many add clauses indicating the need to set the intercessory systems up within weeks or days or even hours of the testator's death. Hence there are many wills asking that the masses begin 'with all possible haste', 'as soon as possible after my death', 'in greatest haste'. Some wills show their makers trying to secure concentrated intercessory regimes which would blast them out of purgatory on a tidal wave of prayer and good works, like the Lavenham testator who provided for four hundred masses 'in the week of my death', or the Mildenhall testator who asked for one hundred masses as soon as possible, if possible all on one and the same day, or the testator from Fornham All Saints, who left 4 d apiece to one hundred chaplains stipulating they should all say mass for him on the same day, 'as soon after my decease as they can be provided', or the more modest Wattisham bequest for thirty masses to be said if possible within seven days, or the Sudbury request for a trental 'on one and the same day if possible'. The degree of organisation required to honour the more elaborate of such requests must have been considerable, and one suspects that many were never fully achieved: so, a good many testators left more realistic bequests for 10 s or more to go to the local houses of friars for funeral prayers and masses, where the concentration of clergy meant there was a better chance of the reasonably speedy fulfilment of requests for multiple masses and diriges.

Yet when one adds together all the wills containing such signs of anxiety about the speed of provision of post-mortem intercession, they are a drop in a bucket. The total number of wills with some hint of haste comes to forty-three out of more than 2,300 wills, or just under 2 per cent of testators. The vast majority of wills leave the timing of the masses and other good works they requested to their executors and families, and many clearly envisaged a regime of intercession which stretched out over time. Many specify the distribution of the masses over a year or even longer, like the testator at Badwell Ash who requested the Dominicans at Thetford to celebrate a trental of masses 'at appropriate feasts, for a year' or the Cambridgeshire testator who left £5 for a trental to be celebrated by a scholar of Cambridge University who would ride over to the testator's home village of Fordham at the major feasts 'that is, the Nativity of our Lord, Easter, Pentecost and such like, to celebrate the masses in the parish church there'. Some testators even delayed the establishment of chantry services or charitable activities until their widow had died and had no further need of their money or property, which might then be used for good works 'for the health of our souls'. For such testators, the religious symbolism of appropriate masses celebrated on the major feasts, in the Fordham case with the added enhancement of securing a learned and dignified priest-scholar from the university, mattered more than any urgency about hastening the soul out of its sufferings in the shortest possible time.

The most elaborate Suffolk example of opulent post-mortem religious provision was the remarkable will of John Baret, an immensely successful Bury St Edmunds cloth merchant who was also a gentleman of the chamber to the abbot of Bury, and who established a lavish chantry in the Lady Chapel of St Mary's Church in Bury. Baret's chantry employed only a single priest, but architecturally it was on a scale which rivalled all but the most sumptuous perpetual foundations in the county. Baret's will, made in 1463, runs to thirty closely printed pages in the nineteenth-century edition which made it famous, and its almost obsessively detailed provisions have struck many modern readers as morbid, an impression strengthened by Baret's famously macabre grave effigy. The tomb, which he commissioned and installed in the Lady Chapel in the south aisle of St Mary's years before his death, portrays Baret himself as a rotting corpse, clutching at his shroud, the stretched skin on his grinning skull caught in the rictus of death, and the body hedged around with inscriptions pleading for prayers. Baret bought both papal and local episcopal indulgences to induce onlookers at the tomb to pray for him, and wanted these prominently placed in wooden display cases above the burial site, together with an English devotional ballad which he had commissioned, presumably like the purgatory poem by Lydgate painted on the roof of the Clopton Chapel at Long Melford. Baret called for the reconstruction and elaboration of the Lady Chapel in St Mary's around his burial place, with a new reredos on the theme of the *Magnificat*, which perhaps means that it portrayed the Annunciation, mirrors set in the ceiling above the tomb, and a new image of the Virgin commissioned from Robert Pyot, with elaborate candle-holders before it. He also paid for mechanical chimes in the steeple and in the Lady Chapel which were to play the tune of requiem *aeternam* at the elevation at both the Jesus and Lady Masses as well as at the requiems celebrated for Baret himself, and to be rung also after the singing of the *salve* at Compline on feast-days and Sundays. Baret also made careful provision for the manning and maintenance in perpetuity of the clock and chimes which were to be played in his memory. He additionally envisaged enlarging the Lady Chapel with a south aisle, and left money to lower the floor and raise the entrance arch to his chapel to encourage the parishioners to process through it with the parish cross and banners on Sundays. The funeral itself was to be spectacular – five poor men vested in black in memory of the wounds of Jesus, and five poor women clad in white for the joys of Mary were to carry torches around his hearse, the requiem masses were to be sung with both plainsong and polyphony, and there were special payments to the clergy, lay-clerks and singing boys in surplices who attended. There was to be a dinner on the day of the funeral for the aldermen, burgesses, gentlemen 'and other folks of worship', and doles to the local deserving poor and to the prisoners in Bury gaol. In the longer term, part of his spinning house was to be converted into a flat for his chantry priest to live in, and those priests were to call in perpetuity for prayers for Baret's repose whenever they were invited to say grace at public dinners in the town. His fellow servants in the abbot's household were all to receive silk and golden purses, and the senior monks of the abbey were given costly sets of rosary-beads.

This meticulous attention to every last detail of his own funeral and post-mortem commemoration, stretching years into the future and involving a vast network of religious, business, social and kinship networks all harnessed to intercession for Baret's soul might well be thought to be the direct result of a religion dominated by fear of punishment and a frantic desire to pre-empt or shorten that suffering. But that is not how Baret's will strikes one on an attentive reading. Here is an immensely rich man, a social arriviste buoyed up by new money made in trade, who has no children of his own, and so whose goods and business and memory will have to be carried by his brother William and his nieces and nephews, and by the various corporations and social and religious groups to which he belonged. Baret was undoubtedly a deeply devout man (though his will contained revealing provisions to compensate at least one business acquaintance whom he had diddled out of a substantial sum of silver), but equally clearly, his fantastically elaborate religious provisions represent a kind of displaced dynastic aspiration, a desire to perpetuate his memory and his influence through a kind of extended family. His centre of operations was one of the great ecclesiastical corporations of late medieval England: personal service in the household of the abbot of Bury was the means by which Baret and his wealth gained entree to aristocratic circles and lifestyle, and it is striking that there is more social than religious anxiety in all his insistence that his emblems and motto (he does not seem to have had a coat of arms) should be emblazoned in his chapel and on the vestments of the priests who celebrated services there in his memory. His lavish commemorative gifts to the abbot's household, to the more notable monks, to the parish, and his erection of a processional cross with a wooden shelter around it before his house for use during rogation processions and so on all suggest a man determined to make and leave his mark on the community in which he had made good.

I would argue that the same is true of the late medieval preparation for death and the afterlife in general. Fourteenth- and fifteenth-century English people had distinctive and daunting beliefs about the afterlife. They thought God was both merciful and just, and they thought that the consequences of sin must be met before they could enter into God's bliss. But they viewed that formidable prospect as another of the facts of life: they provided for it, but only those prone to panic about everything seem to have panicked about this. For the most part, post-mortem provision was a way of extending the network of friendship and obligation which constituted the community of the living: intercession for the dead was less like fire insurance than the extension of the obligations of friendship and family and neighbourhood into the dark world of the dead – purgatory provision helped domesticate death; it did not make it more terrible. A chantry like Wingfield was about many things besides remembrance of the souls of the faithful departed: it was important and worth spending lavishly on because it was also an expression of power, of wealth, of conspicuous consumption and lavish display – it continued de la Pole patronage of the local community into the world beyond.

Above all, perhaps, a chantry was about lineage and family. The English aristocracy of the late Middle Ages, like aristocracy everywhere, were obsessed with pedigree and kin. Prayers for the dead catered for that concern as well, for a perpetual chantry was designed to ensure the permanent commemoration of the ancestors. To put it like that, though, is maybe to empty the doctrine of purgatory of its most attractive feature – its projection of the bond of charity and the obligation of care for friends and kin even beyond the grave. Prayer for the dead was the measure and last proof of our love for them. In the last of all last medieval English evocations of revelations from the souls in purgatory, Thomas More's *Supplication of Souls*, published in 1529, this is the dimension of purgatory most insisted upon. The dead depend upon us, the living, for relief and comfort: they are the beggars at our door, the Lazarus of the Gospel story on whom we must take pity if we in our turn hope for the pity of God beyond the grave. The first and sharpest pain of purgatory, according to More, was the shame of meeting the loved ones for whom we had neglected or forgotten to pray, and according to More it is not fear, but the pathos of the dead and the demands of charity which the doctrine of purgatory embodies. Let us leave the last word to More's souls in purgatory, beseeching us, their friends, for our prayers.

In most pytouse wyse continually calleth and cryeth upon your devoute charite and most tender pyte / for helpe cumfurt and relefe / your late aqauyntaunce / kinred / spouses / companions / play felowes / & frendes / & now your humble and unacquainted and halfe forgotten supplyauntes / pore prisoners of god ye sely soules in purgatory / here abydyng and enduring the grevouse paynys and hote clensyng fyre / that freteth and burneth oute the rustye and filthy spottes of oure synne / tylle the mercy of almighty god the rather by your gode and cherytable meanes / vowchesaufe to delyver us hense.

4

The Foundation and Surrender of Wingfield College

The Texts of the Original Foundation Charter of 1362 and the Surrender Document of 1542, with Explanatory Notes

The Foundation Charter of Wingfield College

Norwich Record Office DN/REG2 Book 5: Diocese of
Norwich Institutions Book 5 (Percy, 1355–69), fol. 88

Universis sancte matris ecclesie filiis presentes literas inspecturis Thomas permissione divina Norwycensis Episcopus Salutem in omnium Salvatore. Majestatis divine celsitudo inscrutabilis illorum merita condigno premio recompensat qui domus dominice sic facultates amplificant ut in ea christo famulautium necessitatibus provideatur uberius etipsorum numerus augeatur. Sane petitio dilectorum Domine Alianore relicte Domini Johannis de Wynfeld, militis fefuncti et Thome de Wyngefeld fratris dicti defuncti executorum testamenti ejusdem nobis exhibita continebat quod prefatus dominus Johannes dum vicit premissa sedula meditatione propensius animavertens optansque cultores dini officii ampliare, laudem et honorem summe et individue trinitatis, glorioseque virginis marie necnon sanctorum Johannis Baptiste et Evalgeliste et beati Andree Apostoli inter ceteros victissimi et omnium sanctorum pro statu suo salubri ac parentum propinquorum benefactorum et onmium illorum quibus ipse seu parentes et progenitores sui quovismodo tenebantur, civitorumque [sic] fidelium animarum salute unum collegium certorum capellanorum secularium in ecclesia parochiali de Wyngefeld predicta nostre diocesis cuius dum vixerat patronus extiterat domino perpetuo famulari debentium dotemque pro collegio huiusmodi et ipsius oneribus supportandis ordinare proposuit set quia non secuto effectu invadens mors pestifera sundem sustulit ab humanis, idem executores ipsius domini Johannis tam pium in Domino propositum considerantes et id exequi summo desiderio cupientes, nobis humiliter supplicarunt ut in ecclesia existere dinoscitur unum colegium trium capellanorum secularium quorum unus sit nominatus magister sive prepositus qui nostro nomine personas collegii huiusmodi corrigere et cetera ad hoc spectantia dum necesse fuerit valeat reformare ita quod beneficium huiusmodi cum alio beneficio crate seu dignitate quacumque compassibilis existat ad presentationem dicte Domine Alianore dum vixerit et post ejus obitum , dominorum seu domini manerij quondam Domini Johannis de Wyngfeld predicti et alius sacrista dicta collegii qui curam parochianorum gerere debebit ad presentationem dict magistri sive prepositi per nos et successores nostros instituendus et omissa juris solempnitate proficiendus in eadem [sic]. Ac tertius capellanus per prefatum prepositum sive magistrum qui erit pro tempore in collegio huiusmodi deputandus ordinare et eam in Collegiatam ecclesiam secularem erigere, statuta et ordinationes ac omnia regimen fieri facere et statutum dicti collegii secundum excrescentiam bonnoveni Capellanorum et trium choristarum proveniatur confirmare dignaremur, quam quidem ecclesiam ut congruentius collegio huius modi conveniret edificari de novo in magna parte et construi fecerunt et facere proponuit solito ampliorum cum campanili, campanis, domitus et aliis officinis necessariis opere sumptuoso: quod cultores in breve augere proponunt at prefertur. Attendentesque quod non nulli ecclesiarum parochialium Rectores clerici seculares nostre diocesis eorum quidam dominorum insistentes obsequiis alii literarum vacantes studio suarum ecclesiarum parochialium curam per conducticios capellanos qui revera mercenarii dici mercentur potius quam pastores, frequenter faciunt exerceri, considerantes eciam in eodem loco divini officii ampliare cultores inquisita primitus et comperta super premissis plenaria veritate dictorum executorum precibus inclinati, predictam ecclesiam de Wyngfeld vacantem habito super hoc cum capitulo ecclesie nostre Norwicensis tractater assensu et concensu omnium quorum interat intervenientibus in hac parte servato processu legitamo Solempmitatibusque juris cum deliberatione diligenti observatis ac concurrentibus precedentibus et subsequentibus de jure seu consuetudive requisitio, auctoritate nostra pontificali in Collegiatam erigimus ecclesiam secularem ac in ipsa ecclesia collegiate Dominum Thomam Sket, rectorem ecclesie parochialis de Asketon dicte nostre dioc. magistrum sive prepositum prepositure dicte ecclesie quam non curatum beneficium neque dignitatem conferi set tenentem eandem tanquam prioritatem quamdam, et ordinationem omnium bonorum juxta sanum consilium suorum consociosum habere, et de bonis communibus secundum facultatem bonorum Collegii huiusmodi et statuti ejusdem dum in loco fuerint et sociis suis presideat honesties vivere in communi. Ac eundem dominum Thomam seu cuicunque successorem suum qui ad beneficium prepositure huiusmodi promoveri contigerit dum absens fuerit nisi in negocio collegii huiusmodi per consilium sociorum suorum constitutus extiterit nichil de bonis collegii huiusmodi percipere debere volumus inter picantes prepositurum huiusmodi cum omni alio beneficio curato compassibilem et pro tali eam decrevimus reputari eundemque dominum Thomam et quem libet successorem in beficio prepositure prefate omnimodam juris dictionem tanquam Commissarium nostrum et cuiuscumque successoris nostri nomine nostro et auctoritate assensu et consensus omnium quorum intererat [sic] in hac parte accedentibus at promittitur ex certa scientia in collegio (habemus?) ordinavimus excercere debere necnon Dominum Robertum de Wortham sacristan qui curam parochianorum dicte ecclesie gerere debebit et Dominum Johannem Budde de Herdwyk capellanum (?capellani) seculares singulos in ordine sacerdotati constitutos quos dicta Domina Alianora nobis ista vice primaria nominaverit seu presentavit ponimus et eciam deputamus.

Statuimus eciam et ordinavimus quod excrescentibus prefati collegii facultatibus pro singulis decem marcharum mercementis capellanorum dicti Collegii numerus augeatur quousque ad numerum Novem capellanorum et trium choristarum secularium sit proventum. Item, volumus et ordinavimus quod cedente vel decetente ipsius collegio magistro seo preposito seu preposituram dimcarere contigerit seu magistro ad prefatam Dominam Alianoram dum vixerit et post ipsius obitum ad heredes Domini Johannis manerii dicti domini Johannis de Wyngefeld dominos presentacio seu nominatio dicti magistri sive prepositi per nos et successores nostros facta fide de vacatione prepositure huiusmodi absque alia inquisicione in ea parte capienda per nos et successores nostros in eodem beneficio instituendo ac proficiendo in eodem perpetuo debeat pertinere, successoremque quemcumque post decessum magistri seu prepositi qui nunc est infra mensem a tempore vacationis prepositure huiusmodi per dictam Dominam Alianoram et post ipsius obitum per heredes dicti Domini Johannis quondam domini manerii de Wyngfeld predicti et ejusdem manerii successores nobis fore presentandum ordinamus per nos canonice ut premittitur instituendum in eodem Alioquin decrevimus collacionem beneficii huiusmodi illa voce nobis fore devolutam illud tamen per nos et successores nostros unum de predicto Collegio conferendum. Volumus eciam quod collegio huiusmodi preposito vacante presentacio sacristarie et deputacio capellani seu capellanorum ad dictam Dominam Alianoram dum vixerit et post ipsius obitum ad heredes dicti Johannis et heredes ac successors ut premittitur spectabunt, spectare etpertinere debebunt fiende [? sciende] tamen infra viginti dies a tempore vacionis sacristarie seu Capellanie seu Capellaniarum huiusmodi continue numerand alioquin extunc volumus sacristarie et capellanie seu capellanii illa vice per nos et successors nostros canonici provideri. Volentes eciam ecclesie nostre Norwicensis cuius est in singularum ecclesiarum parochialium vacationibus annals primos fructose percipere et habere indempnitati precavere et eam in sua justicia confovere de dicte Domine Alianore patrone ceterorumque quorum interest in hac parte consensus et assensu juris ordine ac solempnitatibus in hac parte requisitis debite, secundum juris exigentiam observatis ecclesie de Wyngefeld predicte censum et pensionem annuam viginti solidorum ad synodos Pasche et Sancti Michaelis per equals portiones nobis et successoribus nostris annuatim inperpetuum imponimus persolvend ac Magistrum seu prepositum quemcunque qui erit pro sempore ad solucionem pensionis huiusmodi per suspensionem sequestrationem fructuum dicte ecclesie et aliarum censurarum ecclesiasticarum quarum cunque fulminationem per nos et successors nostros qui pro tempore fuerint in magistrum sive prepositum dicti Collegii qui pro tempore fuerit compelli volumus et etiam obligari ut sic ecclesiam nostram sponsam in ea parte preservemus indempnem cum ptrestacio pensionis huiusmodi valori seu estimacionioni primorum fructuum huiusmodi poterit versimiliter adequari. Item volumus et ordinamus quod dictus Magister seu prepositus in institutione sua juramentum faciat corporale quod infra viginti dies a tempore institutionis et inductionis sue continue numerand secundum suum posse fidele faciat Inventarium inter ipsum et suos consocios de omnibus jocalibus et bonis mobilibus spectantibus ad Collegium memoratum cuius quidem Inventarii per modum indenture conficiendi unam partem penes dictum prepositum, aliam vero penes ceteros capellanos volumus remanere quorum quidem bonorum mobilium preciosiora utputa [?utpota] vestimenta et ornamenta ecclesiastica et omnia huius-modi ad usum cotidianum nullatenus neccessaria cum parte Inventarii indentati capellanis predictis liberata reponi volumus in cista sua communi sub clavibus salvo custodienda per eosdem communit in majoribus festis cum opus fuerit extrahendra et finito usu protunc in archa communi protinus reponenda. Item statuimus et ordi-namus quod prefati magister sive prepositus ac Capellani matutinas et alias horas canonicas secundum usum ecclesie Sarum ac magnam missam de officio diei et de beata maria virgine et summa et individua trinitate et missam pro defunctis ad disposicionem dicti magistri si presens fuerit et in ejus absencia juxta disposicionem et discrecionem dicti sacriste qui erit pro tempore in ecclesia de Wyngefeld predicya pro salubri statu domini nostri Regis Anglie domini Edwardi serenissimi principis Wallie pro pace et unitate ecclesie Regis et regni tranquillitate ac pro salubri statu Domine Alianore de Wyngefeld, Domini Michaelis de la Pole, Katerine uxoris sue, Thome de Wyngefeld ac parochianorum ejusdem ecclesie, necnon reverendi patris Domini Willelmi dei gracia Wyntoniensis Episcopi, nobilis viri Roberti Comitis Suffolcie et Domine Margarete consortis sue veroque statu ac reverendorum Domini David de Wollore et Magistri Johannis de Carleton, necnon Domine Thome quondam Rectoris ejusdem ecclesie ac totius populi dei dum vixerint et animabus eorundem cum ab hac luce migraverint et precipue pro anima bone memorie Domini Johannis de Wyngefeld defuncti, Patris et matris ejusdem, progenitorum liberorum propin-quiorum benefactorum et omnium illorum animabus quibus idem Dominus Johannes parentes pater mater seu progenitors sui in aliquo tenebantur, Domini Ricardi de Brewes, Thome de Verlay et Johanne consortis sue, parochianorumque dicti ecclesie et omnium fidelium defunctorum dicere et celebrare cotidie teneatur. Item volumus et ordinamus quod idem prepositus et capellani in ecclesia superpelliciis alibis et amities [sic] nigris utantur ad modum vicariorum in ecclesiis Cathedralibus ac extra ecclesiam decenter incedant in habitu honeste clericali juxta disposicionem prepositi que pro tempore fuerit collegii supradicti. Item volumus et ordinamus quod omnes et singuli capellani dicti collegii presentes at futuri magistro seu preposito ejusdem qui pro tempore fuerit in licitis canonicis et honestis obediant et intendant. Item volumus et ordinamus quod magister sive prepositus et capellani dicti collegii qui pro tempore fuerint possint habere bona propria a bonis communibus dicti Collegii separata et de huiusmodi bonis suis propriis libere sua poterint condere testamenta, bonis ad collegium huiusmodi pertinentibus vel ratione ejusdem qualitercunque provenientibus semper salvis. Item volumus et ordinamus quod prepositus dicti Collegii qui erit pro tempore sit bonorum dicti collegii cum consilio et auxilio suorum sociorum legitimus administrator et quod justa constitutions Othonis et Octoboni quondam in regno Anglie Apostolice sedis legatorum ad modum Religiosorum semel in anno fidelem compotum de receptis et administratis de bonis communibus coram consociis suis reddere teneatur alioquin ipsum prepositum pene constitutionem huius mora culpa fraude et negligencia procedentibus et causantibus volumus subjacere, et ipsum summarie de plano sive strepitu judiciali beneficio huius demoveri et privari eodem Potestate cum libera ad supplicationem dictorum executorum seu eorum alterius qui diucius vixerit heredum dicti domini Johannis et dominorum dicti manerii augendi vel diminuendi omnia et singula que ad utilitatem dicto Collegii requiruntur ac in competentiorem formam redigendi si et quando opus fuerit aut necesse nobis et successoribus nostris specialiter reservata. Que omnia et singlua observari ey teneri debere modo et forma premittitur omnibus temporibus infu turum decernimus proninciamus et eciam declaramus. In quorum omnium testimonium sigillum nostrum presentibus duximus apponend. Datum apud Hevyngham vj° die Junij, A.D. 1362 et consecrationis nostre septimo.

Et Nos. Frater Nicholaus Prior et Capitulum ecclesie Cathedralis Nowicensis predicti premissa omnia et singula quantum ad nos attinet consensus habito per nos et tractatu ut prefertur approbamus ratificamus et confirmamus et in huiusmodi approbationis ratificationis et confirmationis testimonium atque fidem omnium et singulorum premissorum sigillum commune capitali nostri presentibus est appensum. Datum quoad consignacionem presentium in domo nostra capitalari vij° die Junij A.D. 1362

Et Nos. Alianora de Wyngefeld et Thomas de Wyngfeld executors testamenti prediscti domini Johannis de Wyngfeld militis defuncti suprenominati predictam ordinacionem per dominum reverendum patrem Dominum Thomam dei gracia Norwicensis Episcopum juxta formam petionis nostre eidem patri per nos exposite et porrecte factam ac omnia et singula in eadem ordinatione contenta acceptamus et ratificamus ac huiusmodi ordinationi dicti patris nostrum ut utriusque nostrum consensum expressum et assensum tenore presentium adhibemus. In quorum omnium fidem et testimonium premissorum sigilla nostra presentibus duximus apponenda. Datum apud Wyngfeld quoad consignacionem nostram viij° die Junij A.D. 1362.

Translation

To all the sons of the Holy Mother Church who shall inspect these present letters, Thomas, by permission of God Bishop of Norwich,[1] sends greeting in the Saviour of all men. The unsearchable greatness of the majesty of God recompenses with a fitting reward the merits of those who so increase the resources of His house that

---

[1] Thomas Percy, born c.1332, a younger son of Henry, 2nd Lord Percy; appointed bishop of Norwich by papal provision 1355 while still in his twenty-third year through the intervention of his relative, Henry, duke of Lancaster; consecrated 1356. Died 1369, probably of the plague.

the necessities of Christ's household may be therein the better provided, and their numbers augmented. Now the petition of our well-beloved Dame Eleanor,[2] widow of Sir John de Wyngfeld, knight,[3] deceased, and of Thomas de Wyngfeld, brother of the said deceased,[4] executors of his will, submitted to us, sets forth that the afore-named John, whilst he lived, pondering deeply and meditating upon the truths enun-ciated above, and desiring to augment the number of the ministers of the service of God, to the honour and glory of the supreme and undivided Trinity, the glorious Virgin Mary, and of Saint John the Baptist, St John the Evangelist and the Blessed Apostle Andrew, the most martyred among the rest, and of all saints, for his own salvation and that of his parents, kinsfolk, benefactors and all those for whom he, or his parents and progenitors, were in any way bound, and for the health of the souls of all other the faithful, proposed to establish a college of certain secular chaplains in the parish church of Wingfield aforesaid, in our diocese (of which during his life he was patron) devoted to the service of the lord for ever, and to provide an endow-ment for such college and for the maintenance of the charges thereof; but since he was attacked and carried off from this world by remorseless Death, before he had accomplished his purpose, the said executors of the same Sir John, bearing in mind this his pious purpose in the Lord, and desiring very earnestly to put it into execu-tion, have humbly besought us that we would be pleased to ordain in the parish church aforesaid (which is now known to be of the patronage of the said Dame Eleanor) a college of three secular chaplains, of whom one shall be named Master or Warden, with power in our name to correct the members of such college and to reform, when necessary, other things to the same belonging, so that this benefice (compatible with any other benefice, cure or dignity whatsoever) shall be at the presentation of the said Dame Eleanor for her life, and after her death at the pres-entation of the lords or lord of the manor of the late Sir John de Wyngfeld aforesaid – the second to be sacristan of the said college and to have the cure of souls of the parish, at the presentation of the said Master or Warden by us or our successors to be instituted and professed but without any public ceremony, and the third chaplain to be appointed by the aforenamed Warden or Master in such college for the time

[2] Eleanor was probably the daughter of Thomas de Verlay and married Sir John de Wingfield. She died in 1375 and is buried in Wingfield Church – her brass indent lies on the floor in front of her husband's tomb.

[3] Sir John de Wingfield. A soldier, he fought at the battle of Crécy in 1346 and at Poitiers in 1356. He entered the service of Edward the Black Prince shortly after the Black Death, and from 1351 to 1361 he was the prince's 'business manager' – being variously called his steward, chief councillor and governor of the prince's business; the prince's attorney 1358. Died circa 1361, possibly of the plague and is buried in Wingfield Church; his effigy is in a canopied tomb in the chancel.

[4] Sir Thomas de Wingfield, the younger brother of Sir John, married Margaret, the widow of Sir William Carbonell of Badingham, Suffolk, and the daughter of Sir John de Bovill; she was also the niece and heiress of Sir William de Bovill of Letheringham in Suffolk. Sir Thomas obtained the manor of Letheringham through this marriage. He died in 1378 and is buried in Letheringham church.

being; and also to erect the said parish church into a secular collegiate church, to draw up statutes and ordinances and all necessary regulations for the rule and governance thereof, to determine the same and see them put into due form; and to confirm the statutes of the said college to be increased up to the number of nine chaplains and three choristers according to the increase of the immovable goods or rents thereof; the which church, in order to make it more suitable for such a college, must be in great part built anew; and they have had, and propose to have, it constructed on a larger scale than before, with a belfry, bells, houses and other necessary offices, at a very great expense; and moreover they intend, after the said college has been established, in a short time to augment the same as is set forth above, in order to increase the number of the worshippers of God. And we, knowing that not a few rectors of parish churches in our diocese, being secular clerks (some of them being occupied with the business of their lords, others engaged in completing their studies) frequently commit the cure of their parish churches to hired chaplains whom they pay, and who are rather day-labourers than pastors; and considering also that in this place the number of ministrants of divine worship will be increased – after first duly inquiring and ascertaining the truth of the premises – are inclined to grant the request of the said executors; and therefore, after consultation thereupon with the chapter of our church of Norwich, with the assent and consent of all those concerned in the matter, all necessary legal proceedings having been taken and all customary ceremonies duly observed, and all things concurrent, precedent and subsequent as by law and custom required, by our pontifical authority we do erect the aforesaid church of Wingfield, now vacant, into a collegiate secular church, and in the same collegiate church (appoint) Sir Thomas Sket,[5] rector of the parish church of Hasketon in our said diocese Master or Warden of the wardenship of the said church, which (we declare) is not conferred as a cure, benefice nor dignity, but as holding the same as a priory, and to have the management of all the goods, on which he shall take counsel with his colleagues, and he shall live in common with his said colleagues, over whom he shall preside, upon the common goods, according to the resources of the college, and the statutes thereof, so long as they shall continue in the place. And we will that the same Sir Thomas, and any successor of his who may happen to be promoted to the benefice of such wardenship, during any absence (unless it be upon the business of such college with the advice of his colleagues) shall not be entitled to receive anything of the goods of such college, declaring that this wardenship shall be compatible with any other benefice with cure, and we have decreed that it shall be so reputed; and we have appointed the said Sir Thomas and all his successors in the benefice of the wardenship aforenamed to exercise by right all jurisdiction in the same college as the commissary of us and all our successors, in our name and by our authority, with the assent and consent of all those in this behalf concerned, as is aforesaid; and

5   Sir Thomas Sket, rector of Wingfield 1329–61, Rector of Hasketon 1361 (a church in the gift of the de Brewes family, his former patrons at Wingfield); first master of Wingfield College 1362.

we do also place and appoint Sir Robert de Wortham as sacristan, who shall have the cure of the parishioners of the said church, and Sir John Budde of Herdwyk to be chaplain, both of them being seculars in priest's orders, and nominated and presented to us on this first occasion by the said Dame Eleanor. Moreover we have appointed and ordained that for every ten marks' increase in the resources of the said college the number shall be augmented up to a total of nine chaplains and three secular choristers. Also we will and have ordained that, on the resignation or death of a Master or warden of the College, or in the event of his relinquishing the warden-ship in any way, and as often as the said College shall happen to be without a warden, the presentation or nomination of the said master or warden shall belong to the aforenamed Dame Eleanor, so long as she lives, and after her death to the heirs of Sir John, lords of the manor of the said Sir John de Wyngfeld for ever; and such presentees shall by us or our successors upon oath made of the vacancy of such wardenship, without any other inquiry to be made in this behalf by us or our succes-sors, and shall be therein professed; and after the decease of the present Master or Warden, we ordain that his successor, to be presented to us within one month of the time of the falling vacant of the said wardenship by the said Dame Eleanor, and after her death by the heirs of the said Sir John, late lord of the manor of Wingfield aforesaid, his successors in the same manor, shall be by us canonically instituted therein, as is aforesaid. Otherwise we had decreed that the collation to this benefice shall for that turn have devolved upon us, to be conferred, nevertheless, by us and our successors upon some member of the College. We will, moreover, that when the wardenship of this college is vacant, the presentation of the sacristancy and the appointment of the chaplain or chaplains shall belong to the said Dame Eleanor, so long as she lives, and after her death to the heirs of the said John, and their heirs and successors, as is aforesaid, provided, nevertheless, that such presentation or appoint-ment be made within twenty days next following from the time of the falling vacant of the sacristancy or chaplaincy or chaplaincies; otherwise we will that the sacristan, chaplain or chaplains shall for that turn be canonically provided by us or our succes-sors. And whereas we are desirous of protecting and indemnifying our church of Norwich, whose right it is to have and take the first-fruits in all cases of vacancies of parish churches, and to uphold her just claims, with the assent and consent of the said Dame Eleanor, the patroness, and of all others in this behalf concerned, and with due observance of legal form and the taking of all proceedings necessary for the purpose according as the law demands, so we do charge the aforesaid church of Wingfield with a tax and yearly pension of 20s, payable every year at Easter and Michaelmas synods, in equal portions, to us and our successors for ever, and we will that the Masters and Wardens for the time being shall be compelled and bound to pay such pension by suspension, sequestration of the fruits of the said church and the fulmination of all other ecclesiastical censures whatsoever by us and our succes-sors for the time being against the Master or Warden of the said College for the time being, so that by this means we may save harmless in this behalf the church, our spouse, as the payment of such pension may be calculated in all probability to be equal in value to the first fruits. Moreover, we will and ordain that at his institution the said Master or Warden shall take his corporal oath that, within twenty days following next after the date of his institution and induction, he will, to the best of his power, with his colleagues, make a faithful inventory of all the jewels and movable goods belonging to the said College, which inventory shall be made indented, and one part, we will, shall be retained by the said Warden and the other remain in the keeping of the other chaplains. And we will that the more costly of such movable goods, such as the vestments, ornaments of the church and all such things not required for use every day, together with the part of the indented inventory given into the keeping of the chaplains aforesaid, shall be put into their common chest and kept safe under lock and key by the said chaplains jointly, to be taken out on the greater festivals, as may be necessary, and replaced forthwith in the common chest as soon as their use is finished. Also we have appointed and ordained that the afore-named Master or Warden and chaplains shall be bound to recite and celebrate every day matins and the other canonical hours according to the use of the church of Sarum, and high mass of the office of God and of the Blessed Virgin Mary and of the Supreme and Undivided Trinity, and mass for the dead, at the appointment of the said Master, if he be present, and in his absence at the appointment and discretion of the sacristan for the time being, in the church of Wingfield aforesaid, for the health of our lord the King of England,[6] of the Lord Edward, the most serene Prince of Wales,[7] for the peace and unity of the church, the tranquillity of the King and Kingdom, for the health of Dame Eleanor de Wyngefeld, Sir Michael de la Pole,[8] of Katherine his wife,[9] of Thomas de Wyngefeld and the parishioners of the said church, also of the Reverend Father Lord William by the grace of God Bishop of Winchester,[10] or the noble man Lord Robert, Earl of Suffolk,[11] and the Lady Margaret

---

[6]   King Edward III. Born 1312, became king in 1325, died 1377.

[7]   Edward of Woodstock 'the Black Prince', prince of Wales. Born 1330. Patron and employer of Sir John de Wingfield. Died 1376.

[8]   Sir Michael de la Pole was born circa 1330, the son of Sir William de la Pole, a wealthy Hull wool-merchant. Served in France under the Black Prince; admiral of the North 1376–7; lord chancellor of England 1383–6; had a licence to crenellate his mansion houses in Wingfield, 27 April 1385; created Earl of Suffolk 6 August 1385; impeached by parliament 1386; attainted 1387/8; fled to France and died in exile in Paris 5 September 1389, buried in Hull.

[9]   Katherine, the only child of Sir John de Wingfield, married Sir Michael de la Pole c.1360. She was dead by 1386 and is buried in the Charter House in Hull.

[10]   William de Edington. Elected Bishop of Winchester 1346; treasurer of England 1345–56; chancellor of England 1356–62; archbishop of Canterbury 1366; died 1366. Founded Edington College in Wiltshire c.1347.

[11]   Robert de Ufford, 1st earl of Suffolk, K.G. Born 1298; steward of the royal household 1336–7; created earl of Suffolk 1337; admiral of the North 1337 and 1344–7; fought alongside Sir John de Wingfield at the battles of Crécy in 1346 and at Poitiers in 1356; died 1369.

his consort,[12] and for the Reverend Sir David de Wollore,[13] the Reverend Master John de Carleton,[14] and the Reverend Sir Thomas, late rector of the same church,[15] and of all the people of God living, and for their souls after they have departed this life, and especially for the soul of Sir John de Wyngefeld deceased, of good memory, of his father and mother, of his ancestors, children, kinsfolk and benefactors, and all those whose souls the said Sir John, his parents or ancestors were in any way bound, for Sir Richard de Brewes,[16] Thomas de Verlay and Joan his wife,[17] parishioners of the said church, and for all the faithful departed. Also we will and ordain that in church the said Warden and chaplains shall wear white surplices and black gowns in the manner of vicars in cathedral churches, and out of church they shall go abroad in decent clerical clothes as arranged by the Warden of the said College for the time being. Also we will and ordain that all and singular the chaplains of the said College present and to come, shall obey and submit themselves to the Master or Warden thereof for the time being in all lawful, canonical and reputable things. Also we will and ordain that the Master or Warden and chaplains of the said College for the time being may have their own goods apart from the common goods of the said College, and shall be free to make their wills disposing of such their own goods, goods belonging to the said college or coming in any way by reason thereof always excepted. Also we will and ordain that the Warden of the said College for the time being, with the advice and assistance of his colleagues, shall be the lawful administrator of the goods of the said College, and that he shall be bound once a year to render a faithful account of his receipts and expenditure in the presence of his colleagues, as is done

---

[12] Margaret was the daughter of Sir Walter de Norwich and the sister of Sir John, Lord Norwich of Mettingham Castle; her first husband Thomas, Lord Cailly died in 1316 and she remarried Robert de Ufford c.1320; she died in 1368.

[13] Sir David de Wollore, a king's clerk from Wooler in Northumberland, acting in Chancery from 1329, a 'greater clerk' from 1344 and later principal clerk of Chancery; master of the rolls 1346–70 and frequently keeper of the seal in the same period; a prebendary of Chichester 1345, of St Paul's in London 1349, of York 1352, of Lincoln 1360 and of Ripon 1361; had a licence to found a chantry for one chaplain in Ripon 1368; involved in the acquisition and settling of the manor of Wingfield by Sir John de Wingfield 1357. Died 1370.

[14] Master John de Carleton, LL.D., vicar-general of Norwich 1359; archdeacon of Suffolk 1359–67; died c.1367.

[15] Sir Thomas Sket.

[16] Sir Richard de Brewes was a younger son of Sir Richard de Brewse of Stinton Hall in Salle, Norfolk, which he acquired through marriage to Alice, the daughter and heiress of William le Rus of Whittingham Hall in Fressingfield, Akenham, Clopton and Hasketon in Suffolk and Stinton and Heydon in Norfolk. Alice also inherited Stradbroke and Wingfield, which she settled on Richard, her younger son, in 1296–7. Richard was knighted in 1306. He transferred his manor of Wingfield to trustees for the heirs of Sir John de Wingfield in 1357, reserving a life interest for Katherine, who had been the wife of Sir Richard's son Richard – possibly the same Katherine who was the daughter of Sir John de Wingfield and subsequently the wife of Michael de la Pole.

[17] Thomas de Verlay was a king's yeoman by 1310 and a serjeant in the royal household by 1320. Through his marriage to Joan, who was probably the daughter of John de Glanvill, he acquired lands in Saxmundham and Sternfield in Suffolk which were later settled on Sir John de Wingfield and Eleanor his wife, who was probably the daughter of Thomas and Joan.

by the religious according to the constitutions of Otto and Ottobon, formerly Legates of the Apostolic See in the Kingdom of England,[18] otherwise we shall declare the said Warden by reason of such delay guilty of fraud and negligence, according to the said statutes, and that he shall be summarily removed from such his benefice and thereof deprived as a simple consequence without any clamour in the courts; always reserving full power to us and our successors (at the request of the said executors or the survivor of them, for the heirs of the said Sir John and the lords of the said manor) to augment or diminish all the singular things as are necessary for the good of the said College and to re-establish them in better form, whensoever it may be considered needful or advantageous. All and singular the which things we decree, pronounce and declare shall be henceforth for ever kept and observed in manner and form as aforesaid. In witness whereof we have thought fit to affix our seal to the presents. Given at Hevingham[19] on the 6th day of June 1362, and in the 7th year of our consecration.

And we, Brother Nicholas, Prior,[20] and the chapter of the cathedral church of Norwich aforesaid, having discussed the matter and given our consent, as is aforesaid, do approve, ratify and confirm all and singular the premises, in so far as to us belongs, and in witness of such approbation, ratification and confirmation, and to testify to all and singular the premises, the common seal of our chapter is appended to the presents. Given, as regards the countersigning of the presents, in our chapter house, this 7th day of June 1362.

And we, Eleanor de Wyngefeld and Thomas de Wyngefeld, executors of the will of the aforesaid Sir John de Wyngefeld, knight, deceased, in the above instrument named, do accept and ratify the aforesaid ordinances made by our Lord, the Reverend Father Lord Thomas, by the grace of God Bishop of Norwich, according to the form of our petition to the said Father by us submitted, and by tenor of the presents we do testify the express consent and assent of us and either of us to such ordinances of our said Father. In warrant and testimony whereof we have thought fit to affix our seals to these presents. Given, as regards our countersigning hereof, at Wingfield, this 8th day of June 1362.

---

[18] Cardinal Otto de Tonengo was the papal legate in England 1237–40 and Cardinal Ottobuono de Fieschi was the papal legate in England 1265–8. In 1268 Ottobuono issued a set of canons, which formed the basis of church law in England until the Protestant Reformation. He became Pope Adrian V in 1276 but died little more than a month later.
[19] The moated palace of the bishops of Norwich at Hevingham in Norfolk.
[20] Nicholas de Hoo, elected prior 1357; resigned 1382.

The Surrender of Wingfield College in 1542

Rymer's Fœdera, vol. XIV, p. 748.

Omnibus Christi Fidelibus ad quos hoc præsus Scriptum pervenerit, Robertus Budd Clericus Magister Collegii sive Cantariæ in Ecclesia de Wynkfeld in Com. Suffolciæ, et ejusdem Collegii sive Cantariæ Capellam, Salutem in Auctore Salutis sempiternam.

Sciatis quod Nos præfati Magister et Capellam, Certis de Causis Specialibus ac urgentibus, Nos nostriumque Conscientias ad præsens non parum moventibus, unanimi nosto Assensu et consensus necnon ultraneâ et spontanea Voluntate nostrâ libere et Sponte, Dedimus Concessimus, et has præsenti Cartâ Confirmavimus Excellentissimo, et Præpotentissimo Pricipi et Domino nostro Henrico, Dei gratiâ, Angliæ Franciæ et Hiberniæ Regi Fidei Defensori, ac in Terris Anglicanæ et Hibernicæ Ecclesiæ Supremo Capiti, ejusque Nominis Octavo, totum Collegium et Cantariarum nostram prædictam, Necnon totum illum Situm Septum, Circuitaum, Ambitum, et Præcinctum ejusdem Collegii sive Cantariæ, Ac etiam omnia et singula Maneria, Mesuagia, Teras, Tenementa, Redditus, Reversiones, Servita, Rectorias, Pensiones, ac cætera Hæreditamenta, Possessiones, et Prosicua nostra quæcumq; cum eorum pertinentis universis, jacentia sive existential in villis Campis seu Parochiis de Wyngfeld, Chekeryng, Saxmondham, Selyham, Esham, Walpole, Benhall, ac Rectorias de Myddleton, Chekeryng, Raydon, Wyngfeld, et Stradibroke in Comitatu Suffolciæ, seu alibi ubicumque in eodem Comitatu aut infra Regnum Angliæ, dicto Collegio sive Cantariæ, aut nobis dictis Magistro et Capellanis, ratione ejusdem Collegio sive Cantariæ, quoquomodo spectantia sive pertinentia, Ac præterea etiam omnia Bona, Ornamenta, Vas, Jocalia, Implementa, et Debita nostra quæcumque, Nobis præfatis Magistro et Capellanis ratione Collegii sive Cantariæ prædictæ, quoquomodo spectantia sive pertinentia, Habenda Tenenda et Gaudenda prædicta Maneria, Mesuagia, Terras, Tenementa, Rectorias, Bona, Ornamenta, et cætera singula Præmissa cum eorum pertinentiis, prædicto Excellentissimo Principi et Domino nostro Regi Henrico Hæridibus et Successoribus suis imperpetuùm, Ac ulterias Sciatis quòd Nos præfati Magister et Capellam et Successores nostri prædictum Collegium, Cantariam, Manneria, Messuagia, Terras, Tenementa, Rectoria, et cætera singula Præmissa, cum eorum pertinentiis universis præfato excellentissimo Principi Domino nostro Henrico Hæredibus et successoribus suis contra omnes Gentes Warrantizabimus et imperpetuùm Defendemus.

In ejus rei Testimonium huic præsenti Cartæ Sigillum nostrum commune apposuimus.

Dat in collegio prædicto secundo dei Junii Anno Regni dicti Domini Regis Tricesimo quarto.

Translation

To all the Faithful in Christ to whom this present Writing shall come, [I] Robert Budd,[21] Priest, Master of the College or Chantry in the Church of Wingfield in the County of Suffolk, and the Chaplains of the same College or Chantry, eternal Salvation in the Author of Salvation.

Know you all that We the aforesaid Master and Chaplains, for Certain Special and urgent Reasons at the present time moving Us and our Conscience not a little, unanimously with our assent and consent, also with our spontaneous goodwill freely and spontaneously have Given, Conceded, and our present Charter have Confirmed these things to our most Excellent and most Powerful Prince and Lord Henry, by the Grace of God King of England, France and Ireland, Defender of the Faith, and in the Lands of England and Ireland Supreme Head of the Church, the Eighth of his Name, the whole College and our Chantry aforesaid, also that entire Site, Enclosure, Circuit, Border, and Precinct of the same College or Chantry. And also all and singular the Manors, Messuages, Lands, Tenements, Rents, Reversions, Services, Rectories, Pensions, and all the rest of the Hereditaments, Possessions, and our Benefits whatsoever; with all the whole of their appurtenances, in ruins or in existence, in the towns, Fields or Parishes in Wingfield, Chickering, Saxmundham, Sylham, Earsham Street, Walpole, Benhall, and the Rectories of Middleton, Chickering, Raydon, Wingfield and Stradbroke in the County of Suffolk, or wherever else in the same county or beyond in the Kingdom of England, however situated or belonging to the said College or Chantry, or to us the said Master and Chaplains, by the right of the same College or Chantry. And moreover also all Our Goods, Ornaments, Vases, Jewels, Implements and Debts whatsoever, however situated or belonging to the aforesaid Master and Chaplains by right of the College or Chantry aforesaid. To Have, to Hold and to Enjoy the aforesaid Manors, Messuages, Lands, Tenements, Rectories, Goods, Ornaments and the other separate Premises with their appurtenances, to the aforesaid Most Excellent Prince and Lord our King Henry, his Heirs and Successors in perpetuity. And furthermore know that We the aforesaid Master and Chaplains and Our Successors will Guarantee and Defend in perpetuity, against all Peoples, the aforesaid College, Chantry, Manors, Messuages, Lands, Tenements, Rectories and other separate Premises, with their entire appurtenances, to the aforesaid Most Excellent Prince Our Lord Henry, his Heirs and successors.

In Witness of this we have affixed our common Seal to this present Charter.

Given in the aforesaid college on the second day of June in the Thirty-fourth year of the Reign of our said Lord King [1542]

---

[21] Sir Robert Budd(e), chaplain to Charles Brandon, duke of Suffolk and a friend of Richard Freston, the comptroller of Brandon's household, was made master of the college in 1531 on the death of Master Thomas Deye.

THE MEDIEVAL STRUCTURES

5

Reconstructing Wingfield Castle

Robert Liddiard

Introduction

The use of reconstruction, be it in the form of drawings or physical scale models, is a familiar method of illustrating the original appearance of historic buildings. The detailed artworks that often accompany guidebooks or visitor interpretation boards are a key part in making ruins intelligible to the academic and general reader alike. When well executed, reconstruction drawings and physical models are powerful ways in which to communicate both the form and often monumentality of buildings in their landscapes. Anyone with an interest in historic architecture or archaeology will almost certainly be able to recall a visit in their youth to a museum or ruin where a reconstruction left a lasting impression and where, implicitly or explicitly, they imagined 'maybe that's what it really looked like'.

For the present generation, digital technology offers new opportunities, most obviously the development of virtual reality. The blanket term 'VR' in fact masks a series of different techniques and applications, but a useful distinction can be made between reconstruction modelling – the creation of buildings and landscapes – and virtual reality proper where, depending on the application, there is a level of interactivity between viewer and the virtual environment.[1] Advances in both hardware and software mean that it is now possible to create highly convincing photo-realistic digital models that move beyond the single frame of the artist's reconstruction or the physical constraints of the static scale model. The benefits are immediately apparent: detailed virtual environments can be created that can give the viewer a sense of past buildings and spaces in a totality that cannot easily be achieved by drawings or physical models. Within a computer-generated world, the viewer's standpoint can be altered with relative ease; those experiencing it are not necessarily bound to a single viewpoint. Rather than observing a static model, or looking at an imagined scene from the solitary perspective of the artist's drawing, VR permits a more 'immersive' experience where, depending on the level of interactivity, the viewer can follow a

---

[1] Lock 2003, pp. 152–63.

pre-set route or navigate themselves not just around a building, but also an entire past environment.

The use of VR in the presentation of historic buildings and archaeological sites is so well established that there is now a considerable academic literature as to its benefits and disadvantages.[2] A particular point of interest is the relationship between historical evidence and computer reconstruction. The quality of digital modelling is such that the results can sometimes look almost too good to be true, and, albeit unintentionally, carry with them the air of authenticity.[3] An empirically well-researched computer reconstruction is perhaps inevitably open to the charge of bringing with it a sense that it represents some kind of definitive statement and, unwittingly, implies a set way of 'seeing' the past. The idea that reconstructions, digital or otherwise, carry with them a sense of authenticity tends to sit uneasily with historical or archaeological methodologies. Here limits of the possible (or, to put it another way, whether something is 'right') are defined by evidence that is itself open to interpretation. As anyone who has attempted it will know only too well, the end product of the process of reconstruction, whether a drawing or a physical or digital model – and particularly one of a high visual or technical standard – inevitably conveys a sense of certainty that is frequently belied by the evidence upon which it is based. Nomenclature is undoubtedly important here, as a sense of uncertainty is more readily communicated by the term 'artist's impression' rather the authority implied by the term 'historical reconstruction'.

In some respects the rise of VR has brought back into focus problems of interpretation that have existed for as long as reconstruction itself has been seen as desirable. Issues of objectivity and empirical accuracy have long concerned those who have produced reconstruction drawings or made physical models of historic buildings.[4] Particularly in those cases where reconstructions are themselves the centrepiece of the research, the philosophical and practical issues inherent in the creative process inevitably inform the discussion.[5] The long-standing nature of the issue surrounding historical authenticity is best-illustrated by the widely known anecdote concerning the ground-breaking and inspirational drawings by Alan Sorrel that graced a generation of guidebooks and interpretation boards; here, the standing joke is that the artist's judicious use of smoke hid areas of uncertainty and contentious areas of the subject matter. In fact, it was Sorrel who wanted hard evidence for his illustrations and the archaeologists who requested ambiguity.[6]

The development of VR has brought some of these issues back into view and at the same time raised others. Given its more 'immersive' aspects, how to represent

[2]   Reilly 1990; Higgins et al. 1996; Barceló et al. 2000; Earl and Wheatley 2002.
[3]   Forte and Siliotti 1997.
[4]   Faulkner 1963.
[5]   De la Bédoyère 1991.
[6]   Sorrell 1981.

empirical uncertainty or differing interpretations in a computer-generated model is a problem; in a virtual world Sorrel-like smoke at every ambiguous moment is simply unviable. More fundamentally, some commentators have pointed out that it is incumbent to define what is meant by reality in the present, before we try to recreate it virtually in the past.[7] Such a question is entirely reasonable, given that it is a fundamental tenet of historical studies that there are a myriad of ways in which people perceive their moments and landscapes and so 'see' the world mediated through lenses of age, gender, social class and cultural expectation.

It is against this intellectual background that in 2009 the University of East Anglia commissioned a project to create digital reconstructions of Wingfield College (Bloore this volume) and castle and a programme of research was conducted in order to inform the models. This chapter is intended to give an explanatory commentary on the reconstruction of Wingfield Castle that accompanies this volume and also to relate the results of work undertaken at the castle, which sheds further light on the development and landscape context of the building.

Wingfield Castle

The origins of Wingfield Castle are well known, at least in outline. In 1385 Michael de la Pole obtained a licence to crenellate at Wingfield and at his other manors of Sternfield and Huntingfield, the same year that he became the 1st earl of Suffolk.[8] As Edward Martin has convincingly argued elsewhere in this volume, there were good tenurial reasons for choosing Wingfield as the site for the new castle and in all likelihood the building was raised over an existing manor house; a common occurrence at other fourteenth- and fifteenth-century castles in East Anglia.[9] There seems little doubt that the southern range of the castle that survives today was either the work of Michael himself, or if not, completed by the second Michael de la Pole before the close of the fourteenth century.

The castle remained in de la Pole hands until the early sixteenth century, when it briefly passed via the Crown to the Howards and in turn was leased by Charles Brandon. Following a short period again in the hands of the Crown, in 1544 the castle passed to Sir Henry Jerningham.[10] Thereafter the history of the castle is one of gradual decline and the building assuming the status of a gentry farmhouse, before a programme of restoration after the Second World War.[11] This basic framework masks a degree of complexity that is impossible to elucidate fully without a complete

---

7   See in particular the work by Mark Gillings: Gillings 2002; 2005; Goodrick and Gillings 2000.
8   *CPR 1381–5*, p. 555.
9   Liddiard 2008.
10 Copinger 1909, vol. IV, p. 111; Gunn 1988, pp. 41–3.
11 Emery 2000, pp. 160–4.

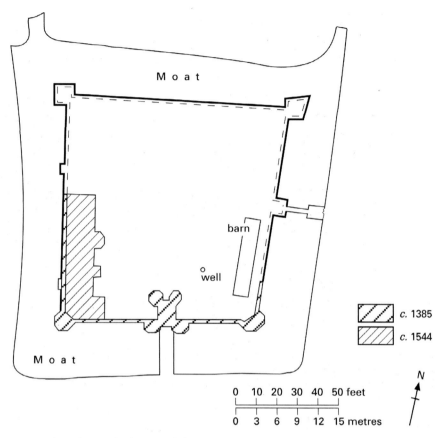

Fig. 5.1. Plan of Wingfield Castle (after Emery 2000).

recording of the building, but a series of observations can be made that shed light on the castle's development.

The castle consists of a large irregular quadrilateral enclosure surrounded by a substantial moat upon which are a series of buildings and ruined structures (see Figure 5.1). The two principal buildings on the platform today both date from the post-medieval period: a sixteenth-century house that sits hard on the western edge of the platform and a post-medieval barn on the eastern side. The only substantive structure to survive from the medieval castle is the southern curtain, chiefly made of flint, which incorporates two corner towers and the central gatehouse (see Figure 5.2). The latter comprises a two-storied central block, with a principal room above a vaulted entrance chamber, with three-storied turrets to the front and rear, the former containing chambers. Today, access to the upper room and roof is via a nineteenth-century wooden staircase that rises through the south-western part of the gatehouse. Although the buildings themselves are now gone, on the interior wall of the southern curtain are the clear remains of a floor levels, doorways, fireplaces and

Fig. 5.2. Southern curtain of Wingfield Castle.

Fig. 5.3. Interior of south-eastern range, Wingfield Castle.

Fig. 5.4. Jerningham House, showing its position on the western side and south-west corner of the main moat.

roof scars of the range that once stood on either side of the gatehouse (Figure 5.3). The absence of any masonry wall footings or foundations from what would have been the interior of this range, together with a lack of any masonry scarring from former walls on the side elevations of the gatehouse, indicates that the original castle buildings were timber-framed. There are no other buildings on any other part of the moated enclosure, which today is chiefly a garden area.

The medieval masonry curtain wall continues for only short stretches along the eastern and western sides of the moated platform. On the eastern side it peters out close to the footings of a rectangular structure that represent the remains of a subsidiary entrance, almost certainly a small gatehouse or entrance tower. On the west there is a short section of upstanding wall, but this is incorporated into footings of the sixteenth-century house. Beyond the house, the revetment is more substantial and incorporates the footings of what is almost certainly a garderobe chute. On the remaining three sides, the curtain wall continues only as a revetment of the moat and in the north-east and north-west corners it runs into the footings of two towers.

Today, the southern curtain and gatehouse bear close comparison to the view shown in the eighteenth century by Samuel and Nathaniel Buck, but this is as much the result of nineteenth- and twentieth-century restoration as it is survival of the medieval fabric. A late eighteenth-century sketch of the castle shows both corner towers and the western section of the southern curtain wall without battlements, so the current arrangement is probably the result of a modern attempt to copy what is shown by Buck.[12] The gatehouse in particular has been the subject of much restoration. The upper parts are the work of G. Baron Ash, who undertook a major programme of works following his acquisition of the castle during the Second World War. During the early 1960s the upper parts of the gatehouse were re-roofed and it is probable that many of the crenellations were replaced at the same time. The original accounts with the main builders, Wm C. Reade of Aldeburgh, indicate that Ash's works were more considerable than has hitherto been appreciated, and extended to the crenellations on the corner towers and probably also other parts of the southern curtain; in short, there is less medieval work here than might imme diately be supposed.[13]

The chief building on the moat today is the sixteenth-century brick-and-timber framed house, which has the Jerningham arms displayed on the main entrance (Figure 5.4). This building retains its original roof and has an exact parallel at Crow's Hall, Debenham, some 15 kilometres to the south, which has been dated to 1559–60 by dendrochronology.[14] A date of 1559 is somewhat auspicious in the case of Wingfield as it was in this year that the prominent courtier Sir Henry Jerningham withdrew from public office and retired to his East Anglian estates.[15] It would there-fore not be unreasonable to assume that the building was probably initiated by Sir Henry in order to meet his new circumstances following his departure from court. An inventory drawn up at the castle during the 1590s, which describes the contents in individual rooms, indicates, some seventeenth-century alterations apart, a spatial arrangement broadly in line with what remains today.[16]

Beyond the main moated enclosure are a series of features that were originally part of the castle complex, but which now survive only as earthworks (see Figure 5.5). To the east there is second, smaller, moated enclosure on to which the subsidiary eastern gatehouse originally gave access. In addition, a second enclosure also existed on the southern side of the moat, opposite the castle gatehouse. The original arrangement of these two enclosures is not entirely clear. Either the two were originally one large outer court which enveloped the moat on its eastern and southern side, or were sub-divided, possibly along the southern line of the eastern enclosure, where the line of the current arm of the moat appears to be truncated by infilling. Whatever the exact arrangement, however, there is no doubt that the main approach to the castle was from the south. Here the modern drive, which perpetuates the medieval line of access, is flanked by a substantial pond, some 60 metres long and extends almost to the modern road. A geophysical survey confirmed that a second pond of the same dimensions lay to the east but this had been almost entirely removed by nineteenth

[12] BL: Add. MSS 8987 fol. 125.
[13] Ledgers now held by M.S. Oakes Ltd, un-catalogued.
[14] Philip Aitkens, pers. comm.
[15] Weikel, 2004.
[16] NRO: JER271, 55X1

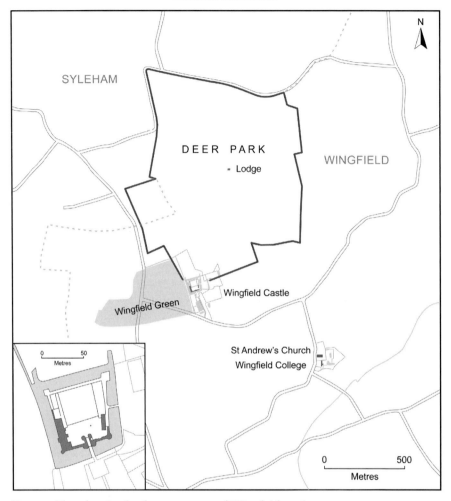

Fig. 5.5. Plan showing landscape context of Wingfield castle.

century, when a relic pond is shown on the tithe award map.[17] To the north of the castle lay the castle park, which was probably initiated at the same time as the castle as imparkment was also specified in de la Pole's original license to crenellate. The approximate location can be gauged from nineteenth-century field-names, and the presence of a former moat in what would have been the centre of the park almost certainly marks the site of a former lodge.

To state an obvious point, but an important one as far as the reconstruction is concerned, the castle as we see it today is one where clearly only a fraction of the original fabric remains. As originally built there must have been a hall, apartments,

[17]   Graham 2009; SROL: HA12/6864/1.

service buildings and so on, and they would have been arranged around a courtyard, but the precise arrangement is more speculative. The closest analogy to the original arrangement at Wingfield is probably Maxstoke in Warwickshire (c.1345), where part of the timber ranges built up against a masonry curtain remain extant, albeit encased in later works.[18]

Perhaps the most important issue in the history of the castle is the date at which the medieval buildings were removed. It is possible that the construction of Jerningham's new house also marked the dismantling of the castle; if this were the case then it would be an indication of the extent to which, by the mid-sixteenth century, the de la Pole residence was simply seen as not fit for purpose for a Tudor gentleman. An alternative explanation is that the castle had been asset stripped in the period following the de la Pole tenure and so when Jerningham took up his occupancy there was little left of the original structure. Even if a slow decline to deterioration in the early sixteenth century is accepted, in any event the medieval buildings seem not to have survived long after the sixteenth century. The only possible exception was a short section of the southern range between the gatehouse and the Jerningham building. A series of illustrations show a complete range of buildings here, and a rare watercolour of the north elevation of the gatehouse (c.1837) shows the buildings, albeit heavily modified from their original medieval form (see Figure 5.6).[19] If these were the last vestiges of the medieval castle then, they were demolished in the late nineteenth century, probably when the present staircase in the western part of the gatehouse was constructed, which was presumably then needed because the removal of the adjacent buildings necessitated a more convenient route to the gatehouse chamber and roof. It was also probably at the same time that some battlements were reinstated and the present bridge into the castle also constructed as photographs of the castle at the turn of the nineteenth century show a building covered with ivy but with battlements on the south-western part of the curtain.[20]

Some light on the fate of the ranges on the southern and eastern side is provided by the date of the barn, which can only have been built after the buildings had been removed. The building sits on nineteenth-century brick footings, but retains a much older queenpost roof and sections of its original timber-framed walls. Local tradition holds that the barn was brought to its current location from somewhere outside the main castle curtilage, which may not be wide of the mark given the antiquity of the roof and the evidence for outer enclosures where it might normally be expected to find such a structure. The barn is shown in place on the mid-nineteenth-century tithe award map and, given the nature of the bricks, it would instinctively follow that it was moved during the nineteenth century. To judge from the structure today, however, the reassembly was conducted to such a high standard it presupposes that

---

[18] Alcock et al., 1978, pp. 195–233.
[19] BL: Add. MS 19092 fol. 387.
[20] SROL: 1300/137/2; 1300/137/3.

Fig. 5.6. Watercolour c.1837 showing northern elevation of the gatehouse (British Library).

it was undertaken by somebody with knowledge of the original method of construction, which would place its re-erection seemingly no later than the end of the seventeenth century.[21] An undated, but probably eighteenth-century, illustration of the castle currently held in private hands clearly shows the barn in its present position, which would also support an earlier date for it being moved.

Whatever the exact chronology, whenever it was moved to its current location any original medieval buildings along the southern and eastern ranges had been taken down, and if the earlier date is accepted this was at some point in the sixteenth or seventeenth century. Pushing the earlier date to a speculative conclusion, it is possible that the re-erection of the barn took place at about the same time as the construction of the Jerningham house, in which case it would mean that it was about 1560 that a dramatic contraction of the castle took place and it began to take on its modern appearance.

In summary, the basic outline of the development of the castle is as follows: the initial establishment of the castle by the de la Poles circa 1385 and which was probably complete by about 1400; a major intervention in the mid sixteenth century that probably saw the removal of large parts of the medieval building and their replacement by the present Jerningham house; a series of piecemeal changes to the southern range before the final removal of the remaining medieval buildings in the nineteenth century; and finally a period of restoration in the late nineteenth century that was concluded by Baron Ash in the twentieth.

Understanding the development of Wingfield Castle requires the use of a number of different approaches – documentary, architectural, archaeological and geophysical. Alongside the fragmentary nature of the original castle, particular difficulties relate to a marked absence of historical documentation from the castle during the late fourteenth and fifteenth centuries. From the point of view of reconstruction, the castle sits between two extremes. On the one hand, if the physical remains were non-existent the reconstruction would, out of necessity, have to draw on (and effectively copy) comparable and better-preserved examples from elsewhere, while on the other, if the physical remains were more extensive, the task of informing the reconstruction from physical evidence would be easier. As it is, as the following discussion makes clear, Wingfield represents a sometimes frustrating amalgam of, to paraphrase the now famous comment by former US Secretary of State Donald Rumsfeld, known knowns, known unknowns and unknown unknowns.

Reconstructing Wingfield Castle

It was decided to place the reconstruction at a date around 1500, a time when the medieval castle was probably complete, but before the major changes that took place

---

[21] Aitkens, pers comm.

Fig. 5.7. General view of Wingfield Castle reconstruction (Virtual Past).

during the sixteenth century. As the castle was the principal residence of John de la Pole and subsequently one of Alice Chaucer's Suffolk houses (see Archer, this volume) it seemed methodologically sound to assume that, while some modernisation might have taken place, the likely appearance of the castle at the end of the fifteenth century was that of a medieval building enjoying an Indian Summer (see Figure 5.7).

It is highly likely that the masonry curtain wall originally extended around the entire moated platform. An undated drawing (but probably from the late eighteenth century) showing the south-east curtain indicates that the wall extended at least to the site of the second gatehouse and that it was the same height as the parts of the medieval curtain that remain today.[22] As this curtain originally extended up to this second gatehouse, it is not unreasonable to suppose that it also continued further north along the eastern arm of the moat, particularly given the survival of the masonry footings of the north-east and north-western towers. The Suffolk antiquarian David Elisha Davy, who visited the castle circa 1837, recorded that on the east and north sides of the moat 'it is choked up by the fall of ruins' and the modern recovery from this part of the moat of a substantial figured corbel of a style consistent with those on the extant southern curtain is suggestive of a masonry wall of some solidity.[23] The presence of the stone garderobe chute on the western arm of the moat, but beyond the Jerningham building, suggests that this too is a legacy of substantial

[22] SROI: K446/1.
[23] BL: Add. MS 19092 fol. 386.

masonry works on this, western, side. This is not to say, however, that the height of any curtain walls was uniform; given that it faced the park it is possible that the walls were lower on this side in order to provide a view and this arrangement was indicated in the reconstruction.

One of the chief difficulties of the reconstruction was deciding how the timber-framed buildings should be arranged on the main moated platform. Some kind of subdivision of the main moat is highly likely but, while geophysical survey on the moat a revealed a series of cut features, it yielded nothing to suggest the presence of a subdividing wall of medieval date running in any direction. On the assumption that there was some division but in the absence of definitive evidence, two scenarios are possible. The first is where the interior is divided north–south. This would have meant any visitor coming through the main gatehouse would have entered the lower court and then had to dog leg through some kind of dividing wall to reach the principal rooms. Such an arrangement would be analogous to the original build at Baconsthorpe in Norfolk, where the main buildings were arranged around a small courtyard.[24] This type of reconstruction would envisage the eastern half of the main platform as a service court, something supported by the presence of a well in the south-east corner and it would also mean that the subsidiary eastern gatehouse would connect the service court with the base-court enclosure. Militating against this interpretation, however, is the fact that any such subdivision would have to sit up against the north-west gatehouse tower and where one would reasonably expect to see traces on the building today, as is the case at Baconsthorpe, but no such evidence exists and is also not suggested by the earliest historic image of the gatehouse.

The second scenario is one where the main moat was subdivided east–west. This would mean the southern part of the enclosure containing both a service court and also the main apartments. The evidence for such an interpretation rests on a broader sense of the ideal medieval high-status residence. If it is accepted that there is a tendency for higher status Tudor buildings to follow the footprint of earlier high-status medieval lodgings, then it would follow that the castle's principal medieval apartments lay on the western side, in the place now occupied by the Jerningham house and as suggested by Emery. This would logically place the great hall at ninety degrees to this range, which would mean that it faced the visitor as they came through the main gatehouse, a classic medieval arrangement. There is certainly nothing problematic with an east–west subdivision as far as the services are concerned. It is perfectly conceivable that the eastern gatehouse led directly into a service range on the eastern side of the castle. This would leave the problem of what was present in the northern half of the enclosure. This is not easily resolved, but it may be signifi-cant that in such a disposition this part of the moat would have faced the castle deer park. If an east–west division is posited then it would mean that the overall spatial

---

[24] Dallas and Sherlock 2002, p. 16.

Fig. 5.8. Reconstructed courtyard of Wingfield Castle (Virtual Past).

ordering of the castle in its landscape was one of an approach across water, into a base court, then into a lower court with great hall and apartments, then a more private enclosure and then the deer park. Such a grouping would not only be classically medieval but one that accords with the broader pattern established by landscape archaeologists both across the country and East Anglia in particular. In the end, it was decided to go with this interpretation, with the northern part of the main moat given over to a garden (see Figure 5.8).

The precise form of the timber-framed buildings is more speculative, but to judge from the fenestration and fireplaces on the extant southern range, two-storied apartments once existed along the whole of this side. The most likely scheme is that of accommodation for servants and lower members of the household on the ground floor, with more senior members on the floor above. Emery plausibly suggests that to the east of the gatehouse the first floor comprised an inner and outer chamber, with the former leading into private rooms in the south-east tower. To the west of the gatehouse was more high-status accommodation for the de la Poles themselves, as there is evidence for a fireplace on ground floor level and more elaborate fenestration.[25] The fact that during the sixteenth century it was the south-west corner and western side of the moat that was re-used as the site for the Jerningham house also suggests that this was where the original medieval high-status suites were located.

In the design of the timber-framed buildings arranged around the southern courtyard a ready source of inspiration is provided by the surviving structures at Wingfield

[25] Emery 2000, p. 162.

Fig. 5.9. Aerial view of Wingfield Castle showing Wingfield green and deer park (Virtual Past).

College. The reconstructed castle buildings reflect the hierarchy of space, with lower status windows arranged around the southern and eastern sides, which represent the services and servants' lodgings and higher status windows on the western range. The design of the hall itself draws heavily on the surviving example from the college.

Perhaps one of the more unusual aspects of the castle reconstruction – and which reflects a concern that existed at the start of the project – is the attention also given to the landscape context. Work on the surroundings of medieval castles has drawn attention to the importance of environs, both in terms of the constituent elements such as parks and ponds that made up the castle landscape, but also in turn as being something more than the sum of its individual parts: it was the placing of elements in such a way as it reflected on the dignity of the owner.[26] This is particularly applicable to Wingfield where the placing of fishponds on either side of the main approach in order to frame the gatehouse hints at a deliberate attempt to create a particular visual effect. Traditional reconstructions of castles tend, quite naturally, to focus on the buildings, and the landscape is usually something of an afterthought, whereas at Wingfield there was a concern to reflect both the broadening of academic interest to include castles in their landscapes, but also give some sense that castles extended beyond their immediate walls (see Figure 5.9).

The siting of the castle also reflects the wider pattern of settlement in this part of East Anglia. Here, the process of 'common edge drift' – a phenomenon whereby from the eleventh to the thirteenth century farms clustered around the sites of parish

[26] Creighton 2009.

Fig. 5.10. The basecourt (Virtual Past).

churches gradually shifted to the margins of common and greens – led to a distinctly regional settlement morphology. Castles that were in residential use for a considerable period – as opposed to those that were more temporary – tended to adhere to this broader pattern and there is a close correlation in Norfolk and north Suffolk – where common edge drift tended to be at its most pronounced – between castles and common edges.[27] Wingfield is in fact an excellent example of this, where the western arm of the moat abuts directly on to Wingfield Green. It is to give this distinctive regional character that the flythrough begins with a perspective that includes the castle in the context of its immediate landscape.

From here the flythrough takes the visitor along what would have been the principal medieval approach to the castle along the causeway between the two fishponds. The elongated form was undoubtedly intended to act as a visual device to raise the appearance of the castle as well as representing an exaggerated form of production. The base court is conjectural and based upon what might reasonably be expected at a castle of this status (see Figure 5.10). A barn is prominently displayed on the edge of the court, with the suggestion that this was the structure later moved into the main platform and re-erected. Fortuitously, a barn is shown in a similar position on a rare illustration of a base court at Holt Castle (Denbighshire) and its conspicuous location so as to be seen on the main approach is a reminder that barns were symbols of status during the Middle Ages.[28] The gatehouse and interior of the base court itself are conjectural, with the inclusion of animals, carts, barrels and ancillary

[27] Liddiard 2008.
[28] Goodall 2011, p. 222.

structures in the latter is, out of necessity, a 'best guess' at how this area might have looked, something that points up how, historically and archaeologically, base courts are relatively poorly understood.

The castle itself has been shown with the central moated platform divided east–west, with a further subdivision provided by a cross-wing at the east end of the hall, which gives a sense of a smaller courtyard around the principal apartments. Service buildings stand in what was effectively a service court and which sits on the eastern side towards the secondary gatehouse and in turn out to the base court. The northern side of the moated enclosure has been reconstructed as the castle garden, again divided between a more utilitarian area for the production of food and a more private garden for the occupants.

The final element in the castle landscape is the deer park. The reconstructions show it as a 'compartmented' park, that is, one where the area of the park is internally divided, principally to facilitate the production of coppice. In the reconstruction, the coppice lies towards the extremities of the park, with the central area comprising an area of grazing known as a 'laund' being managed as woodpasture, with oaks scattered across the turf. In the centre, at the site of a probable moat, is a hypothetical lodge building, based upon the late fourteenth-century lodge at Odiham park in Hampshire, which represents one of the best-documented examples of a lodge in England.[29]

The structure of the animation specifically asked the viewer to consider a number of themes. First, the bird's-eye view at the start showing the castle with its adjacent green and deer park is intended to make the point that no castle existed in some kind of ether, divorced from its physical surroundings; rather, it was intimately associated with both high-status and 'vernacular' landscapes that lay beyond the curtilage. Secondly, the approach both into and through the castle invites discussion of differential access to castle buildings. What was the social status of the base court? Was this as much of Wingfield Castle as those not directly associated with the de la Pole household ever saw? Questions of exclusivity also relate to the castle park. Hunt servants and members of the household would have had access, but for others was this a landscape of exclusion where illicit poaching was the only time when it was entered? The final scene shows the southern curtain, which must always have been the centrepiece of the castle, slowing fading to what can be seen today.

Wingfield Castle: Reconstruction and Reality

Wingfield is best seen alongside a group of late fourteenth-century castles built by 'local knights in the spirit of self-promotion' that are often noteworthy for a bullish or exaggerated form of military architecture.[30] The rise of the de la Poles had taken

---

[29] Roberts 1996.
[30] Coulson 2000; Goodall 2011, p. 314.

them beyond knighthood and into the peerage, however, something that throughout the Middle Ages was usually marked by the building or re-building of a castle, embodying as it did unequivocal membership of the aristocratic caste. The castle has variously been described as a 'power base and retirement home' and as a place strategically sited between a riotous Bury St Edmunds and a coastline vulnerable to French raiding.[31] Mono-casual explanations only rarely come close to the plurality of interests that castle-building was intended to serve, but the former comment draws attention to the kind of image (and kind of power) the castle was intended to project, something highly relevant to the reconstruction.

For the de la Poles, the acquisition of the new title did not automatically bring with it the wealth needed for lavish building, however, and while they may have technically been earls, the foundations of the castle were not built on decades of income from extensive landed estates. The diminutive scale of the gatehouse with its modestly heated and lit chambers betrays the mercantile origins of the de la Poles and has the hallmark of a family attempting to pressure up. As a castle of the late fourteenth century, Wingfield bears comparison with Bodiam, Maxstoke, Scotney and Cooling, buildings raised by the knightly class, not by earls. That Thomas Walsingham commented that the new Earl Michael de la Pole was 'a man more suited to the world of commerce than to knighthood, and had grown old peacefully among bankers, not on the battlefield among soldiers' echoes the idea that whatever else the recipient was and notwithstanding his considerable achievements, he was not old money.[32]

As has been noted before, the architecture of Wingfield Castle is not particularly demonstrative. The design of the window tracery is anachronistic in comparison to that of the contemporary parish church, and the addition of flushwork on the gatehouse gives the whole ensemble a much softer feel. Whatever else it may be, Wingfield cannot be described as belligerent. The emphasis is rather one of a productive estate, albeit a grand one, with a nostalgic sentiment. While a certain economy of scale is understandable, the reasons behind this particular image, while subjective, are not difficult to imagine. As Mark Bailey has demonstrated in this volume, the social context of the construction was one of a society rocked by climatic deterioration, epidemic disease, political instability and social unrest. For Michael de la Pole, a less demonstrative, but nonetheless still potent, expression of his new power and status, and one which, with its architecture framed by watery approach and parkland setting, evoked the sentiments of chivalry was evidently more suitable.

It is perhaps this last element – the *ideals* of Wingfield Castle - that the reconstruction captures and it is here that VR (at least in this case) comes into its own. When viewed in this light, positivist concerns over factual accuracy do not really matter and the exact arrangement of the buildings or precise line of the deer park

[31] Emery 2000, p. 160; Platt 2007, p. 95.
[32] Taylor et al. 2003, p. 236.

pale are less significant. What is inescapable from a study of the castle is that it confirmed to an ideal, one that is attested in contemporary literature, manuscript illustration and archaeological survey. As an aspirational construction project, the castle and its landscape conformed to the sense of what such a building *should* look like. The depiction of Sir Bertilak's castle in *Sir Gawain and the Green Knight*, written at about the same time as Wingfield's construction, and with similar *mores* of chivalry and knighthood, is instructive:

> Scarcely had the knight crossed himself three times, when he became aware of a dwelling in the wood surrounded by a moat, on a knoll above a glade, shut in under the boughs of many massive trees round about the defensive ditches: the fairest castle that ever a knight owned, erected in a meadow, surrounded by a park, set about by a palisade of close set spikes, which enclosed many trees in its circuit of more than two miles. The knight gazed at the castle from his side of the moat, as it shimmered and shone through the lovely oaks.[33]

It is in this spirit that the reconstruction, hopefully, is successful. The virtual part of late medieval Suffolk presented here hopefully takes some of the best elements of both the traditional artist's reconstruction and virtual reality and invites the viewer to image that, *just maybe*, that is what it could have looked like.

Acknowledgements

I should like to thank the following for their help with various aspects of this chapter. John Charmley, then head of history at UEA, provided the initial impetus for the reconstruction. I am heavily indebted to Philip Aitkens who kindly put at my disposal his encyclopaedic knowledge of timber-framed buildings, to Edward Martin on matters tenurial and John Goodall for his many inspiring conversations about the castle and college. Michael and Inga Lyndon-Stanford generously facilitated access to the castle and lastly thanks must go to Peter Bloore for his boundless enthusiasm for Wingfield and without whom the project would not have happened.

---

[33] Barron 1974, p. 69.

6

Historical Digital Reconstruction: The Role of Creativity and Known Unknowns – A Case Study of Wingfield College

Peter Bloore

> In my beginning is my end. In succession
> Houses rise and fall, crumble, are extended,
> Are removed, destroyed, restored, or in their place
> Is an open field, or a factory, or a by-pass.
> Old stone to new building, old timber to new fires,
> Old fires to ashes, and ashes to the earth.
>
> T.S. Eliot, *The Four Quartets: East Coker* (1943)

Wingfield College is a good example of a medieval building that has gone through many changes of use during its lifetime, from a religious college of priests to a Jacobean gentleman's residence; from a Georgian squire's Palladian mansion to a Victorian farmhouse; from a 1970s arts centre to a family home. Changes of use are not unusual in historic buildings, which have adapted to survive. Whilst the heart of the medieval timber frame of Wingfield College has survived inside, each period has brought new uses and fashions, including adding and removing a quadrangle, extending and knocking down different wings, endlessly re-decorating on the inside and re-facing on the outside. This has often involved demolishing and then re-using the old materials – for example, the current kitchen was added as an extension in the Jacobean period (when it was not the kitchen but a high-status parlour with an impressive bay window); however, it was built from re-used medieval bricks and beams, probably taken from a dismantled range on the same site. A classic example of T.S. Eliot's line 'old stone to new building'.

So with all these alterations and the cannibalising of old materials, how much do we know is definitely authentic? How much do we assume was originally there, when there are so many absences in the record: historical, documentary, archaeological and architectural? When it comes to creating a digital reconstruction of the medieval site we have to employ a mixture of surviving evidence, supposition based on other similar sites and regional conventions, and creativity. So what kinds of questions are raised by the digital reconstruction process, and what ultimately does it tell us about the nature of contested notions of authenticity, creativity and our relationship with the past? The purpose of this chapter is to raise key issues and problems that confronted the reconstruction team of researchers, experts and computer modellers, as we designed the digital reconstruction of the college; and it will reflect on how these issues may be relevant to other historical reconstructions and wider debates about recreating the past.

This will be done in three parts, the first of which elucidates the concepts around reconstruction and the role of creativity. The chapter then goes on to explore the vacillating fortunes of the de la Pole patrons and their endowments of the college, and how this raises the question of how far the building was resourced and 'finished'. The third part of the chapter reviews the remaining structural evidence at Wingfield College, describing in detail the choices made during the reconstruction process. As we shall see, new technology has been used to make the reconstruction look 'authentic' to modern eyes, but behind it lies old-fashioned historical research and creative decision-making.

Reflections on the reconstruction process

Reconstruction, absence and truth

So, what do we *mean* by reconstruction? The original sense of *re-* in Latin is 'back' or 'backwards', and is also used in words like recede, return and recover. So *re-*construction means to go back to construct something as it was in a previous state. In its current modern usage reconstruction could be described as the act of making a model, artist's impression or re-enactment of a past event or place, using informed supposition based on the available evidence. But this makes it sound easier than it is, because the available evidence is often incomplete, contested or unreliable; and in this case a reconstruction can never be more than a probability or even a possibility.

For a reconstruction to be necessary there must be something missing. It requires an absence: a building or landscape must have decayed or successive generations must have destroyed or substantially altered it (perhaps in the name of 'improvements'). This absence can be threefold:

1. A space where something was: a total physical absence of a previous structure, or the partial replacement of it with later structure?

2. A space or ambiguity in the historical record:
   a. How many records survive? What is missing?
   b. Can they be trusted as impartial and accurate?
   c. Are there multiple possible interpretations of the record?

3. A space in our cultural and societal understanding of the past. How did people

at the time perceive and understand these objects or structures? What were their cultural references and preconceptions, and how do they differ from ours? What preconceptions do we ourselves bring to bear? This will be discussed more in the next section.

This absence at the heart of reconstruction is also the central problem: how do you fill that gap in our knowledge? Sometimes plans or images survive and a reasonable reconstruction of a lost building is possible; although even then a building would have visibly changed at different stages in its life, and the original architect's plans may not reflect the later reality of the building's use. But sometimes there are lots of gaps in our knowledge and we have to use informed supposition, using comparative examples based on conventions in use in other buildings in that part of the country at that time in that type and status of building. One example is the medieval monastery, which usually followed a relatively consistent layout and plan: a church with a chapter house and other buildings set around the rectangular cloister on, usually, the south side of the church. From this it can often be possible to reconstruct the likely layout of a lost monastic site. However this means we are creating an indicative and likely typology, rather than a genuine *re*-construction; and reconstructions based on typology can by their nature become over conventional. In the absence of evidence the norm becomes all-powerful, probably more so than it was in real life. In the reconstruction rooflines become level, walls become upright, and structures become symmetrical and regular. However, look at a real surviving medieval monastic complex or manor house and they are usually an accretion of different phases and styles of work, with plenty of wonky angles, sloping rooflines and strange abutments. They have often been created piecemeal and over time (rare exceptions are places like Salisbury Cathedral which were built under the plans of a master mason in one relatively well-funded and consistent phase). To try to imitate this appearance of accretion, some reconstructions introduce an intentional element of discord and irregularity. For example, in the Wingfield College reconstruction it was decided to introduce different architectural phases into the northern range, to give the appearance and feeling that the building developed over time in an organic and haphazard way (and to reflect things we do know about different phases of the building, for example the gable of the west range was in existence before the completion of the cloister).

This leads us to the question: how do you reconstruct the atmosphere or 'truth' of a vanished place or object? Is there one accurate single truth to be shown in a reconstruction, or is it a series of possibilities and variables, depending on the views and interpretations of different experts, the use of different comparative examples, or the changing appearance of the site at different stages in time? One solution to this conundrum is to make a range of different reconstructions, showing possibilities that the remaining evidence or expert opinion could support, drawing attention to the academic debate and ultimately the subjective nature of reconstruction of the past. On the downside multiple versions might confuse the audience and it would certainly increase the costs of the reconstruction (multiple reconstructions are an expensive use of the computer programmer's time, resources and expert opinion). On the upside it might be a more honest approach to representing conflicting academic opinions of the interpretation of the evidence, and a representation of the elusive nature of truth in reconstruction.

Reconstruction, creativity and realism

There is a further additional way to fill the absence left in the historical record, and that involves creativity.[1] Creativity in digital reconstruction involves the generation of a new audio-visual artefact designed to communicate to the viewer information, a mood, and an experience of what the past may have been like. It can include the following issues:

1. The creative craft skills of the computer programmer, producing surfaces, textures, shapes and the play of sunlight and shade that trick us into thinking that what we see is real.
2. The use of imagination, to try and put ourselves into the past and the lives of the people alive then, to try to see it through their eyes.
3. Decisions around taste and decoration, trying to research their taste and cultural context, and trying to be hermeneutically aware of our own taste, as we try to reconstruct the appearance and meaning of the site.

This last sentence raises the complex issue of personal taste. As the novelist L.P. Hartley famously put it: 'The past is a foreign country: they do things differently there.'[2] In his novel the character is reflecting on his memories of his own childhood. It is much harder for us to try and transport ourselves back to a world we never knew, and where many tastes and values could be alien to us. In the process of reconstruction we constantly have to ask ourselves: how much are we reflecting our own taste, culture and beliefs; rather than theirs? For example, our austere post-reformation sensibility has been conditioned by centuries of Protestant thinking that rejects showiness and ostentation; so we tend to take pleasure in bare wood and stone surfaces, whitewashed plaster and clear glass. However, the average medieval visitor

---

[1]   The word creativity has different values in different cultures, and there are many definitions. Professor Margaret Boden has suggested the following definition: 'Creativity is the ability to come up with ideas or artefacts that are new, surprising and valuable ... Ideas here include concepts, poems, musical compositions, scientific theories, cookery recipes, choreography, jokes – and so on. Artefacts include paintings, sculptures, steam engines, vacuum cleaners, pottery, origami, penny whistles – and many other things you can name.' Boden 2004, p. 1. In the case of reconstruction, 'valuable' can be seen partly as its ability to communicate with a viewer or visitor to the site an idea of history and the past.
[2]   Hartley 1953, p. 1.

to a church or a great hall would instead have been impressed by vibrant colours and ornate surfaces, the wall paintings and the stained glass, and would probably view these decorations as a legitimate worship of God and a reflection of the wealth of the patrons. Even if we accept that the college hall was coloured, painted and decorated, how far do we go in redecorating it, given the total absence of physical remains of colour (the surviving crownpost roof, for example, does not show evidence of paint fragments)? It was decided to strike a balance between plain surfaces (such as the wooden seats and pillars) and conjectural coloured decoration. However, the truth would almost certainly have been more colourful, cluttered and possibly quite garish. Again the ideal reconstruction could contain several versions of the same room, from a bare simple hall (reflecting what it may have been like when the de la Poles were not at the height of their fortunes, or where the tastes of the master may have been influenced by austere Franciscan taste), to a highly ornate and decorated hall, full of colour and statues (reflecting what it may have been like in the heyday of William and his son John, or where the master may have been more influenced by the Cluniac Benedictines, who embraced art and splendour as a key element of worship).

But what do you put into the reconstruction when the historical or physical record is patchy, or even when there is really nothing known at all? Does creativity again have a further role to play here? For example, we know from a brief documentary reference of 1493 that Wingfield College had a north gate (see later discussion), and from the geophysics surveys we think we know where it was likely to have stood, on the north-east corner of the perimeter wall; but we do not know when it was built or what it looked like. We felt we could not just leave a grey block on the reconstruction video saying 'north gate', because that would have looked odd compared to the rest of the reconstruction, and would interrupt the 'reality' of the experience of viewing the reconstruction. However, leaving a grey block may be the most honest thing to do. We chose instead to put in an example of a timber-framed gatehouse from a nearby similar domestic ecclesiastical site of that period: Archdeacon William Pykenham's gatehouse to his courtyard house in Northgate Street in Ipswich.[3] Its construction date of circa 1471 is potentially late for our purposes, but we decided a gatehouse would not be a top priority in the college's construction process, so it may have been added later. Yet there is absolutely no evidence that the Wingfield College gate or gatehouse actually looked like that at all. It is a supposition based on a comparative example, so we are in effect saying that it 'could have looked something like this'. But the casual viewer of the digital reconstruction could not know this, and may assume that the appearance of the gatehouse is based on fact.

This also raises a crucial issue about digital reconstruction, as opposed to other forms of reconstruction (such as drawing and model-making), and that is the consistency of the perceived reality of the completed artefact, a reality that does not allow

---

[3] For a detailed discussion of Pykenham's gatehouse and his other building projects, see Tracy 2007, pp. 289–322.

for contested areas to be left unrealised or left out, because they look like lapses in the reality. Everything visible has to be completed to the same level of detail. A digital reconstruction is a computer-generated impression, either a single still image or more often moving multiple images, exploring the space in three dimensions. Early digital reconstructions often showed simple three-dimensional lines and the flat planes of surfaces. The limitations of the technology meant it could not attempt to imitate reality, so it was honest about its limitations in representing the past, and it was clear that it was a computer simulation of reality. Improvement in technology over the last twenty years means that Computer Aided Design (CAD) programs are now able to model textures, like bricks, wood, grass and water realistically; and imitate natural effects on those textures, like sunlight, smoke, mist and even glittering water. This means that digital reconstructions are now imitating reality more closely, and even though we subconsciously know that we are watching a computer-generated image our eyes and minds are increasingly tricked into imagining that we are looking at something real. We have become used to the high-quality special effects in feature films and television, and digital reconstructions are having to adopt this technology in order to remain convincing and satisfy an increasingly discriminating and audio-visual experienced audience. As this apparent realism increases, we put more credence into the digital images we are looking at, believing them to be a more accurate and a true representation than if we are looking at a wooden model or an artist's painting or drawing, where the media is drawing attention to itself and therefore to its partiality. This leads to a growing belief amongst the general public that a digital reconstruction is an 'accurate" one, partly due to this realism and partly because the medium itself was popularised in the 1990s by factual television programmes on respected channels like BBC2, Channel 4, the History Channel and the Discovery Channel. The digital reconstruction was often the climax of episodes of Channel Four's influential and popular television series *Time Team* (1994–2013). This chapter is trying to draw attention to the fact that the ordinary viewer should be more suspicious and questioning of the appealing reality presented by digital reconstructions – they have no greater claim to being authentic or true than any other method of reconstruction.

In fact, moving 3D reconstructions are much more methodologically complex than static images because the journey of the fictional camera does not allow a single convenient viewpoint to be chosen by the illustrator. As the viewpoint pans, tracks and flies through the computer-generated space, every single thing that it 'sees' has to be given form, light, colour and texture. When going inside buildings, the thickness of the walls and internal space of the rooms have to look and feel convincing to the human eye. In the case of the Wingfield College reconstruction some walls and spaces that looked reasonable on a two-dimensional ground plan became cramped and out of proportion once rendered into three moving dimensions, and had to be re-modelled. Ground plans do not communicate internal space in the way that a three dimensional image does.

And when artificial reality is concerned, no item can be taken for granted. In the Wingfield reconstruction we decided to show the great hall in preparation for a feast day, because it would look more interesting and inhabited than if the hall was totally empty (see Plate VII). However, this simple decision became a can of worms, because all the things that we take for granted in a dining room (like tablecloths, cutlery, plates and cups) had to be reconstructed based on pictures in medieval manuscripts or from rare surviving examples. So these table dressings are now ostensibly 'authentic', in that they are based on genuine medieval examples, and yet not one of them is *known* to have existed at Wingfield College. They are all authentic but indicative, designed to give an impression of an imagined reality to the viewer.

There were further issues of custom and behaviour to consider. Originally the digital modeller included forks at every person's place, but medieval people very rarely used forks (they have existed since Roman times, but were mainly used in this period for serving not eating). So the forks were removed, apart from a serving fork on the top table. In this status-conscious society the high table was more likely to have objects made from gold and silver, whereas the lower tables had them made from base metals and wood. Strictly speaking, ordinary people probably brought their knives with them to the table, rather than having them laid out in advance, but this made the tables look too bare, so it was decided to put knives in place on the tables.

To conclude, because the digital reconstruction is purveying an imagined form of reality, considerable work has to be expended on creating that simulation; and as the viewpoint moves through the digital model a larger number of creative and academic decisions and suppositions come into play during their manufacture than drawings which need only present one viewpoint. And the larger the number of decisions the greater the opportunities for error or supposition, since parts of the reconstruction cannot simply be left blank due to absence of hard evidence.

Reconstruction as a new creative artefact

The above issue of the table dressings of the great hall takes us back to the nature of reconstruction and the previous example of the Wingfield gatehouse. The question is: at what point is reconstruction actually the creation of a totally new artefact (in the case of a digital reconstruction an audio-visual experience) that is designed to communicate the perceived feel of the original site, as *inspired* by the original building and comparative examples? Maybe it is not a reconstruction as much as a creative re-imagining. In the pre-digital twentieth century these interpretive images of historic buildings were often referred to as *artist's impressions*. This is a more honest title than the current one of reconstruction, because it is explicitly stating that it is only one person's interpretation (the artist) and it is only aspiring to provide an impression, not a reality. Even the published names of those impressions drew attention to their subjectivity; for example, the paintings by the artist Alan Sorrell in the 1960s and 1970s often had titles like: 'Castle Acre Priory From the South West as it Might Have Appeared Shortly before its Suppression in 1537'. The title flags up the fact that the whole illustration is a supposition ('might have appeared') and a single snapshot in time.

Maybe we now need to re-introduce the idea of the artist-visualiser into debates around digital reconstruction. Furthermore, if as suggested we consider the reconstruction as an entirely new artefact then the 'truth' of it can be judged not just in relation to the historical past and the lost object but also whether it is true to the coherent vision of the artist-reconstructor, through the prism of their own creativity and historical–social–cultural context. The final role of creativity in digital reconstruction (to add to the list above) is maybe the creation of a coherent vision that satisfies the viewer and draws them into the experience in a holistic way.

We could use the parallel of the digital reconstructor and the film or television director working on an adaptation: both are interpreting an original object or text through their own vision. A film or television adaptation of a novel is never a perfect copy of the author's original work, but an interpretation of it. Both film-making and reconstruction are a translation of a source material into a totally different medium, expressing the vision and judgements of the director and screenwriter (who could be compared to the reconstructor and the academic experts providing advice). The existing academic field of screenplay adaptation studies considers the screenplay as a text in relation to other texts, examining the source text of the screenplay (often literature: a modern novel or a classic such as Jane Austen) and comparing it to the adapted screenplay and the completed film or television artefact. It focuses on issues such as the fidelity of the adaptation to its source-text; the complexity and subjectivity of value judgements about different versions; the nature of appropriation, interpretation, inter-textuality and authorship; and the relative cultural and historical contextualisation of the various texts.[4] All of these issues and debates are relevant to what we could perhaps now call 'historical reconstruction studies'. We could define this as the academic study of the intellectual and creative process of reconstruction and the analysis of the completed artefact, including its relationship to the original historical source materials, and relative cultural and historical contextualisation. The audio-visual reconstruction artefact could also be read as a media studies text in its own right; using many of the traditional approaches of that academic discipline, including issues of taste and reception; audience reception studies; analysis of the context of the intent of the commissioning authority (the museum, broadcaster or other cultural industry organisation); and the sociological study of cultural production and aesthetics.[5] This radical suggestion is not trying to set the reconstructor up as an *auteur* figure (the powerful creator status that is often according to directors in media studies and film studies); however, it is raising the issue that there often has to

4   Bloore 2014, p. 25.
5   These issues around taste and cultural production have been well debated from the work of Bourdieu onwards. See Bourdieu 1984, 1993 and 1996, and for a brief overview of Bourdieu see Grenfell 2008.

be one final person providing overall vision, and that person is making decisions over creative issues and taste as much as over the historical evidence of the site. The 'voice' of the reconstructor is currently uncredited and sublimated in the presentation of the reconstruction (on television or at a historical site), but in reality that role and that voice is present in the artefact. In some reconstructions the team is more powerful and decisions are more collegial, but in some the leader's decision has more sway.

To conclude, the aim of creativity in reconstruction is to create a more immersive and 'realistic' experience, to engage the viewer and to communicate an idea of a sense of the past; and through that to educate and inspire them to understand more. But this means that the final interpretation or reading of the reconstruction is made not by its creator(s), but by those viewers, who bring their own understanding, precon-ceptions and cultural values to bear as they watch the reconstruction. In the case of a historical site the audience then use their experience of the reconstruction to fire their own imaginations as they walk around the real site. Hopefully it may help them 'see' into the past, even if that view is influenced by their own imagination and the vision of the reconstructor-artist. So the viewer is yet another step on the process between the absent artefact in the past, and the creation and reception of the reconstruction artefact in the modern day.

And how strange that reconstruction may look in a hundred years' time, when a new audience looks back at today's reconstruction and thinks how much 'of its time' it looks, compared to what they then think the medieval past was like. Galileo thought that the nature of observed reality depended on the position of the observer, and the same is true of the past.

The process of the Wingfield College reconstruction

In the case of Wingfield College, the methodology was fourfold. First, to examine and document the remaining physical structures, carried out by Edward Martin, formerly of the Suffolk County Archaeological Service, and Philip Aitkens, an expert on timber-framed structures in medieval East Anglia, with further input from Dr John Goodall. Secondly the landscape surveys, carried out by Edward Martin, Dr Rob Liddiard of the University of East Anglia (UEA) and Dr Lucy Marten, formerly of UEA. Thirdly radiography and geophysics surveys of the site (Stratascan), including test pits over any potential anomalies. And fourthly desk research undertaken to identify relevant medieval documents (Dr Chris Bonfield of UEA); other regional similar timber-frame structures (Philip Aitkens); and comparative chantry colleges (Dr Peter Bloore of UEA). This research into comparable types meant the recon-struction could be representative of a Suffolk timber-framed college of that period, even if the absence of evidence in parts meant it could not always be wholly authentic to this particular site.

Each step of the reconstruction design was discussed by the relevant members of the group, and decisions were usually made on what was reasonable to assume based on the evidence, often using what is known as 'Ockham's Razor'. William of Ockham was a Franciscan friar and philosopher from Surrey (c.1288–c.1348) and his process was to select from competing hypotheses that which makes the fewest assumptions and thereby offers the simplest explanation of the effect. At every step consensus was sought, although final decision rested with Peter Bloore as overall project director. Philip Aitkens drafted a floor-plan and suitable elevations for the lost sections, using old-fashioned pencil and paper. He redrafted several times according to the rest of the team's feedback, and these drawings were then loaded into the CAD digital reconstruction software (the work of John Williams of the Virtual Past team at UEA). These drawings were combined with photographic evidence of surviving structures (like the great hall), and the surface textures of the surviving building (bricks, plaster, timbers etc.). Some of the team discussions about the three-dimensional space of the college made us carefully question our assumptions and beliefs, and made us consider whether the reconstruction process was actually a research method in itself.

During the desk research it was necessary to consider the vacillating fortunes of the patrons and the likely extent of the buildings. This chapter will now go on to look at both these areas in turn, and consider how our findings informed the final reconstruction.

How wealthy was the college and its patrons

The vacillating fortunes of the de la Poles

Early in the research process it was questioned whether the newly ennobled de la Pole family had the resources to build the college to the same level as their aristocratic competitors, such as the more established dukes and earls with substantial fortunes. To inform the scale and ornamentation of the reconstructed buildings it was important to establish how well endowed the college was, after Sir John Wingfield's initial substantial investment (see Bailey, this volume). If it was mainly built in the late fourteenth century then it may have the look of one period; however, if it was re-funded regularly then it may have the appearance of additions and modernisations. The de la Poles certainly lived in interesting times: some left further wealthy endowments of money and land to the college, but others lost their money and status in their own lifetimes, died in exile or were arraigned as traitors.

However, the first twenty-five years of the college's existence were stable and successful for the patrons, and their fortunes rose inexorably. Sir John's widow Eleanor oversaw the carrying out of her husband's dying wishes, until her own death and burial next to her husband thirteen years later in 1375 – a good period of consolidation for the foundation. Michael de la Pole then finally gained personal control of his mother-in-law's wealth, and his receipt of the Wingfield family's manors via his wife Katherine included many estates in Suffolk, including the manors of Wingfield,

Stradbroke, Syleham,[6] Fressingfield, Huntingfield, Saxmundham and Sternfield; and, in Norfolk, the manor of Saxlingham, and in Essex the manor of Langham.[7]

Michael de la Pole's political fortunes rose until he was sworn in as chancellor of England in 1383. Richard II made him earl of Suffolk in 1385, along with a grant of most of the lands that had belonged to the previous earl, William de Ufford.[8] His promotion was in part due to his work arranging the marriage between King Richard II and Anne of Bohemia.[9] However, in 1387 his fortunes declined as he was accused of treason and corruption and had to flee the country to evade trial (he died in exile in 1389). Some of his lands were seized by the Crown, and the fall in the de la Pole's political and financial fortunes lasted for more than ten years (the title of earl of Suffolk was initially withheld from his son Michael, who was not made earl until 1398).

For the architectural history of the college the question is: how much had already been built by the first earl's downfall in 1387? And if it was not already physically substantial then does this hiatus in the patron's fortunes mean it was never fully completed and therefore not as large as some other contemporary colleges founded by men of equal wealth?[10] We will never know for sure, but the dendro-dating of the great hall at Wingfield to the early 1380s shows that this at least was completed before or around this date (the hall's north arcade plate timber was felled in 1379 and the upper tiebeam in 1383, five years before Michael's exile[11]). Furthermore, the great hall overlaps the decorative wind bracing of the earlier phase of the east-facing wall of the lodgings, so it is definitely a replacement (larger) hall to the original hall. The question is whether all the attendant buildings were also completed, such as the rest of the cloister. In the 1380s Michael certainly spent time and money in Wingfield, including fortifying his manor house into a castle to match his newly acquired noble status.[12] So it is possible that builders were working on the castle and the college at the same time (again in keeping with the dendro-dating). He also created the deer

---

[6]   This was the manor of Syleham Comitis, which contained the main Syleham manor house and the chapel at Essam/Esham; rather than the manor of Monks Syleham, which was owned by the monks of Thetford. Gray 1996.

[7]   Roskell 1984, p. 207.

[8]   CPR 1385–9, p. 24. The grant was in reversion after the deaths of Queen Anne and Isabella de Ufford, dowager countess of Suffolk.

[9]   Emery 2000, p. 160.

[10]   This potential hiatus makes it difficult to achieve direct comparisons with the nearby and roughly contemporaneous Mettingham College. The latter had consistent patronage throughout its growth, as shown by Ridgard 2009.

[11]   Bridge 1999a. Oak timbers in this period were often used 'green' rather than seasoned, so they contracted in situ.

[12]   He was granted a royal licence to crenellate on 27 April 1385 (CPR 1381–5, p. 555). It is possible that the building of Wingfield Castle had already started, because some crenellation licences were granted retrospectively. How much time Michael personally spent at Wingfield is unclear, since he spent most of 1361–75 fighting in France and when he was in the country he spent time in London at court or in Hull.

park at this stage, so a lot of the landscape and buildings in the area were being substantially modified in this period. Furthermore, he was certainly not backward at funding big religious building projects. In Hull he founded a substantial Carthusian house in 1379,[13] and a hospital for twenty-six poor men and women in 1384. To conclude, twenty-six years since the death of the founder (1361 to 1387) is a reasonable period of time for a substantial quantity of work to have been completed, and the dendro-dating of the hall suggests major building extensions were undertaken well before Michael's exile.

The return of the seized lands in 1398 and the return to royal favour may have meant that building work on the college and castle could start again. Simon Walker, in his biography of Michael, has asserted that 'At Wingfield, Suffolk, the centre of de la Pole influence in the region, he completed his father's ambitious building plans, augmenting the endowment of the family chantry college and considerably enlarging the church of Wingfield itself.'[14] This could have included the addition of the chancel clerestory and the lady chapel.[15] We have documentary evidence that in 1401–2 Michael granted 'land and rent in Stradbroke, Wingfield, and Earsham Street in Wingfield and Syleham to the Master and Chaplains of the Church of Wingfield',[16] which was worth 10 s yearly.[17] In 1406 Michael chose to commemorate the death of his brother Richard (d.1403) with a grant to the college in 1406 of the manor of Benhall and rent from the east Suffolk manors of Sweffling, Cransford, Great Glemham, Rendham and Farnham.[18] These manors were granted to fund a priest to pray for Richard's soul at the altar of Holy Trinity in Wingfield church. The font in the church was donated in about 1405 by Michael de la Pole and his wife Katherine Stafford.[19] There were grants from other patrons too: licence was granted in 1401 to the provost or master and the chaplains of the collegiate church of Wingfield, for Thomas Doupe to grant in mortmain land in Stradbroke, Wingfield and Earsham Street.[20]

Evidence of ongoing enrichment of the college comes with two further de la Pole burials in the church: the aforementioned Richard in 1403, whose will left to his executors all his goods to dispose of 'to the glory of God and the salvation of the soul of the same Richard'; and John de la Pole in 1414 (canon of York and Beverley), who was buried in the church next to the altar and whose will left money …

---

[13] Emery 2000, p. 156.

[14] Walker 2012.

[15] Aitkens et al. 1999.

[16] Aldwell 1925, p. 81.

[17] *VCH Suffolk*, II, p. 152.

[18] Aldwell 1925, pp. 38, p.81; also in Davy MS p. 374. Benhall in Suffolk is just south of Saxmundham. In 1538 the manor house was leased by Charles Brandon, so it seems likely that the manor went from Wingfield College to Henry VIII when the college was dissolved, and then to Brandon.

[19] Fripp 1896, p. 9.

[20] *VCH Suffolk*, vol. II, p. 152.

to the high altar of the Church of Wingfield aforesaid twenty shillings. Also I leave to the Sacrist of the College there six shillings and eight pence. Also I leave to the Sacristan there three shillings and four pence ... Also I give and bequeath the rest of all my goods, moveable or immoveable, to the Chantry or College of Wingfield aforesaid for the transferring for ever of certain lands for the support of one Chaplain at the Altar of the Holy Trinity in the aforesaid Church to say masses for my soul as well as for my parents and all other faithful departed for ever.[21]

When Michael de la Pole himself died in 1415 of dysentery at the siege of Harfleur he willed 'to the College of Wyngfelde one vestment of white cloth of gold with everything belonging, viz., 3 copes, 1 amictus, 1 chasuble, 3 amices, 3 albs, 3 stoles, 3 fanons, 2 altar cloths with 1 frontal, 2 pillons, 1 canopy, 2 curteynes of Tartaryn and 2 towelles'. His body was parboiled at Harfleur to be transported back to be buried in the church. In circa 1420 Michael's son William de la Pole gave to the College of Wingfield the income from the manor of Chickering Hall or Chickering-cum-Wingfield and a moiety of the Manor of Walpole and land therein, presumably to help pay for the masses for his parents.[22] This is the fourth of the Wingfield parish manors and contained the chapel of Our Lady of Chickering that features in some wills, and was serviced by the college chaplains.[23] Again this is a substantial parcel of land and rental income

William and Alice de la Pole

All the above evidence of money left to the college shows it was a place of some status and income. This was enough to be able to keep funding the building work as well as the salaries, and it would surely not have fitted the status of the de la Poles for the accommodation next to the family mausoleum to appear only half finished by the early fifteenth century. But in 1429 the de la Pole fortunes took a dramatic turn for the worse. Two of William's brothers (Alexander and John) died fighting in France and a third brother (Thomas) died in captivity there in 1433. More problematically, William himself was captured by the French at the siege of Jargeau, and over the next three years the family had to sell many manors in Suffolk to pay the huge ransom of £20,000, including even William's own birthplace at Cotton in Suffolk.[24] This may explain why when he came to build a tomb for his parents he could only afford to pay for the effigies to be made out of wood (unusual for a tomb this late).[25] However, once William de la Pole returned to England he was soon enriching the college again,

[21] Aldwell 1925, pp. 28–8. He suggests that John's stone is at the entrance to the chancel.
[22] Ibid., p. 81. At William's death in 1450 the college received the full right to the manor.
[23] The chapel was probably in *Church Field* next to the old Chickering Hall on the road to Hoxne. Ibid., p. 3.
[24] Curran 2011, pp. 138–47, 178
[25] Badham, this volume. However, once painted and seen from the other side of the rood screen they would have still appeared very impressive. According to Scarfe 1986, William's father Michael had previously laid under a plain slab.

because in 1438 he got royal permission to endow the college with lands and rents worth 100 s a year for two chaplains to say mass at the altars of St Mary and St Nicholas in the church at Wingfield, in memory of his mother Lady Katherine; and mass at the altar of the Holy Trinity for his uncle Richard de la Pole.[26]

It is likely that William's improved fortunes were in part through his marriage in 1432 to the wealthy heiress Alice Chaucer, who has been estimated to be 'by the standards of her day one of the wealthiest inhabitants of England';[27] and was also a substantial patron of education and literature in her own right, including a substantial grant to the Divinity School at Oxford University.[28] William and Alice have been described as 'exceptionally lavish patrons of religious foundations';[29] and a few months before the Wingfield College endowment they got royal permission for the foundation of a charitable hospital and school at Ewelme in Oxfordshire, and William gifted more money to his grandfather's Charterhouse monastery in Hull. William was also a benefactor of Eton College Chapel and was to become Protector of Oxford University in 1447.[30] Clearly, William and Alice are investing in other religious institutions in this period (perhaps out of feelings of guilt at the deaths of William's brothers, especially since he had been leading the English army when Alexander and John were killed at Jargeau); so by now it seems unfeasible that the Wingfield College buildings would have been left incomplete, especially in the de la Pole's home manor. Given this evidence of financial investment activity in the late 1430s it was decided that the reconstruction of the college would show a timber frame range of this period of studding and window design on the north side of the quadrangle. This was potentially the last side to be completed, but would have been relatively high status in its decoration since it faced towards the church itself.

William's political and financial fortunes continued to improve during the 1440s, including negotiating the peace treaty with France and the resulting marriage of King Henry VI with Margaret of Anjou in 1444. In 1447 he was made lord high admiral and earl of Pembroke, and in 1448 he was elevated to be duke of Suffolk, so this was a man of considerable status and a need to display patronage that reflected that status. After the murder of William in 1450 his wife Alice spent a lot of time consolidating her control of her ex-husband's fortunes,[31] and by the early 1460s she had sufficiently secure funding to spend the substantial sum of at least £75 8s 4d on the extension of the chancel and the chapels at Wingfield Church to house 'my Lord's fader's and his moder's tomb'.[32] These works required 38 tons of Lincolnshire stone to be trans-

---

[26] Goodall 2001, p. 33.

[27] Archer, this volume.

[28] Goodall 2001, pp. 11–12, 143 and 273–7.

[29] Ibid., p. 31.

[30] For a detailed analysis of William and Alice's charitable endowments see ibid., pp. 31–5.

[31] Archer, this volume

[32] The estimate for the work survives in the Ewelme Muniments and is discussed and dated to the early 1460s in ibid., pp. 57, 267–77. He argues that it is Alice's work, since the estimate was found

ported to Wingfield, presumably by boat up the River Waveney and then over the fields. The question is why did she do it at this stage, apart from simply making the collegiate church grander? College churches and chantries were often expanded to allow for extra tombs to be inserted, and yet here there are no extra tombs of this period in the church. The tomb of William's parents Michael and Katherine was moved eastward and their tomb had a new grander table-top tomb created, with niches for statues of their children around the sides.[33] Their aggrandisement may have been part of the motive, but it is a lot of work to carry out, especially when Alice decided to move to Ewelme in 1466. The north chapel (now the vestry) was also extended by a bay at this stage,[34] and may have then been a private chapel for Alice herself to worship in privacy,[35] or a separate chantry chapel, maybe originally intended for William himself. Badham and Goodall argue that William was buried at Charterhouse in Hull in 1459, in accordance with his will,[36] but that might not have been Alice's original plan. The use of this space as either a chantry chapel or a private chapel would explain the richness of the decoration of the windows and their glass. This space was altered in the late fifteenth or early sixteenth century by the insertion of a partial timber upper floor with a relatively simple but painted screened front overlooking the altar below; and in the north wall two small simple lancet windows and a small unadorned external door. Two roughly shaped first-floor

amongst her papers of the 1460s and seems synchronous with others in that package. The estimate is the source of the above quote about the tomb. Scarfe 1986, pp. 157–8, previously argued that this work was the work of William de la Pole in the 1530s, while at the visit of the Suffolk Institute for Archaeology and History in 1998 a date of 1430–50 was preferred, though allowing that it could be later (Aitkens et al. 1999). The total spent would have been greater than £75, because the estimate does not cover either the conversion of the vestry into the larger chapel structure or the creation of the table-top tomb for Michael and Katherine.

[33] Goodall 2001, p. 62. The existing stone plinth is apparently too wide to fit between the arches and the plinth mouldings of the original canopy.

[34] Previously this chapel (perhaps the Holy Trinity Chapel) had two tall decorated windows with similar internal and external frames to those of the nave south aisle windows that, stylistically, could be as early as the 1330s, but because of the avowed intent in the 1362 foundation charter that the church 'must be in great part built anew' are perhaps as late as the 1360s. An extra bay was added in Alice's commissioned works, with a new window that may have originally gone the same length of the others – the later addition of a simple north door truncating it. The editors of the book believe that this increased length of the chapel may have allowed for the insertion of an Easter sepulchre, like the ones at Bures St Mary and Long Melford in Suffolk; and referred to in three wills (Thomas Dade als. Rushey of Wingfield 1477 (Norwich Consistory Court): to support of sepulchre light 5 s; John Deye of Wingfield 1453 (Suffolk Archdeaconry Court): to light of sepulchre of body of Christ 6 d; Thomas Stratford of Wingfield 1502 (Suffolk): increasing of the sepulchre light 12 d). The sepulchre alcove may have subsequently been filled in on the north side and the original sepulchre replaced by the tomb of John and Elizabeth de la Pole, which is cramped in its present position and shows signs of re-assembly, perhaps indicating that it has been moved from its original position elsewhere in the church – perhaps more centrally in the chancel.

[35] Goodall, this volume.

[36] Badham, this volume; Goodall 2001 pp. 297–8, 270. There is a charter referring to the planned burial of William and Alice dated 1462. However, Goodall thinks he was buried by 1549 (ibid., p. 10).

squints were also inserted and these would have enabled the occupant(s) to see the more important altars in the main parts of the church (a frequent feature of chantry chapels, anchorite cells, watching-chambers and parcloses).[37] This structure could have been an upper parclose for the de la Poles,[38] or given the comparative simplicity of the design and decoration of these additions it is likely that it was a sacristan's watching-chamber.[39]

Either way, if Alice was spending large amounts of money on the church in the 1460s it means that the college as a whole was very much in her thoughts and receiving substantial patronage, and not a foundation in decline. The odds are that she would at least have maintained the college accommodation to match its church, if not also actively making it grander (maybe she paid for work on the gatehouse facing the church, mentioned in the bishop's visitation?) She carried out a lot of work on church porches and towers in the area in this period, including the porch at Syleham Church (which was operated by the college priests), and the very substantial church tower and new south porch at the nearby town of Eye (carried out in 1454, and in memory of her dead husband).[40]

Throughout the late fifteenth century Alice's son John de la Pole was duke of Suffolk, married to Richard III's sister Elizabeth Plantagenet. Although historically under-researched, John is said to have avoided high politics in London (not surprisingly given the fate of his father), and spent most of his life at Wingfield Castle. In 1493 the college received a deed of gift from Elizabeth, duchess of Suffolk, of various

[37] See Roffey 2007, 2008, for a detailed discussion of squints and their possible different uses.
[38] Goodall, this volume.
[39] In favour of a sacristan's chamber are Cautley 1954, p. 346; Scarfe 1986, p. 159; Jenkins 1999, p. 667. In Anon. 1891, pp. xxxiv–v, there is a discussion of the parclose option versus the sacristan's chamber option, and deciding on the latter as follows: 'While researching through some of the old records of a neighbouring parish, he [the historian and antiquary, the Rev. Dr Augustus Jessopp] had come across a complaint that the Custos Capelli did not sleep in the church, and this fact opened his eyes to the conviction that this chamber was the place of residence for one of the chaplains of the church, whose business it was to watch over the light that burned perpetually on the altar, to sleep in the church, and also to guard it against robbers. Dr Jessopp said there was a similar chamber at Hingham, in exactly the same position as this ... Dr Raven remarked how delighted he was to accept Dr Jessopp's explanation of the use of the chamber, more especially because he was able to support it by stating that he recollected that one of the nonjuring clergy had actually died on a portion of the rood screen, that he might die in the sight of the altar.' James Willoughby (2012, p. 340) cites a number of collegiate churches which had inhabited sacristies, especially when the lodgings were away from the church and outside the cloistered enclosure, as Wingfield is. In his case study of St Mary's collegiate church at Warwick the first-floor sacristy was evidentially both a private chapel for the earls of Warwick *and* a dwelling place for the Sacristan, and like Wingfield it had an external door to the churchyard. However, the Warwick sacristy has a higher ceiling and four larger ornate windows, clearly overseeing the whole high altar area, which are more suited to the status of an earl of and his family than the rough cut and narrow squints at Wingfield.
[40] Goodall 2001, p. 34; and Martin 2013.

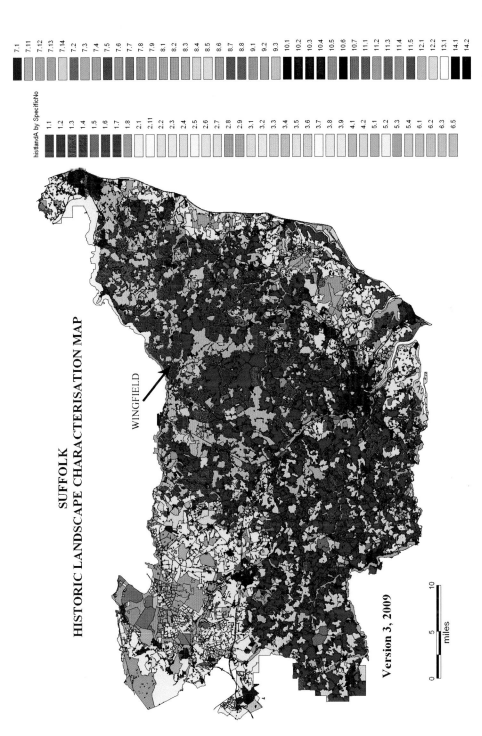

Plate I The Suffolk Historic Landscape Characterisation map (version 3, Suffolk County Council Archaeological Service, 2009).

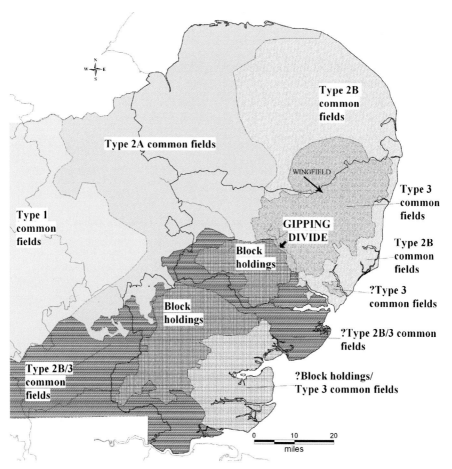

Plate II Map of the medieval farming regions of 'Greater' East Anglia, showing the 'Gipping Divide'.

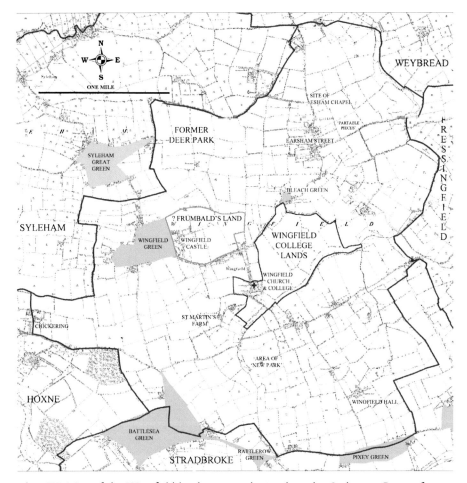

Plate III Map of the Wingfield landscape, as depicted on the Ordnance Survey first-edition map of 1886.

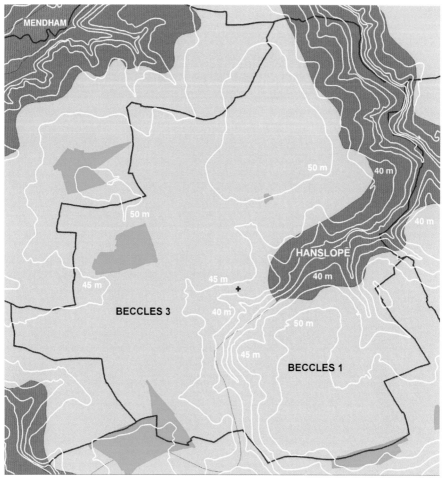

Plate IV The topography and soils of Wingfield. Soil mapping based on the Soil Survey of England and Wales, *1:250,000 Soil Map of England and Wales* (Harpenden 1983)

Plate V The Wingfield College complex from the south.

Plate VI Digital reconstruction of the exterior of Wingfield College as it may have appeared in the 1490s, looking from the north, with the east end of the church on the right of the picture (see pp. 115–16).

Plate VII Digital reconstruction of the interior of Wingfield College great hall as it may have appeared in the 1490s, looking west, as though prepared for a feast day. The de la Pole shields are taken from the tomb of Alice de la Pole at Ewelme. The crest above the high table is based on the extant college seal.

Plate VIII The great hall of Wingfield College, as it appears today, looking east. This shows the 1380s crown post roof and the Tudor tie-beam. The linenfold panelling shows Charles Brandon, Duke of Suffolk, and Mary Tudor, Queen of France. The end wall is a later replacement (see pp. 123–25).

Plate IX Digital reconstruction of the exterior of Wingfield College as it may have appeared in 1378, looking west, towards the accommodation range, before the rest of the quadrangle was presumably added. The first storey decorative fan bracing largely still survives in the college. The presence of an external staircase has been extrapolated from surviving first floor studwork, which implies two external doorframes, and mortises that may have supported a roof. The staircase structure is conjectural (see p. 120).

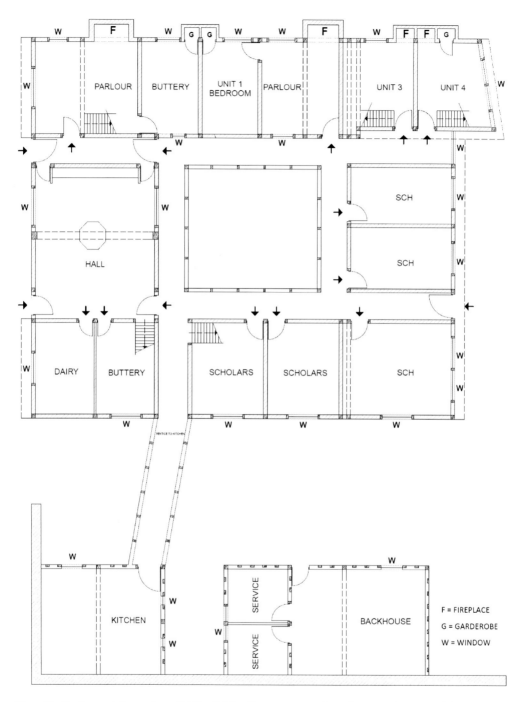

Plate X Conjectural floor plan of Wingfield college as it may have been in the 1490s. This was produced to help inform the digital reconstruction.

Plate XI Digital reconstruction of the south front of Wingfield college as it may have appeared in the 1490s. This would have been the view of the college if approaching the great hall from the barns court – the usual approach for most ordinary visitors (see p. 126).

Plate XII Digital reconstruction of the western exterior of Wingfield college as it may have appeared in the 1600s (see p. 129). The west side has now become the front of the house. Many of the illustrated mullion windows survive *in situ* inside the house, but were filled in by the Georgian Palladian facade. The reconstruction chimneys and the porch have been taken from Monks Hall Syleham, Suffolk.

Plate XIII Digital reconstruction of the western exterior of Wingfield college as it appeared in the 1790s (see p. 130). This is as it looks today, however the circular window in the portico has now been filled in.

Plate XIV Charles Stothard's coloured
study of Sir John Wingfield's effigy.
Wingfield (Suffolk).

Plate XV Detail of effigy of Sir John Wingfield (d.1361). Wingfield (Suffolk), showing surviving surface finishes below head.

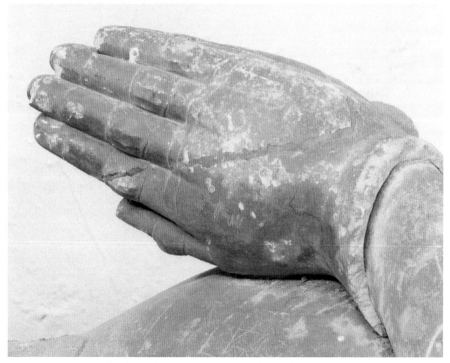

Plate XVI Detail of effigy of Sir John Wingfield (d.1361). Wingfield (Suffolk), showing surviving gold leaf on gauntlets.

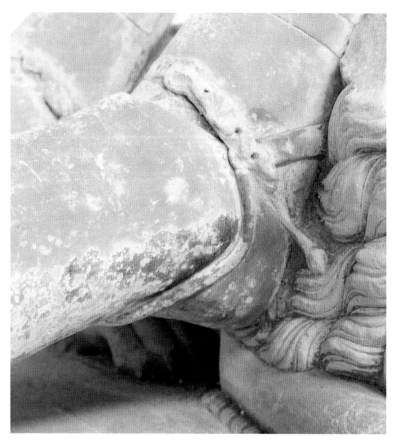

Plate XVII Detail of effigy of Sir John Wingfield (d.1361). Wingfield (Suffolk), showing surviving gold leaf on sabatons.

Plate XVIII Detail of tomb monument of Michael de la Pole, 2nd earl of Suffolk (d.1415) and his wife Katherine showing remains of names of children, Wingfield (Suffolk).

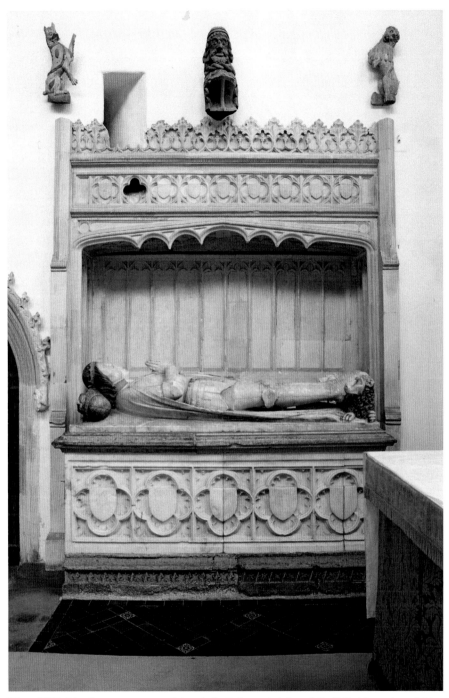

Plate XIX Tomb monument to John de la Pole, 2nd duke of Suffolk (d.1491), and his wife, Elizabeth of York (d. ?1503). Wingfield (Suffolk).

Plate XX Charles Stothard's coloured study of tomb effigies of John de la Pole, 2nd duke of Suffolk (d.1491), and his wife, Elizabeth of York (d. ?1503). Wingfield (Suffolk).

Plate XXI Detail of effigy of John de la Pole, 2nd duke of Suffolk (d.1491), showing hair and crest. Wingfield (Suffolk).

Plate XXII Detail of effigy of John de la Pole, 2nd duke of Suffolk (d.1491), showing lion at foot Wingfield (Suffolk).

Plate XXIII Detail of effigy of John de la Pole, 2nd duke of Suffolk (d.1491), showing traces of the blue of the garter robe. Wingfield (Suffolk).

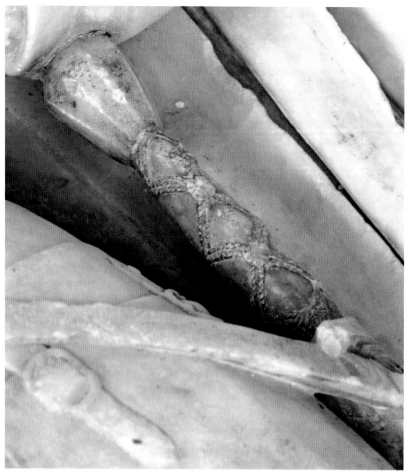

Plate XXIV Detail of effigy of John de la Pole, 2nd duke of Suffolk (d.1491), showing the grip of the sword. Wingfield (Suffolk).

Plate XXV Detail of effigy of John de la Pole, 2nd duke of Suffolk (d.1491), showing the dagger. Wingfield (Suffolk).

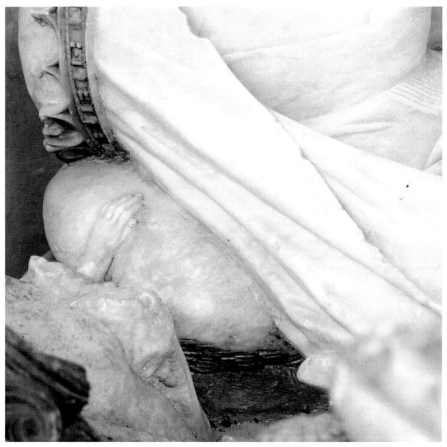

Plate XXVI Detail of effigy of Elizabeth of York (d. ?1503), showing colour on coronet and pillows. Wingfield (Suffolk).

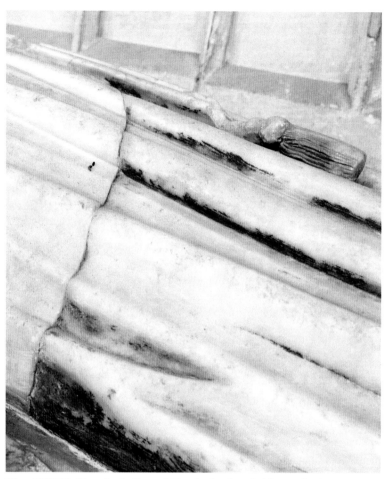

Plate XXVII Detail of effigy of Elizabeth of York (d. ?1503), showing colour on *surcote ouverte* and on tassel of mantle. Wingfield (Suffolk).

tenements and lands in and about Wingfield. In 1491 John was buried in the church, followed by Elizabeth Plantagenet in 1503. They have substantial alabaster tombs, and the fact that they lived at Wingfield Castle and were buried here (rather than in London or Hull) shows that the college was still very powerful and of high status – not run down or in decline.

The downfall of the de la Poles

Some of the sons of John and Elizabeth were claimants to the English throne, since their claim through their Plantagenet mother was stronger than that of Henry VII. Richard III apparently named their son John de la Pole as his heir to the throne in 1484; and as such he was granted the revenue of the lands of the Duchy of Cornwall,[41] an income of about £500 a year, and the role of president of the Council of the North.[42] The de la Pole sons variously met their ends in their struggle against the Tudors (John at the Battle of Stoke, 1487), executed by the king (Edmund in 1513) or in captivity in the tower of London (William arrested in 1499, died in 1537). Therefore, doubtless the first decade of the sixteenth century was a low period for the prestige of the college – dedicated as it was to the memory of the now traitorous de la Poles. However, eventually the college was not abandoned, but in fact updated, which shows that it must have been considered worthy of continued use and modernisation. There were a series of major building investments during Henry VIII's reign, probably triggered by the arrival of the new Duke of Suffolk Charles Brandon (patron of the college from 1516 to 1542) and his Wardens Thomas Deye and Robert Budde (the latter was previously Brandon's own chaplain, which shows how important Brandon considered the appointment). These modernisations include the building of the great barn (c.1527)[43] and considerable work to the great hall, including removal of the aisle pillars and their replacement with a huge Tudor tie-beam to give more space and allow more light (see plate VIII), plus the insertion of larger windows on both sides of the hall, including a high status oriel window on the east side. They also commissioned some fashionable linenfold panelling, depicting portraits of the new Tudor patrons: Charles and his wife Mary Tudor (sister of Henry VIII and previously queen of France), and their son Henry as a boy.[44] This was almost certainly created as part of the re-branding of the college, as it switched from being the de la Pole's college to Charles Brandon's college.

---

[41] Wagner 2001, pp. 211–12.

[42] Ross 1981, p. 159.

[43] Key timbers have been dendro-dated to have been felled in 1527; Bridge 1999b.

[44] The panelling (not *in situ*) can be dated by the simultaneous presence of Mary and one of her sons, either the first son Henry (1516–22), or their second son Henry (1523–34). Mary died in June 1533, so this panelling has a window of commissioning from 1520 to 1533. Robert Budde was made master by Brandon in 1531, and the panelling may have been commissioned after his arrival.

Around 1530 there were five priests at the college,[45] and in 1532 there were still five (though one claimed that they were two short).[46] In 1534 the *Valor Ecclesiasticus* surveyed the wealth of all the religious houses as preparation for dissolution, and Wingfield College was included. This gives us one of our few accounts of how much the college owned and what it was worth. It was endowed with the temporalities of the appropriated churches of Wingfield, Chickering, Syleham-cum-Esham, with the chapel of Esham, and Stradbroke; the manors of Benhall, Syleham, Stradbroke, Walpole, with Chickering, and Middleton Chickering; and with lands and rents in other parishes. Page (1907), Aldwell (1925) and Knowles and Haddock (1953) interpret *Valor Ecclesiasticus* as stating an annual net income value of £19 14 s 5 d, and gross income over £47.[47] Among the deductions from the gross value was the sum of £8 per year paid to the three poor boys charitably supported at the school.[48] Knowles and Haddock (1953) suggest that this net income of £19 places it in a lower income category overall compared to some of the larger secular colleges in the rest of the country, such as Attleborough in Norfolk, Bere Ferrers in Devon and Bredgar in Kent. However, some of its income may have been lost when the de la Pole's lands were confiscated and given to Brandon, and the size and scale of the buildings would have been paid for more by the de la Pole's occasional largesse than by the annual income from land holdings (which would instead have paid salaries). This net income places it below Mettingham (income of £202 at 1534, with thirteen priests and fourteen choristers); and closer to the Ufford Chantry at Campsey Ashe (net income of £35 with five priests) or Jesus College at Bury St Edmunds (£20 net income and seven priests). At the dissolution in 1542 the college surrendered to the king the college site and all its estates.[49] Shortly afterwards, on 10 December 1544, a lease of the college was granted by Henry VIII to Sir Richard Freston of Mendham, the receiver and surveyor of Brandon's East Anglian estates.[50] The fact that such a senior figure in

---

[45] Aldwell 1925, p. 91.

[46] Jessopp 1888, p. 296.

[47] The gross figure is more debatable and could have been higher. Davy (MS, pp. 374–5) interprets *Valor Ecclesiasticus* as valuing the college 'after the deductions were made agreeable to the instructions of £69.14.5 per annum'. Page (1844) interprets its gross value in *Valor Ecclesiasticus* as £82 10 s 4 d. Page adds that the site of the college itself, and the attached estate of arable, meadow and pasture land contained about 60 acres, was valued (including rents payable) at £8 6 s 2 d.

[48] *VCH Suffolk*, vol. II, p. 152.

[49] See the surrender document in this volume.

[50] The lease was twenty-one years. Freston was comptroller of the household to Brandon (effectively the manager of his estates) until 1537 and then receiver and surveyor of his Norfolk and Suffolk estates. Brandon had already conveyed Mendham Priory to him in 1536 for £300 and Freston subsequently lived in the converted priory buildings, so presumably Wingfield College was rented out. Freston was an officer of the Green Cloth under Mary I and was present in her coronation procession. He had two wives (Anne Coke was his second wife) and was interred at Mendham in Suffolk in 1558. The monument still survived in 1848. Haslam 1982; Aldwell 1925, pp. 91–2; MacCulloch 1976, p. 239; Gunn 1988, p. 164; and MacCulloch, this volume.

Brandon's household received the college from Henry VIII implies that it was still a desirable and well-maintained building, and not a declining shell.

Reconstruction as a snapshot in time

The purpose of this lengthy examination of the monies left to the college and church is to prove that it did not peak at one period and decline, but was in continual use and in receipt of regular endowments of money and land. However, the changes in fortunes may have meant that parts of the college may have been built or repaired in the mid fifteenth century and therefore looked stylistically different from the earlier phases. This would be borne in mind during aesthetic discussions of the college's appearance, so that instead of looking very simplistic and coherent to one period, different walls may date from different periods, and roof lines may not be uniform, but more indicative of extension, accretion and repair.

A crucial reconstruction choice is which point in the past we decide to reconstruct at. This raises another interesting methodological issue about reconstructions: they are only ever a snapshot in time; or else a series of chronological snapshots to demonstrate how the building has altered; so another issue where a decision is required. Do we choose to take the college back to its original state, for example a possible Saxon manor house;[51] or do we choose the college's most important moment, when it was at its largest and most developed state? Man is by nature a storytelling creature, and historical reconstructions often therefore try to create a story or look at a building in a key moment in its history, such as a battle or the visit of a monarch. For example, in the recent English Heritage redecoration of some of the interiors at Dover Castle they chose to reconstruct a new series of the rooms as they would have looked for the visit of King Henry II, even though there is no evidence that the king ever actually visited the site. In the Wingfield reconstruction we chose to show the college in 1493, just before the feasting to celebrate the visit of the bishop. This was because it was presumably in a mature stage of its development (there had been forty years of stability after the death of William, and the de la Poles were related to the Plantagenet king); the church could be shown after Alice de la Pole's eastern extension in the 1460s (thus avoiding complex supposition about what it may have looked like before); and the college was known to already possess its northern gatehouse. Inside the great hall this date told us which shields we should display with which familial coats of arms.

Having chosen this date as the snapshot, we then decided to create an architectural story where different parts were added in different periods. This is in keeping with reality, because the surviving great hall and west range tell us that there were at least three phases of work and extension between 1360 and 1390 alone, so it was

---

[51] See Martin in this volume.

possible that the rest of the structure developed in a similarly piecemeal fashion. With this in mind it was decided to create the main east wing in the style of 1380 (because it must have been built when the larger great hall was built, and a hall without a crosswing would have been an extraordinary departure from convention at the time). But then we chose the 'story' that the north side of the lost quadrangle and the gatehouse was added further into the next century, a time of success for William de la Pole. He was carrying out building works at other religious foundations that he was the patron of (including the school and almshouse at Ewelme in Oxfordshire) – so it made sense that he continued his work at Wingfield College. Therefore, the reconstruction of that north range was carried out in the timber-framing style of the 1440s instead of the 1380s. This makes for a slight visual mismatch between the two phases, which makes the building look as though it has evolved over time – however, it is entirely fake because we have no idea how that range appeared or if indeed it existed for sure. But the important thing is that it looks and feels convincing; looks like other buildings of a similar date and function elsewhere; and enables viewers to get an impression of the typology of the classic medieval chantry college. To achieve that an internal story or narrative was created of the different phases of work, and being consistent to that internal story enabled the artwork to be developed.

We shall now examine the remaining physical evidence and look at how it informed the decisions we had to make during the reconstruction process.

Evidence and supposition for the size and scale of the college site

The biggest problem is that no financial accounts or written records of the college survive from medieval times. We only have the foundation charter, its surrender, a valuation before its surrender, a few notes of the bishop's visitations and the builder's estimate for Alice de la Pole's extension of the collegiate church's east end in the 1460s.

How many people

So how many people lived at the college? There would have been priests, school-children, servants to tend the priests and cook their food, and people to manage and tend the estates. Let us look at each of these categories in turn. We know that there were initially three priests, later expanded to nine priests and three choristers.[52] To start with they were possibly housed together in a dormitory, like the smaller monastic foundations of that period; but by the mid-fifteenth century they would have expected more privacy and in a foundation of this size and prominence would probably have had their own rooms or cells, or at least partitioned subdivisions of the former dormitory. In the reconstruction we have assumed that they were in the

---

[52] This was codified in the foundation charter.

west range of the cloister, off the side of the great hall. The warden or master of the college would have had his own rooms, and almost certainly his parlour and above that his bedroom (or solar) would have been behind the high end of the hall – the usual location for the room's manorial lord or warden in a hall structure of this type. These rooms still survive (one is an upstairs bedroom and the other was panelled by the Georgians c.1710), and they still have some of their original 1362 medieval walls and roof beams, including the slot for a lost crownpost in the top of one tie beam. We know that the master of the college also had a personal buttery, where the more valuable foodstuffs were kept under his own lock and key.[53] The warden was sometimes also a man of personal financial means, since the foundation charter allowed that priests 'may have their own goods apart from the common goods of the said college, and shall be free to make their wills disposing of their own goods';[54] for example, the will of Master Thomas Deye in 1531 left to the college the wall-hanging in his bedroom.[55]

The college did not always retain its full contingent of nine priests and its surrender on 2 June 1542 was signed by Robert Budde as master, and four other priests. However, it shows the college had not been run down in later years, since there were still five of the potential nine priests. Robert Budde received a pension of £21 (a reasonable sum in those days).[56]

The college was also a school, but at no point do we know how many schoolchildren there were. Three poor boys were also supported at the college, and the funds for their maintenance were valued, at the dissolution, at £8 per annum. These poor children would presumably have been among the pupils, but some of the children would have been fee-paying. Some historians have come up with more information about the school, although sadly without revealing sources. Aldwell (1925) suggested that it was 'one of the noted schools of Suffolk and gave a very good education for the times and sent young men up to the Universities' (although being Wingfield's vicar and local historian he had possible reason to exaggerate the school's importance).[57] In 1895 the Suffolk antiquarian Dr Raven referred to the similarity in foundation and operation between Mettingham (near Bungay) and Wingfield, and said they were both boarding schools. He stated that the fees at Mettingham were £2 a year for boarding, clothing and food, and this was probably similar at Wingfield.[58] L. Steele Hutton's 1908 paper on medieval Suffolk schools states:

---

[53] Aitkens et al.1999, p. 392.
[54] See the foundation charter in this volume.
[55] The wallhanging was 'in the chamber over the parlour and the buttery' (Aitkens et al. 1999, p. 392).
[56] Aldwell 1925 p. 90. Four chaplains also received pensions. There may also have been other grants of land or positions in addition to the pension.
[57] Ibid., p. 4. See Orme 2006, pp. 312–24 for a valuable summary of the dissolution of the chantries and their schools.
[58] Raven 1895, pp. 77–84; discussed in Aldwell 1925, p. 80.

Mettingham and Wingfield were the great boarding-schools of the fifteenth century for Suffolk; their endowments were more liberal than those of other foundations, their buildings were better ... The classes seem to have been of two kinds, corresponding more or less to our elementary and secondary departments. There were the choristers, little tonsured boys, who began as abecedarians and advanced to the technical studies of 'prick song' and illumination ... At Mettingham, Wingfield and Sudbury more advanced teaching was also to be had, and these Colleges were, in their best days, along with the episcopal schools, the regular feeders of the Universities.[59]

Although uncorroborated, this suggests the buildings and facilities may have been substantial, with a fair number of resident boys. However, over a hundred years later the standards must have slipped, for in his 1493 visitation the bishop of Norwich complained that the master of the college was 'too slack in administration and discipline' and had not ensured that there was someone appointed specifically to teach grammar (music was the other main subject taught in medieval schools).[60]

It is impossible to know how many servants there would have been, and how many lived on site as opposed to in the village. However, the previously mentioned will of Master Thomas Deye gives us a glimpse, in that he had two personal servants as well as the servant who was part of the college. If the master alone had three servants there is no telling how many other people worked in the kitchens, brewhouse, stables and other ancillary buildings. There were also staff to work on the estate that provided fish from the fishponds, fowl from the dovecotes, and meat and crops from the fields that the college owned immediately to the east of the site (most of these fields stayed in the college's possession right up until the 1950s, as shown by the tithe map of 1841[61] and the sale details of the college in 1861[62]). The large Tudor queenpost barn was also part of the college's outbuildings (it pre-dates the college's dissolution, with a dendro-date of 1527 and certainly replaces an older medieval barn[63]). It is impossible to know how many more buildings were on the site that have since been lost: accommodation for the estate workers and other outbuildings for foodstuffs and farm equipment. The college would have needed an estate manager to oversee the numerous manors and estates all across Suffolk that were owned by the college (mostly left by the Wingfields and de la Poles to fund the salaries of the priests); all of which would have needed maintenance, business

---

[59] Hutton 1908. Unfortunately Hutton does not provide his sources for this information.

[60] Jessopp 1888, p. 52. The bishop declared that the warden 'ought to appoint someone to teach grammar to the confratres'. Confratres is a general term for 'brethren' and could just mean the adult community in the college, but could in some senses include children.

[61] SROI: FDA 292/A1/1a and 1b.

[62] Sale announcement 27 December 1861. The land is specifically exonerated from the payment of tithes and this is the evidence that it is a survival from the college's medieval lands.

[63] Bridge 1999b.

management and rent collection. This may have been a separate post or may have been the work of one of the priests.

So in terms of how many people were resident at the college we can only say that it was at its height at least nine priests and a bare minimum of three grant-supported schoolchildren, probably more who were fee-paying (nearby Mettingham had fourteen chorister/schoolchildren in 1534), and an indeterminate number of servants and estate workers. So what do we know from our records of the buildings?

Surviving evidence of buildings

The most important college building was the old church itself, which was purposefully 'vacant' at the time of the college's foundation.[64] The foundation charter gives instructions that it should be 'in great part built anew … on a larger scale than before, with a belfry, bells, houses and other necessary offices, at a very great expense', to provide a fine enough setting for the tomb of Sir John and his wife Eleanor. It is impossible to know whether the church absorbed so much funding that the construction of college accommodation suffered, but the fact that funding for the building was not always forthcoming could be inferred by the truncated height of the tower, which is more squat and less impressive than many other de la Pole-funded church towers in the neighbourhood (such as Stradbroke, Eye and Laxfield).[65]

Sadly the foundation charter does not refer to the scale of the college accommodation, so we are left to surmise from the remaining structures and occasional documentary clues. Surveys of the remaining college range show a first phase (in either 1362 or possibly earlier in which case pre-dating the official foundation) with a two-storeyed range with exposed fan-bracing and a crownpost roof extending 36 feet towards the north. This was probably attached to the previous manor house hall, or a 1362 hall, which has been lost. This was followed by a second phase in circa 1380–5 when the range was extended to 61 feet (its current length) terminating in a gable overlooking the churchyard;[66] and the hall was enlarged, as previously

---

[64] See the foundation charter in this volume. The last rector, Sir Thomas Sket, had transferred temporarily to Hasketon, another church living in the gift of the de Brewse family, his former patrons at Wingfield. Sket returned to Wingfield in 1362 as the first master of the college.

[65] The tower has been suggested to be 'earlier fourteenth century', and may therefore be part of the pre-collegiate church; Aldwell 1925, Aitkens et al. 1999.

[66] The following is an excerpt from an unpublished survey by Philip Aitkens 2009, which explains the reconstruction: 'The north gable end has original exposed framing, but the roof and upper gable have gone, and the studded wall at ground floor level has been rebuilt in brick … The studwork spacing must have been similar (to the first floor), and we can assume there was a central crownpost. The braces could have risen upwards from the crownpost, or downwards. I have chosen the latter because they are then parallel with the other braces lower down. It seems to have been normal to have carved bargeboards in the gables of late medieval wings at this social level. This ogee form was popular but there would often be sunk spandrels and cusps as well … Because the north-east corner is jettied on two sides, there was a corner post beneath the massive diagonal brace. It was traditionally called a dragon post.'

mentioned.[67] Surveys of the phase one 1362 range by Philip Aitkens and Edward Martin have identified studs and doorframe features which imply two doorways at the first floor level, providing access to upper-storey bedrooms and apparently reached by a wooden exterior staircase, where mortise sockets suggest a projecting roof-type structure.[68] Plate IX shows Philip Aitkens' hypothetical reconstruction of what an external wooden staircase of this period may have looked like, located on these features. It was decided that the moving version of the digital reconstruction should illustrate this earlier structure by dissolving from the 1493 phase to the 1382 phase; then dissolving in the reconstruction of the external staircase; then returning to 1493. The aim of this was to illustrate how the evidence has shown that the college structure has changed.

When the hall was rebuilt on a larger scale in circa 1382 it is likely that an eastern range and a northern range were added to create a quadrangle, with the hall along one side and the western range on the other. This would have meant the removal of the staircase, which would have been in the way of the surviving western cloister passage. Anthony Emery visited the college for his book *Greater Medieval Houses of England and Wales* and was convinced that 'the college was built round a quadrangle of which one and a half ranges survive, the hall and residential range … two sides of a small brick cloister'.[69] This view is also supported by Aldwell (1925) and by the Suffolk Institute of Archaeology and History during its visit in 1998.[70] From other surviving chantry colleges of this size, period and scale of foundation a cloister court-yard is extremely likely (and maybe even a second one to the west). These courtyard structures were following the design of most monastic accommodation, including the

[67] Aitkens 1997 and 1998, Aitkens et al. 1999, Emery 2000, Bettley forthcoming, and further architectural surveys carried out by UEA as part of the 2010–12 Wingfield Virtual Past Research Project, involving Rob Liddiard, Philip Aitkens and Peter Bloore.

[68] Aitkens 2009: 'The studwork module has gaps of about 1.1 metres between each with studs and posts uniformly 180–200mm wide. A small extra stud indicates a door jamb for a doorway. It keeps the door a little away from the post and tiebeam beside it. There are two wide doorways, about 900mm wide, indicated by this. They are only about 1.5m apart and they open into a single room, at least 5 metres long. If they are doors, they are too wide for garderobe doors. They must lead into a structure to the east … Two mortises in the east flank of the wallplate suggest that there was a wallplate or tiebeam tenoned into each of them. There is a third smaller mortise. Could they be for the roof?'

[69] Emery 2000, p. 136. Emery also suggests that the west range on the first floor was in large part a dormitory structure, and only subdivided into rooms in the 1600s; presumably due to the lack of evidence for internal partitions that pre-date that period. However, Emery is wrong on a couple of counts about the rest of the structure. First, dendro-dating has disproved his suggestion that the hall is part of an older structure that pre-dated the college, and secondly that the master's brick lodging (now the kitchen) was added in medieval times. The latter was suggested by the presence of medieval bricks in this lodging (Kennett 1973). However, recent closer examination of this structure has revealed that it dates from the 1600s. The bricks were re-used and not *in situ*, and are in the context of later bricks and structure, including re-used medieval joists and Jacobean mullion windows.

[70] Aitkens et al., 1999, pp. 392–7.

smaller ones of East Anglia;[71] many manorial buildings of the period;[72] and also the bigger chantry foundations such as Edward III's college at Windsor in 1348, which is large enough to have a double cloister.[73] In terms of more local colleges, the earliest in the Norwich diocese was Rushworth College (1342) near Thetford, and it too had a hall on one side of a small quadrangle cloister.[74] This was followed by Aske College in 1346, and Thompson College in 1349 (a hall on one side of a quadrangle cloister), and Raveningham College in 1350 (moved to Mettingham Castle in 1394, but without a cloister), and Wingfield College in 1362.[75] In Suffolk the Campsey Ash chantry college was founded in 1347, contained five chaplains, and it too had a quadrangle pentice cloister, with the church on the north side and a dwelling house on the south.[76] The earliest known reference to the existence of the Wingfield quadrangle is by Thomas Cromwell in 1819: 'the west side of its quadrangle was converted into a farm-house'.[77] It was also referred to in *White's Directory* of 1844, where it states: 'The west side of the quadrangle of this college yet remains, on the south side of the church, having been converted into a farmhouse.'[78]

Furthermore, surveys of the site have revealed a number of pieces of corroborative evidence. First, there is enough space for a cloister here, including space for the return eastern range and a further courtyard and kitchen structures before the eastern perimeter boundary wall by the fishpond. Secondly, that the internal ground floor corridor on the east side of the surviving range is almost certainly a cloister walkway, previously with a lean-to roof covering it projecting from the surviving wall of the range and with the walkway connecting to the exit doors from the high

---

[71] In the 1520s Cardinal Wolsey dissolved twenty-nine of the smaller monastic houses around East Anglia and central England, and reference is made to a cloister at all the sites. O'Sullivan 2006, p. 242. Halls were usually entered from the cloister. All sites contained kitchens and brewhouses, and most contained gatehouses, outbuildings and fishponds.

[72] Many Cambridge college quadrangles may have drawn their inspiration from manorial courtyard structures of this period, as argued by Willis and Clark 1886. See also Cobban 1988, Chapter 4 for the structures of colleges and hostels.

[73] For a detailed discussion of the St George Windsor college quadrangle cloisters and their construction see Munby 2005, pp. 229–33, and for the foundation of the college and its historical context in both the political situation and other collegiate foundations of the fourteenth century, see Burgess 2005; both in Saul 2005.

[74] Emery 2000, p. 136. Rushworth is now Rushford. See Cook 1959, for discussion of a number of quadrangle-based colleges; Quiney 2003, pp. 217–33 for the courtyard structure of hospitals, almshouses and colleges; and Wood 1965, pp. 183–8 for a discussion of college lodgings and the partitioning of larger spaces into cells or studies.

[75] Aldwell 1925, p. 77. There were a total of six chantry colleges in Suffolk (Bury St Edmunds, Denston, Stoke-by-Clare; Sudbury; Mettingham and Wingfield – Blackwood 2001).

[76] Gilchrist and Olivia 1993, pp. 45, 90. Like Wingfield, Campsey Ash also had extensive fishponds and a large barn. They point out that most Norfolk and Suffolk convent communities were also built on a courtyard/quadrangle system (ibid., p. 45). However, Campsey Ash was both an existing nunnery (1195) and a college of chaplains, so it was a larger community than Wingfield.

[77] Cromwell 1819, p. 18.

[78] White 1844, p. 572.

end of the great hall. Thirdly, that the surviving door at the east end of the cloister walkway is in exactly the right place for access to where a northern cloister walkway would have been (the return of the cloister). Furthermore, there used to be another door at the southern end of the cloister walkway, only removed in the 1970s, which was in the right place for the cloister walkway to turn east to go along the side of the hall.[79] Fourthly, on the surviving range the old first floor external wall (now an internal corridor wall) survives intact with its 1362–80-phase decorative windbracing all the way along until the point where a north range of the cloister would have been attached. At this point the wall has been untidily repaired at a later stage with close upright studs. This implies that the cloister north range was removed and the junction repaired, but the studs were not intended to be seen and were immediately plastered over, probably when the whole range was externally pargeted in the 1600s (substantial quantities of this pargeting survive at the far north end of the east range on both the ground floor and first floor). This implies the removal of a range, and is the right distance for the width of a range matching the surviving range, and is in the right place for the door mentioned above. Finally, the great hall has on its cloister side a large extant high-status Tudor window that was glazed only in the top square panels. The lower three quarters was never glazed and was instead covered by shutters.[80] This means this window aperture was likely to have been shielded from the elements, and the fact that this line between glazed and unglazed occurs at the level of the likely cloister roof position implies that it was indeed facing into the cloister passage, so the unglazed section would have been protected.

This cloister idea also explains an unusual (possibly unique) feature of the Wingfield site. The great hall is not attached directly to the range, as would be expected if it was built in a single phase, but is separated from the range. The hall has its own west wall and a passage between it and the range. The previous hall must have abutted up against the range, as was normal, but the decision to add a quadrangle (and therefore a cloister passage at ground floor level) meant that the new hall had to be built further to the east, so that the cloister passage could lead into the access doors behind the high end of the hall. Thus the back wall of the hall becomes a form of screens passage, preventing drafts coming in from the cloister walk. This hypothesis explains why the cloister passage unusually goes behind the great hall, instead of into the side of it.

To conclude, a cloister on the site is highly likely, given the surviving evidence from the site; the nineteenth-century documentary references; and the conventional structure of other colleges and communal dwellings of this period. Therefore, in the

---

[79] This southern cloister doorway used to have a projecting porch that went up to the first-floor level. It is visible on 1970s floor-plans of the building and old photographs, but was removed in the 1970s restorations. The porch window was moved back and re-embedded in the east wall.
[80] Aitkens et al. 1999, p. 394.

reconstruction a cloister is shown, and the entrances and exits to the central cloister courtyard are shown rising from ground floor to first floor, as was typical of the period and visible at the cloister at Ewelme School and almshouses in Oxfordshire. Ewelme was built under the patronage of William and Alice de le Pole, and there is evidence that the church and cloister there may have been influenced by the Wingfield site;[81] so therefore the Ewelme site has influenced a number of the aesthetic creative/historical judgements made in the reconstruction. We were also influenced by the extant fragment of pentice cloister at Suffolk's Clare priory (see below).

The east side of the cloister has been shown running into the screens passage of the hall, as is likely to have been the case and matching the measurements on the ground (see plate X for a floor plan of the reconstruction). However, this assumes that it was a two-bay hall rather than a three-bay hall – an assumption which was debated in a lot of detail by the team. The current hall is definitely truncated short of its original length, since there is no surviving evidence of the eastern doors and screen passage. The current east end wall is much later, and the junction of the horizontal arcade plate with the east wall is evidently not medieval (unlike the west end). Also the hall is one and a half bays in length which would not have been the intention of the builders, and feels short and out of proportion compared to its height. There is no date for the truncation but it was after the Tudor phase, shown by surviving Tudor modernisations (for example, one Tudor window now abuts right up against the east wall, which would not have been intentional). It was probably shortened as part of the substantial alterations in the 1600s or the 1790s.[82]

The arguments in favour of a two-bay hall are first that all the extant examples of timber-framed halls in rural Suffolk are two-bay, not three-bay halls; and secondly that a two-bay hall means the cloister quadrangle would have been square in shape, if the east side of the cloister connected with the entrance door on the north of the low end of the hall (a three-bay hall would result in a larger oblong quadrangle – not impossible, but more unusual).

The arguments in favour of a three-bay timber framed hall is that three or more bay halls *were* sometimes built in East Anglia in the larger sites in towns and castles, for example the enormous Dragon Hall in King Street, Norwich (a seven-bay crown-posted hall, 85 feet long, c.1427). Wingfield was an aspirational high-status devel-

---

[81] Goodall 2001, pp. 166–9.
[82] By the time of the restoration of the 1970s the great hall had been filled with two stories of subdivisions. Downstairs was a dining room with a Georgian or early Victorian bay window in the east wall overlooking the garden, plus a series of service rooms and boot rooms; and upstairs was a bedroom which was dominated by the kingpost roof structure (and above part of that was an apple loft). Sadly, when removed in the 1970s, these internal additions seem to have not been examined and dated – they may have given us a likely date for the truncation of the hall. However, the decline of the use of great halls by the 1600s and the extending of the western range to add a new downstairs chamber in the 1600s implies that the hall was probably surplus to requirements and subdivided during this phase, rather than waiting until the 1790s. One of these subdivision walls contained as infill the linenfold panelling from the Tudor Brandon phase.

opment, and the size and status of the communal hall may have been as much of a statement of the wealth of the patrons as the size of the church. A comparable example is the hall at nearby Mettingham College, which seems to have been three bays in length, and was providing accommodation for the same number of priests. Mettingham was 46 feet long by 30 feet wide with 6 foot-wide aisles; and Wingfield (assuming a three-bay hall) was smaller but similar in proportion at 42 feet long by 23 feet wide with 4 foot-wide aisles.[83] Secondly there is no surviving evidence of a Tudor chimney and fireplace. The Tudor patrons would not have added the latest design of mullion bay window and not also added the latest design of fireplace (the old method of a fire in the centre of the hall had gone out of fashion). This means the Tudor fireplace must have been in the lost section of the hall. However, if it was a two-bay hall then the lost section would only have contained the screens passage, and entrance doors from the north (the cloister entrance), the east (the kitchen entrance) and the south (the base court entrance from the barns complex). Therefore there would not have been the space for a fireplace and it would have been a very odd placement for one (at the low end of the hall, away from the high table).

Thirdly is the issue of *why* the hall was truncated. It could have been because of a general reduction in the size of the property, as the house was adapted for its new use as a gentleman's residence; or the result of damage due to fire (although there is a lack of evidence for this); or instability and collapse due to subsidence or structural failure. The latter is perhaps most likely. The whole hall subsides to the east (the verticals lean visibly) and the surviving Tudor tiebeam contains a substantial internal fissure, where the weight of the roof vault is putting excessive strain down on to the tiebeam (this had to be reinforced by a steel plate in the 1970s). If it was a three-bay hall then there would have been a further tiebeam to the east, so one likely scenario is that this easternmost tiebeam gave way, bringing down part of the roof and the old east wall.

The final argument in favour of the three-bay hall is the amount of work involved in truncating it. If it was a two-bay hall then removing the old east wall, shortening the horizontal arcade plates and roof plates and building a new east wall would be an illogically large amount of work for the removal of only half a bay. In the case of Wingfield each bay is 14 feet long, so you would be reducing the hall by only 7 foot. However, if it was a three-bay hall, then truncating to the current position would be halving the length of the hall, saving 21 feet. This would have been a considerable rationalisation of the structure.

Regrettably, neither geophysics surveys nor archaeological test pits provided any evidence for the location of the original east wall, and therefore the original length of the hall, probably because the ground had subsequently been very disturbed (the

---

[83] However, Mettingham had brick walls not timber frame. For a detailed discussion of the Mettingham site, including whether the hall building was part of the college or a Tudor post dissolution structure, see Martin 1990.

whole area later became a farmyard) and because timber-framed halls of that period did not have deep footings but often rested on a small brick course. Eventually the decision was made to follow the two-bay system in the reconstruction, in large part to keep the cloister square. However, the reconstruction modelling process itself was insightful as a research method. Once the pillars and their base capitals had been inserted, and the top table put in place, there was remarkably little space to insert enough tables and benches for the likely size of the rest of the community. The difficulty of fitting the tables and benches around the pillars helped us to appreciate why the Tudors decided to do away with them and insert the tiebeam. So by the end of the reconstruction process of a two-bay hall it was felt that the three-bay version was a likely option (and a three-bay hall was included in the castle reconstruction, on the advice of castle experts Dr John Goodall and Dr Rob Liddiard). Either way, the process of discussion and decision about the hall's length highlighted clear issues around what is known and what is unknown and the relationship between the two; what could be surmised from other examples; disagreements between the team and how they should be resolved; and the balance between personal judgement and surviving physical evidence.

The rest of the inside of the great hall has plenty of extant medieval evidence, including an intact crownpost roof, and west wall with exit doors and decorative bracing plus a few later Tudor modifications (as described on page 113).[84] The reconstruction was based mainly on the surviving structure, with the extant decoratively fan-braced west wall repeated at the east end, with the addition of three service doorways. The west wall shows there were no louvred vents in the top of the wall to allow the fire's smoke to escape, which points to the existence of a louvred chimney in the roof above the rafters. The current Tudor windows have been replaced in the reconstruction with smaller medieval examples of suitable size, as designed by Philip Aitkens based on contemporaneous examples and the surviving evidence of the earlier wall studs. It was originally a twin aisle hall, so the Tudor tiebeam has been removed and the capital and footing mouldings of the pillars follow the design of the moulding of the extant crownpost.

No great hall would have been without some colour and paintwork, especially a hall of this level of patronage. There is no surviving evidence of decorative paintwork (the walls and woodwork have been extensively cleaned), so to give an indication of decoration we inserted an image of the genuine college seal on the west wall, as though it was a painted device (decorated with suitable colours, although the only certain ones are the white Wingfield wings against red background); an image of the patron saint of the college, St Andrew, shown as a wall hanging; and a row of de la Pole heraldic shields against the high table (these are based on the shields on the tomb of Alice de la Pole at Ewelme). This is probably an under-estimate of the

---

[84] For a detailed discussion of the architecture of the hall see Aitkens 1997 and 1998, and Aitkens et al. 1999.

sumptuous colourfulness of a high-status medieval hall, especially on a major feast day (such as the foundation day of the college – celebrated with great festivity every year on 8 June). All the depicted furniture and tableware are inspired by extant examples or manuscript illustrations, and a distinction was made between the ordinary knives and plates on the ordinary tables, and the higher quality decorative ware, serving equipment and salt cellar on the top table (see plate VII).

Leaving the great hall by the south entrance, the de la Pole coat of arms above the door into the hall is taken from the pulpit of the church, and the herb and flower gardens are based on manuscript illustrations. It was decided to add chimneys and garderobes on to the west side of the college. Although this is now the front of the house, facing the road, in medieval times the college would have been approached via the hall entrances, either from the barns base court or from the church via the cloister. Therefore the south side facing the barns has been shown as a decorated double-gabled frontage, typical of the period and region (plate XI). Both garderobes and external chimneys would have been expected in a substantial building of the late fifteenth century, especially for the master's apartments; but there is no evidence of them on the east side (because the cloister would be in the way) or internally, so it was decided to put them on the west side. This also highlights the fact that the west was not the decorative front, so it could contain useful features like chimneys.

The kitchen, gatehouse and chapter house

The location of the kitchen and brewhouse are supported by the areas of burning identified by the 2009 geophysics survey commissioned by the University of East Anglia (Graham 2009). These were in exactly the area we expected to find the kitchen, beyond the great hall and next to the fishponds. These are shown based on typical brewhouse structures with chimney vents in the end walls, as advised by Philip Aitkens. Kitchens in this period were often separate to the hall, so in the event of a fire taking hold in the kitchen the main house was less likely to burn down, especially on large rural sites where space was not at the same premium as urban sites. Therefore the kitchen was often linked to the hall by a covered passageway, so food could be carried through without getting too cold. This reconstruction shows a covered cloister-style corridor, influenced by the extant fragment at Clare Priory of a lean-to pentice cloister that used to go from the hall to the kitchen. It was open on one side to the court, with a wall on one side (masonry) and a lean-to wall on the other side, with a low plinth wall and moulded mullions like the side of a timber-frame porch.

As for other college buildings, the account of Bishop Goldwell's visitation on 27 September 1493 gives us vital information:

> That day the Right Rev. Father in God in the course of performing his visitation in his Diocese of Norwich went out of his way to visit the aforesaid College and was received *at the north gate* of the said College [*ad portam borealem ejusdem collegii*]

by the Master and all the Fellows of the College in solemn procession. He then proceeded to the High Altar, while the bells were rung and the organs pealed forth and the Master and Brethren sang praise to the Holy Trinity. When prayer had been piously performed and the customary ceremonial carried out, the Episcopal Blessing was given, all humbly standing before him. The Bishop afterwards went straight to *the Chapter House* [*domum capitularem*] of the College and entered.[85]

(My emphases.)

This tells us, first, that there *was* a north gate facing towards the church. This might have been nothing more than a private door like a postern gate in the north wall, used by the priests and boys to walk across to the church; however, since the bishop was met there it was presumably an important approach to the college, and not just a minor entrance. According to Cook (1959, 1963) most chantry college foundations of this size did have a gatehouse. The reconstruction shows both possibilities, depicting a small door in the north wall of the north range, lining up with the cloister passage into the hall; and further over to the east a more substantial north gatehouse with a room above (based on William Pykenham's Gatehouse in Ipswich, see previous discussion). It has been placed on the north-east corner of the college precinct, so that it avoids the churchyard. This is because a gatehouse would have been approached by a track, for carts and horses, so was unlikely to abut right on to the churchyard (no other examples could be found of East Anglian gatehouses facing straight across the churchyard). In the reconstruction the gatehouse is accessed by a track that skirted the east side of the churchyard, coming down from Butt Lane (an old lane that used to run from the church to the archery butts, and then on towards Fressingfield).

There are other good reasons for this gatehouse site at this eastern end of the north wall. First, a considerable amount of disturbed and reburied brick and flint has been found on this spot, as recorded by Aldwell in the 1920s and traced by the 2009 geophysics survey, in the right place for the footings of a substantial gatehouse. Secondly, the north wall joins up here to the surviving eastern college precinct wall, which is an extant substantial flint and brick late mediaeval or Tudor structure that used to skirt the side of the second fishpond (and is now partially subsided into the pond). Finally, there is no geophysical disturbance or remains on the west end of the north wall, so the eastern end of the north wall is the likely site for a north gatehouse.[86]

---

[85] Jessopp 1888, pp. 52–3. The account states that the bishop met William Baynard, the master, three other *consocii* (fellows) and four *conducti* (stipendiary priests); so there were nine priests in residence in total at that stage.

[86] Another possibility is that the church was also contained within a wider college precinct wall, and the gatehouse was actually on the north side of the church (instead of between the church and the college buildings), which is still the commonly used village approach to the church. Or the chronicler got his north alignment wrong, and there was instead a west gate of the college, looking on to the road to the west of the west range, where the entrance now is. However, this is

The specific reference to the *north* gate of the college could imply there was a further gatehouse or entrance to the precinct in another direction, possibly to the south (between the barns court and the hall, although the land is sloping here); or to the west, either where the current entrance to the college drive is, or more likely further down, to provide access to the base court of domestic buildings and frame the approach to the decorated south face of the great barn. The reconstruction has selected this place for a second gatehouse, providing access to the barns court.

Secondly, the visitation tells us that there was a chapter house. The chronicler would have known a great hall when he saw one, so this must be another separate structure or a large room within one of the timber-frame wings. In order to be conservative about the scale of the buildings, we decided to make it a room within the north range of the college quadrangle, and not a grand separate structure. This fits the fact that there were only nine priests, who would not have required chapter house accommodation on the scale of the monasteries of the period.

So what about the wider college precinct and other outbuildings? Edward Martin has argued in this volume that the college occupies a classic late Anglo-Saxon manorial hall and church site, possibly with a perimeter fence. In the surrender document of 1542 the priests state that they are surrendering to the king: 'the whole College and our Chantry aforesaid, also that entire Site, Enclosure, Circuit, Border, and Precinct of the same College'. This implies there was an enclosed precinct of some form (not just a simple house next to the church). This enclosure concept is worth considering further, since the Peasants' Revolt of 1381 occurred during the construction of the college, and a number of ecclesiastical establishments across the county were attacked by rioters, including the abbey at Bury St Edmund where the prior was murdered. Michael de la Pole himself addressed parliament in October 1381 referring to ongoing unrest in Suffolk and 'acts of disobedience and rebellion ... which continue from one day to another'.[87] Unrest and further local uprisings continued through to 1383, when the duke of Norfolk's properties in Parham and Framlingham were attacked.[88] Michael obtained his license to crenellate Wingfield Castle and his other Suffolk manors in 1385,[89] and it is possible that the college may have had a perimeter wall and gatehouse partly to defend itself against a future uprising, especially since the college owned manors across Suffolk, as we have seen, and the target of some medieval rioters was the destruction of manorial land deeds. Any defensive walls would not have been expected to withstand a full-scale attack, but to keep rioters at bay long enough for reinforcements to arrive. There is the remnant of a substantial late medieval perimeter wall alongside the main fishpond, made of flint and brick and as

less likely given the alignment of the entrances of the great hall, which instead faced north (towards the church) and south (towards the barns complex), rather than west.

[87] Ridgard in Dymond and Martin 1989, p. 90.

[88] Ridgard ibid., p. 204.

[89] The royal licence to crenellate granted on 27 April 1385 included his manor houses at Sternfield, Huntingfield, and Stradbroke.

thick as a church wall. The wall has now subsided in parts into the pond, as a result of subsequent wind and water erosion undermining the wall. Its close proximity to the water may have been as an extra defensive barrier. The geophysics survey strongly implies that the east wall previously met the churchyard wall coming from the north (see above and the site of the north gatehouse). To conclude, if the wall in the pond is anything to go by, the whole precinct may have been enclosed with quite a substantial defensive wall, more than just a boundary fence to keep livestock in (or out).

The reconstruction of post-medieval phases of the college

The late Elizabethan/early Jacobean period saw a substantial investment in the post-dissolution building, including new fireplaces and chimneys; the latest mullion windows, complete with expensive glazing; a new large roof with two gable windows;[90] and the extension of the west range, to add a brick ground floor parlour and an upstairs master bedroom with a suspended plaster ceiling (probably decorated) and walls painted with fashionable pale green paint. Both floors in the extension had a splendid projecting bay window with large mullions, facing the westward setting sun. These and other mullions are evidenced in the surviving fabric and have been shown in the reconstruction. A few other conjectural mullion windows have been inserted in likely positions (see plate XII).

It is known that by the 1600s the building had been re-oriented so that its main front entrance was to the west (rather than the southern approach to the great hall), so the later phases of the reconstruction have added a typical example of a two-storey entrance porch in the Tudor to Jacobean fashion, as would have befitted a house being lived in by the landed gentry, such as the prosperous Edgar family from Glemham and John Cornwallis, a deputy lieutenant of Suffolk.[91] It was still surrounded by considerable land and outbuildings, as shown by a survey in the 1640s:

> The site of the college consisting of a fair house with barns, stables, dovehouses, and other ouhouses, with the yards, gardens, orchards, and backsides thereunto belonging containing by estimation four acre ... also 13 closes of land, meadows etc., the total number of acres 110 ... The full yearly value of the aforsesaid particulars as they were worth in 1641: £66. There is growing upon the Premises certain Timber trees and Pollings.[92]

Another indicator of its external appearance in this phase is that in 1674 the returns from the hearth tax record that the college had twelve hearths. It currently has a total

[90] Philip Aitkens surveyed the west range roof as part of the UEA research project and found that it was entirely rebuilt in a style consistent with the 1600s.
[91] The porch used in the reconstruction was taken with permission from the owner from photographs of Monks Hall, Syleham, a nearby timber-farmed house of comparable age and status. The chimneys also come from that building.
[92] Davy MS, p. 390; the original document is in the Cambridge University Library: MM. II. 19, pt 2, pp. 25–7.

of seven fireplaces, so others (or the buildings that contained them) have since been removed.[93] In the late 1600s/early 1700s the medieval master's parlour was rebuilt with Georgian panelling painted pale green; and a substantial walled garden was added, on the site of an earlier garden or a lost range or agricultural outbuildings.

The next phase we chose to show in the reconstruction was the 1790s (plate XIII). This saw the sweeping away of the 1600 windows and other features on the west side, and the addition by John Rix Birch[94] of the current Palladian-esque façade containing new sash windows; the lowering of the ground level on the west to increase the height of the front;[95] the hipping of the previously gabled 1600 roof (which otherwise stayed intact); the replacement of the ornate Jacobean chimneys with simple brick chimneys; the addition of a first-floor back corridor above the cloister walkway on the east side of the west range to provide access to each of the bedrooms; and very considerable internal modernisation, including a system of servants' bells. The only change between the 1790s and the present day is the filling in of the round window that was almost certainly in the centre of the portico, so this has been reinstated in the reconstruction (lots of Georgian porticos of this period contain a window to light the interior attic space). The Victorian period saw the addition of outbuildings, but no identified changes to the main building, only internal redecoration.[96]

This brings us to the modern day, and the building as it stands now. The architectural historian and journalist Simon Jenkins has recently called the college 'a truly historic house, its skeleton a maze of medieval woodwork';[97] and yet most of what he was looking at was the result of a major 1970s *restoration* (like reconstruction, restoration is another word derived from the Latin *re-* to go back). The owner Ian Chance chose to strip the interior of the building to reveal much of its historic

93 Photos show that until the 1970s there was a chimney in one of the rooms built within the hall, with a fireplace at ground and first-floor level. This was removed in the 1970s.

94 John Rix Birch (1769–1811) inherited the college from his grandfather Samuel Jessup. Birch's father John Rix Birch (1739–93) of Redgrave married Mary Jessup at Wingfield in 1768. Samuel's wife Mary died in 1770 and is buried in the church, but Samuel's death date is uncertain. John Rix Birch junior was certainly at the college by 1796 when Gillingwater recorded the 'elegant modern built house, rebuilt by Mr Birch, who came to reside there a few years since'. By 1798 Birch was 'late of Wingfield' and living in Norwich as a lieutenant in the Cambridgeshire Militia. He sold up at Wingfield in 1809 and died in 1811 in the West Indies.

95 Chance 1985. The current horizontal series of brick courses were inserted under the timber-frame structures to the west when the ground was lowered. The lowering of the ground level was not attempted in the reconstruction film. It would have looked complex and would have required a voice-over to explain.

96 By 1861 the outbuildings were described in sale details as: 'Coal, Tub, and Sand Houses, and other minor Offices; and the Pleasure Grounds, Orchard, and Gardens, which are partly protected by massive brick walls, are in good keeping with the Residence, and in excellent order. The Agricultural Homestead Includes spacious Wheat and Barley Barns, Riding and Cart Horse Stables, seven-bayed Waggon Lodge, Gig House, Granary, Neathouse, Walled-in Stackyard, and ample Cattle and Shelter Sheds and Yards.' There are other Victorian inventories of the interior fittings.

97 Jenkins 2003, p. 728.

past, but decided to focus particularly on the medieval phase. Therefore he removed most of the Victorian and Georgian wallpaper and plasterwork, re-exposing Jacobean mullions and medieval wall struts; and he demolished room partitions to re-open the medieval great hall. This exposure of old structure can also be critiqued – it is driven by an educated middle-class taste for the visible effect of age and *shabby chic*, as well a conscious antiquarianism. So was it really a restoration, or actually a reinvention and representation? Further, it does not wholly reflect what any of the previous ages intended when they made their changes to the building. For example, the medieval builders usually whitewashed or plastered over the upright wooden studs inside, rather than leaving them exposed as bare wood, as they are now. One bedroom has visible evidence of no less than five different types of window from different historical periods, only one of which is now open. They were never meant to all exist exposed side by side in this way. So this 'restoration' results in a palimpsest of different periods, where the building is self-consciously wearing its history on its sleeve. Such a knowing exposure of the past is therefore also a modern cultural construct, and the building sits simultaneously between the modern day and different phases of the past, without sitting authentically in any of them. Perhaps it is now almost like the memory of a building – with disjointed fragments of its past bound up with its present.

Conclusions: reconstruction as research method

One of the things that became apparent to us during this project was that reconstruction was not just an outreach artefact to communicate research findings to the public and fellow academics. The reconstruction process itself was part of the research; especially since attempting to answer the endless awkward questions of the computer programmers made us question many of our assumptions. We now argue that reconstruction is potentially a research method in itself: a questioning process of learning and re-discovery, testing our own knowledge, preconceptions and misunderstandings, as well as our understanding of the past. We found ourselves asking questions about the building's size, location and day-to-day practical usage that we would not have done if we were drawing up a simple two-dimensional ground plan. The archaeologist Professor Barry Cunliffe once said of the process of working on a reconstruction with artist Alan Sorrell: 'We were all made to think hard and (certainly in my case) to learn something new of the building we thought we knew.'[98] The artist creating the reconstruction is also mirroring the creative act of the designers and builders of the lost edifice, and through that parallel creative process we can maybe gain insights into the past which an archaeological survey of the standing remains cannot. In a

[98] Cunliffe in Sorrell 1981, p. 17.

speech to the Institute of Archaeology in 1972 Alan Sorrell argued for the importance of the creativity of the artist, and concluded:

> reconstruction drawing … can be the vital final step in an archaeological study. By taking this step we can get inside the minds of the old builders, and savour something of their problems and achievements. The visual apprehension of the artist, disciplined in the most rigorous manner by the facts assembled by the archaeologist, can make a valuable contribution to the search for the truth about the past, which, I suppose, is what archaeology is all about.[99]

As an increasingly popular interpretive and outreach tool and a growing research method in itself, digital reconstruction could now be said to be part of historiography and the study of historical research methods.

To conclude, hopefully we have shown that reconstruction is an inexact science, dealing with issues like material absence, snapshots in time and shifting elusive value judgements like truth, taste and aesthetics. Reconstruction is a series of academic decisions, suppositions, creative choices and re-imaginings; made within the limits of available project materials, budget, timescale and access to specialised expertise. There are often negotiations within a team of people to find common ground, and sometimes there has to be a deciding vote: one person with a decision and a vision, perhaps similar to the director of a film. At the heart of reconstruction is a very human process of trying to understand the past and make sense of conflicting interpretations of evidence, as well as making sense of our own position in the timeline of history, culture and subjective taste. The result is a new creative artefact that can itself be interpreted as a media text: an adaptation of the past, designed to communicate with a modern audience.

And yet we can only reconstruct what we know was once there. What if there were other things there that we do not know about the existence of? The chance survival of one documentary reference to a north gatehouse meant that we had to explore what the college gatehouse could have looked like. How much more could there have been on the site that we do not know about? Could there have been another chapel, within the college? Was the lost Chapter House a standalone structure of some grandeur and ostentation? Was there another western quadrangle of buildings between the surviving range and the road? With these questions in mind, we would like to finish with this famous quotation from a recent American secretary of defence, which may hold more truth for historical reconstruction than it did for weapons of mass destruction …

> There are known knowns: there are things we know that we know. There are known unknowns: that is to say there are things that we now know we don't

[99] Sorrell 1972, pp. 20–6.

know. But there are also unknown unknowns – there are things we do not know we don't know.[100]

Perhaps that is the hardest challenge – trying to reconstruct the unknown unknowns, when we do not even know what we are reconstructing. All we can do is to create our own consistent version of a story, and be honest about what we do and don't know. We must accept that reconstruction is an inexact science and we are only ever looking at the past 'through a mirror darkly'.[101] And sometimes what we see is just a reflection of ourselves, looking in.

Acknowledgements

I would like to thank everyone who worked on the UEA Wingfield Project in all capacities, especially John Williams of Virtual Past for his skill and perseverance; Philip Aitkens for his huge knowledge; Edward Martin for his patience and kindness, Jane Greenwood for her endless support; Rob Liddiard of UEA for his enthusiasm and making the whole thing more enjoyable; Lesley Jackson at Wingfield Barns and Eleanor Goodison and the 1362 committee, for making the 1362 Wingfield commemoration the success it was; and above all John Charmley of UEA, without whose support and energy this project would not have happened. The UEA Wingfield Project was partly supported by the Ann Ashard Webb bequest.

---

[100] United States secretary of defence, Donald Rumsfeld, at a press briefing on 12 February 2002, discussing weapons of mass destruction in Iraq.
[101] 1 Corinthians 13:12. This can also be translated as 'through a lens darkly'.

7

Medieval Monuments to the de la Pole
and Wingfield Families

SALLY BADHAM

In 1362 Wingfield College was founded in memory of Sir John de Wingfield III (d.1361), although the initial work on his chantry had been carried out in his final years.[1] Sir John was the son and heir of John de Wingfield II (d.1327), who was descended from a family of administrators and who rose to prominence through service to the de Brewse family.[2] His father, John I, first established the family at Wingfield through the purchase of the manor of Wingfield Frombalds to which John II had added the manor of Wingfield Hall. Sir John had a distinguished career; he was chief administrator to Edward the Black Prince and a veteran of Crécy. He provided in his will for the building of the large collegiate church near the site of the old church.[3] This was presumably motivated at least in part by the fact that he was the last male of his line, having had only a daughter Katherine by his wife Eleanor de Verlay. There are many examples of men without direct male heirs choosing to be commemorated by a grand tomb monument, quite often associated with a chantry, although few went as far as to rebuild an entire church and set up a collegiate foundation. The act may also have been a form of thanksgiving for having survived the Black Death in 1349, although, as fate would have it, it was probably the 1361 outbreak which caused his death. It was stated in Sir John's will that in order to make the church suitable for the college, it must be 'in great part built anew ... and constructed on a larger scale than before ... with a belfry, bells, chapels, at a very great expense'.[4] He was buried in his new church, which was to act as a mausoleum for his family and many of their de la Pole heirs until the close of the fifteenth century. The tomb monuments at Wingfield are, along with those at Framlingham, arguably the finest collection of medieval carved tombs in Suffolk, two of them being of national importance. However, in order fully to understand the tombs in their context, especially the

---

[1] See the chapter by Mark Bailey in this volume.
[2] See the chapter by Edward Martin in this volume.
[3] Aldwell 1925, pp. 96–107.
[4] Ibid., pp. 77–93.

de la Pole monuments, it is also necessary to examine the other known monuments to family members at their other mausolea in Kingston upon Hull (Yorkshire) and Ewelme (Oxfordshire). In the survey which follows considerable reliance is placed on antiquarian notes, which record the state of the monuments at various times over the past four hundred years and throw hitherto unrevealed light on their appearance.

The Wingfield family monuments

Sir John's monument, which is carved from chalk (commonly called clunch), is a sophisticated monument almost certainly from a metropolitan workshop.[5] It comprises an effigy in armour lying on a Purbeck marble slab on a panelled tomb-chest with four quatrefoils enclosing shield, above which is a crocketed ogee gable with buttressed shafts either side and a cusped and sub-cusped arch (see Figure 7.1).[6] In the oculus of the arch is a support on which there would originally have been an image, perhaps of St Andrew to whom the church is dedicated. Sir John holds his hands in prayer and his feet rest on a lion, which is split in two and has most of the head missing (Figure 7.2). Sir John's head, which rests on his helm, is covered by a pointed bascinet with mail aventail below; wire can be seen passing through the vervelles or staples attached to the bacinet. His torso and limbs are protected by plate armour. Over his body he wears a close-fitting coat armour, the so-called 'jupon', which has a scalloped edge, and a mail fringe protrudes below. His arms would have been painted on the coat armour. Over it he wears a hip belt, properly called an arse-girdle, which formerly supported his sword and dagger, although both are now missing. The spur straps are decorated with circular bosses and have small oval buckles, but the functional parts of the spurs are missing. All these damaged parts are shown in an identical broken state in the earliest known drawing of the effigy, sent in 1780 to the antiquary Richard Gough by one of his correspondents Michael Tyson.[7] The figure had presumably been damaged at some stage and the remains of the sword and dagger were dressed away at a restoration.

Nowadays the effigy and its setting show almost entirely bare stone, but this was not originally the case. A painted scene with a religious theme might well have adorned the back wall of the tomb recess; it is now bare plaster but it is possible that this might cover the original decoration. In addition, the architectural detail and the effigy would have been entirely covered with polychromy and other surface finishes.[8] The shields on the tomb-chest would have been decorated by Sir John's arms and those of his forebears. According to the church notes of circa 1673 compiled by the

---

[5]   Roberts 1974.
[6]   For Purbeck marble, see Blair 1991.
[7]   Bod: Gough Maps 223c, between fols 250–1.
[8]   For polychromy on medieval sculpture, see Boldrick, Park and Williamson 2002.

Fig. 7.1. General view of tomb monument to Sir John Wingfield (d.1361). Wingfield (Suffolk).

Fig. 7.2. Effigy of Sir John Wingfield (d.1361). Wingfield (Suffolk).

antiquary William Blois of Grundisburgh (1600–73) John's arms were painted on his chest, by which he meant on the coat armour.[9] Charles Stothard, an outstanding antiquarian artist who died in 1821, visited Wingfield in the summer of 1812 and spent a fortnight there making eleven carefully observed drawings. Regarding the Wingfield effigy, he wrote to his father that it was 'very singularly painted – red knee and elbow pieces gold; the surcoat, greaves and helmet silver. On the red thigh pieces are golden spots, placed at regular distances; from what I have seen since, I think these were meant to represent studs. The whole of the arms, down to the gauntlets, might have been ornamented in the same manner; but as the paint was nearly effaced I could not ascertain this fact.'[10] From the traces of paint he found, Stothard painted a reconstruction of the colour scheme together with studies of some details (Plate XIV).[11] It cannot be regarded as totally reliable. For example, the arms shown are *Azure on a bend gules cotised argent three pairs of wings argent*, which is contrary to the rules of heraldry; the correct blazon is *Argent on a bend gules three pairs of wings argent*.[12] However, the drawing gives a reasonable overall impression of how such effigies originally appeared.

To modern eyes such reconstructions look repellently garish, but in reality the effect would have been more subtle than Stothard shows. By his time, coloured glazes which modified the final appearance would undoubtedly have worn away. The effect would still have been striking, especially with all the applied gold and silver leaf, but the medieval audience for which this was designed would have regarded such an appearance as exuding wealth, beauty and, above all, realism, all highly desirable qualities. For medieval man, it was essential that the sculpted image was empowered by the application of polychromy into what Michael Baxendall has characterised as

[9]   SROI: CG17–775, fol. 75.
[10] Bray 1851, p. 58.
[11] Stothard 1832, pl. 92.
[12] Corder 1965, p. 100.

'a surrogate person'.[13] Completed sculptures were viewed as existing in the world of the living, not the world of art. This is confirmed by a Middle English sermon writer's words: 'It is nececarie that thou be-have ye as a peyntur behaweth hym in ys peyntynge an ymage. A peyntur penteth now is ymage with white colours, now with blake, now with red colours, not with mydle colour *aftur that it be-commes ye ymage* [my italics].'[14] It was for this reason that religious images were singled out for such destructive ire at the Reformation, even though the 1550 Act which ordered the destruction of all religious images made a specific exception for tomb monuments.[15] In the words of one contemporary critic 'Ye peyntour makith an ymage forgid wth diverse colours til it seme in foolis izen as a lyveli creature' [that is a living being].[16]

Evidently yet more of the surface finishes have worn away in the two hundred years since Stothard observed the effigy, but traces survive, particularly underneath the figure and in crevices. The bascinet on Sir John's head looks black but that is actually tarnished silver leaf; it would originally have had a layer of glaze over the metal leaf to protect it. The attached aventail has remains of *pastiglia* or gesso, which, when still pliant, was moulded to give the impression of mail (Plate XV). It would then have received several layers of paint and finishes. Stothard shows it as being red, and some tiny specks of red still remain on the underside of the head. However, these specks are to be seen only where the moulded mail has fallen away. This shows that the red was actually a ground on top of which the mail was moulded and had applied to it glazed silver leaf. There is more tarnished silver leaf on the leg defences and gold leaf is still present on the gauntlets and the heels of the sabatons (Plates XVI and XVII). The underside of the helm has a large area of red paint with evidence of patterning. The lion was painted golden colour, with a dark mane. As yet, no paint analysis has been carried out to establish exactly what layers are present, although the effigies in Wingfield Church would make an interesting study. I have worked on the assumption that what can be seen is the original paint, but it is possible that any or all of these effigies could have been repainted at some stage. A recently conserved early fourteenth-century military effigy in Exeter Cathedral was shown to have had four successive medieval paint schemes, and a mid-fourteenth-century effigy at Much Marcle (Herefordshire) conserved in 2012–14 has received four re-paintings.[17]

The Rev. Aldwell suggested that Sir John's tomb, now on the north side of the chancel, might once have been within the chantry chapel dedicated to the Holy Trinity on the north side of the chancel but now used as a vestry and that, following the Reformation, this became ruinous, thus necessitating the removal of the tomb monument to its present position.[18] His case is unconvincing. As is explained below,

---

[13] Baxendale 1999, p. 46.
[14] Ross 1940, p. 283.
[15] Deacon and Lindley 2001, pp. 24–37.
[16] Marks 2004, p. 244.
[17] *Ex inf.* the conservators Eddie Sinclair and Peter Martingdale.
[18] Aldwell 1925, pp. 71–2.

Fig. 7.3. Indent of lost brass to Eleanor de Wingfield (d.1375).
Wingfield (Suffolk).

the evidence suggests that the Holy Trinity chapel did not become a de la Pole chantry chapel until the early fifteenth century. Moreover, the tomb shows no sign of having been taken down and reconstructed and was certainly on the north side of the chancel when the unknown antiquary known as the Chorographer of Suffolk visited the church around 1600.[19] The present position of the tomb is a prestigious one, conventionally associated with founders or dominant lords of the manor, which would be an obvious choice for the founder of the collegiate church.

Sir John's effigy is not the only monument to a Wingfield in the church. Beside it is a Purbeck marble slab with the indents of a once-fine monumental brass showing a lady resting her head on a pair of cushions under a canopy, with shields above and below the canopy arch (Figure 7.3). The composition was completed by a marginal inscription with quatrefoils at the corners, on which would have been engraved the symbols of the four evangelists. The brass was obviously a prestigious one to a high-ranking lady. Even though no inlay remains, there are sufficient clues to support a case that it commemorates Eleanor de Wingfield, Sir John's wife. The position at the foot of Sir John Wingfield's tomb monument is highly suggestive of a relationship between the two. There is a similar synchronicity to be found in Lincoln Cathedral in the Cantelupe chantry chapel, where the high tomb to Nicholas, 3rd Lord Cantelupe (d.1355) has adjacent to it an indent of a lost brass commemorating his widow Joan.[20] The outlines of the missing inlay at Wingfield mark out this lost brass as a product of the London B workshop dating from the 1370s.[21] The shape of the canopy and positioning of the shields are similar to the brass of Sir John de la Pole (d.1380) and his wife from a different branch of the family at Chrishall (Essex), while the figure compares very well indeed with that to Elizabeth, lady Cobham (d.1370), at Lingfield (Surrey), likewise near her husband's high tomb.[22] Significant features include the cushions with tassels only on the upper one and the outline of the foot of the effigy. Sir John's widow died in 1375, right in the middle of the likely date span for the lost brass at Wingfield. Conclusive proof of this identification is provided by Blois's church notes; these were principally concerned with heraldry and contain after his description of Sir John's monument the observation 'And nigh unto it A grave-stone upon his wife, Glanvil's daughter, her arms upon stone', followed by a

---

[19] MacCulloch 1976, p. 273, although the Chorographer mistook the identity of the man commemorated, noting that 'On the North side of the Chauncell lay buryed by himself John de la Pole duke of Suff. according to the common opinion of the Inhabitants in the towne.' This can refer only to Sir John Wingfield's effigy as it is the only single effigy extant or known in the church.
[20] I am grateful to Jennifer Alexander for information about the Cantelupe tombs at Lincoln. The fashion of someone placing their brass near a high tomb extended beyond husband and wife relationships. Paul Cockerham has argued that in Exeter Cathedral the proximity of Canon William Langton's brass to his kinsman Bishop Stafford's tomb enabled Langton to bask in Stafford's reflected glory. The position was specified in Langton's will. Cockerham 2010, pp. 8–11.
[21] For the London workshops, see Kent 1949, passim.
[22] Lack, Stuchfield and Whittemore 2003, vol. 1, p. 160; Saul 2001, p. 169.

Fig. 7.4. Simplified pedigree of the de la Pole family showing places of burial and commemoration.

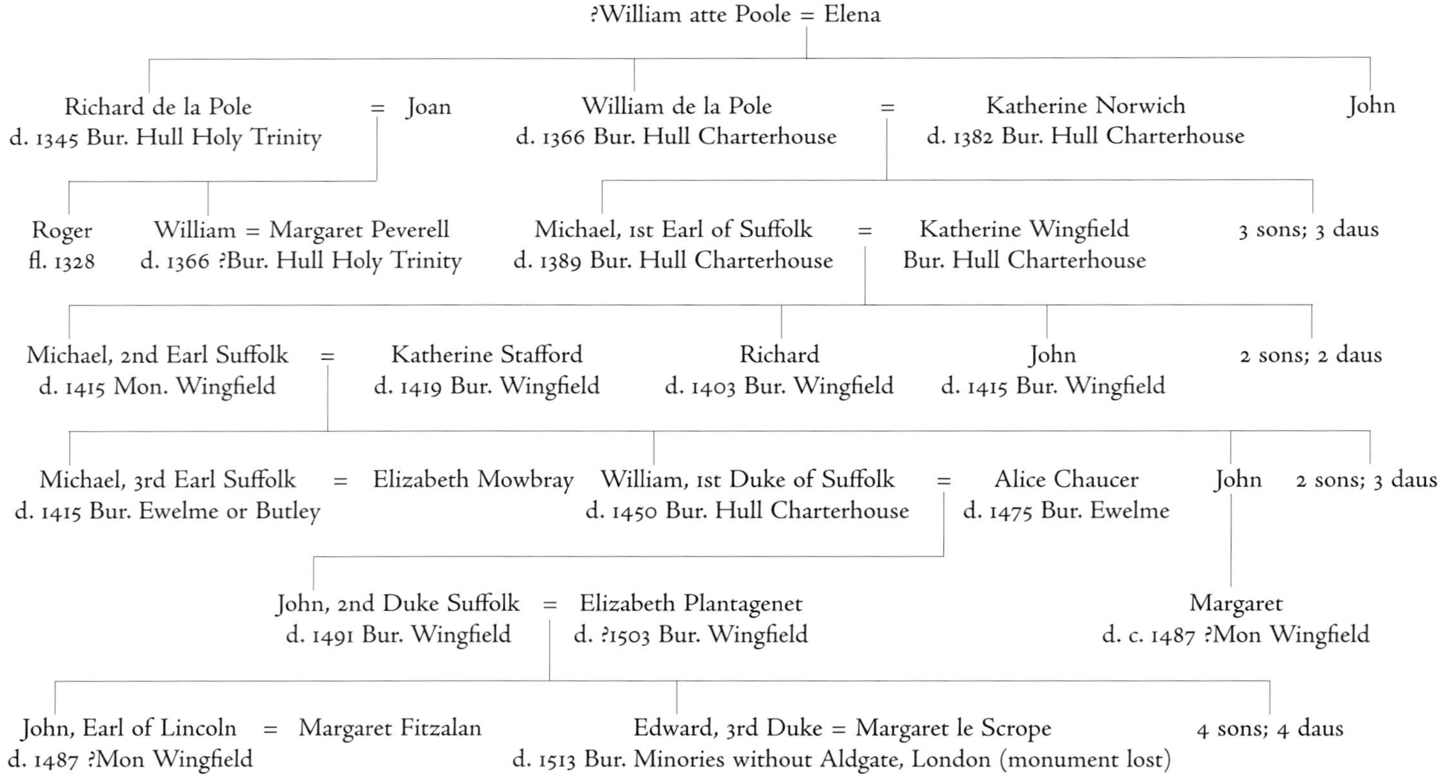

?William atte Poole = Elena

Richard de la Pole = Joan
d. 1345 Bur. Hull Holy Trinity

William de la Pole = Katherine Norwich   John
d. 1366 Bur. Hull Charterhouse   d. 1382 Bur. Hull Charterhouse

Roger   William = Margaret Peverell
fl. 1328   d. 1366 ?Bur. Hull Holy Trinity

Michael, 1st Earl of Suffolk = Katherine Wingfield   3 sons; 3 daus
d. 1389 Bur. Hull Charterhouse   Bur. Hull Charterhouse

Michael, 2nd Earl Suffolk = Katherine Stafford
d. 1415 Mon. Wingfield   d. 1419 Bur. Wingfield

Richard   John   2 sons; 2 daus
d. 1403 Bur. Wingfield   d. 1415 Bur. Wingfield

Michael, 3rd Earl Suffolk = Elizabeth Mowbray   William, 1st Duke of Suffolk = Alice Chaucer
d. 1415 Bur. Ewelme or Butley   d. 1450 Bur. Hull Charterhouse   d. 1475 Bur. Ewelme

John   2 sons; 3 daus

John, 2nd Duke Suffolk = Elizabeth Plantagenet
d. 1491 Bur. Wingfield   d. ?1503 Bur. Wingfield

Margaret
d. c. 1487 ?Mon Wingfield

John, Earl of Lincoln = Margaret Fitzalan   Edward, 3rd Duke = Margaret le Scrope   4 sons; 4 daus
d. 1487 ?Mon Wingfield   d. 1513 Bur. Minories without Aldgate, London (monument lost)

trick of the Glanville arms in confirmation.[23] Although Eleanor was descended from the Glanvilles it was more likely on her mother's side and not her father's.[24] There are four indents for shields on this stone, but Blois does not mention the others. The Chorographer, who visited earlier, failed to record the brass, perhaps because he was less expert in heraldic matters and the monument had no surviving inscription to guide him. Eleanor would have helped to oversee the implementation of Sir John's bequest to establish Wingfield College and rebuild the church, and she was the first patron of Wingfield College, earning her the right to be buried and commemorated in the chancel of the new church.

These two monuments are the only ones to members of the Wingfield family in Wingfield Church. If there were earlier memorials, they must have been swept away when the church was rebuilt. However, many tomb monuments to other members of the family are found elsewhere in Suffolk, a notable collection being in the remote church of St Mary, Letheringham.[25] Sir John de Wingfield's brother, Thomas, gained the manor of Letheringham through his marriage to the heiress, Margaret Boville. He directed in his will 'my body to be buried in the choir of the church of Letheringham Priory on the lower step before the high altar'.[26] Following his death in 1378, he and Margaret were commemorated by a brass, the upper part of which survives only in indent form. Their heir, Sir John Wingfield of Letheringham, died on 1398 and was similarly commemorated, although his armoured figure survives. The church has many other monuments to their successors, right through to 1638.

The de la Pole family monuments at Hull and Ewelme

Sir John Wingfield's personal and dynastic fortunes had been bolstered by marrying his daughter and heiress into one of the *parvenu* families which rose to prominence in the fourteenth century. The de la Poles, originally merchants and traders in Kingston-upon-Hull, rose ever higher until they got too close to the throne for the Tudor dynasty's comfort.[27] Sir John Wingfield's daughter and heiress married Michael de la Pole, later 1st earl of Suffolk, and many of their descendants are buried in Wingfield Church, although they had other mausolea in Hull and Ewelme. Yet before turning to the tomb monuments in Wingfield Church, the burial and commemoration of earlier members of the de la Pole family merit attention.

Richard de la Pole (d.1345), the oldest of the three de la Pole brothers, asked in his will to be buried in Holy Trinity Church, Kingston-upon-Hull.[28] The subject of the

[23] SROI: CG17–775, fol. 75.
[24] See the chapter by Edward Martin in this volume.
[25] Blatchly 1974.
[26] Ibid., p. 178.
[27] Horrox 1983.
[28] Raine 1836, p. 7.

Fig. 7.5. Monument to Richard de la Pole (d.1345) and son Richard (d.1366) linking de la Pole chapel with south aisle. Hull (Yorkshire).

family tombs there has been subject to much dispute and confusion. Two parts of the south aisle are traditionally connected with the de la Pole family. One is the chapel at the west end of the south choir aisle which has an arch over a tomb-chest linking it to the aisle (Figure 7.5). The other, located further east, is a tomb monument with effigies of a civilian and wife, probably carved from the local Ledsham alabaster, resting on a tomb-chest decorated with shields within quatrefoils (Figure 7.6). The whole is within an ornate canopied niche, which is cusped and subcusped and has an ogee gable with blank panelling to the left and right. The effigies are carved in a singular way suggestive of local workmanship. The monument has been subject to some restoration. An engraving made by Basire for Richard Gough before 1786 shows the man's hands as having been broken off, but they have been replaced and

Fig. 7.6. Effigies of Robert de Selby (d.1390) and wife Emma in south aisle. Hull (Yorkshire).

the broken figures of supporting angels smoothed off.[29] The book held between his hands may not therefore reflect the original design, although a heart held by his wife is authentic.

This monument has traditionally been attributed to a member of the de la Pole family but, as argued below, the evidence does not support this. This issue is important to address as the outcome affects the analysis of who is commemorated by the other monument. The notice in the church accompanying the tomb with alabaster effigies is headed 'the de la Pole tomb' and quotes the opinion of many antiquaries. Candidates include various de la Poles and their Wingfield connections; the two most popular suggestions are Richard de la Pole (d.1345) and his wife, and his brother William de la Pole the elder (d.1366) and his wife Katherine Norwich. Yet both can be ruled out. Civilian costume is not always easy to date with precision but a date

[29] Gough 1786–96, vol. 1 (2), p. 121.

in the range 1380–90 for the closely gathered over-gown with straight sleeves of the female effigy seems likely. The bulky veiled headdress of the lady is remarkably similar to that shown on the female effigy on the Marmion tomb of circa 1387 at West Tanfield (Yorkshire).[30] Hence a date of circa 1380–90 seems indicated. Such a late dating would exclude Richard de la Pole as a candidate, as he died in 1345, and probably also William the elder. Moreover, William's wife, Katherine Norwich, like other later members of the family, chose burial in God's House Hospital at Hull, commonly called the Charterhouse, which, according to her will, was planned by her husband, but not actually established until a decade after his death.[31] William left the choice of his own burial place to the discretion of his executors.[32] Whether he was temporarily buried in Holy Trinity and subsequently removed to the Charterhouse is uncertain, but what is clear is that their joint tomb is recorded as having been placed in the choir of the Charterhouse church. In the College of Arms is an account dating from before 1491 in the hand John Wrythe, Garter King of Arms, of founders and benefactors and of burials of several Yorkshire churches, including the Charterhouse church at Hull, which records 'Anno dni M ccc lxx vij … primo fundata erat domus Sancti Michaelis juxta Kyngeston super Hull ordinis Cartusien cujus primus fundator extitit dominus Willielmus de la Pole miles strenuus qui cum uxore sua domina Katherina filia domini Johannis Norwyche comitis nobilissimi sunt sepulti in choro ecclesie dicte domus [in 1377 … was first founded the Carthusian house of St Michael near to Kingston-upon-Hull of which the first founder was Lord William de la Pole, a strenuous knight, who with his wife the Lady Katherine daughter of the most notable earl of Norwich are buried in the choir of the church of the said house]'.[33] The form of the monument is unknown but a carved tomb with effigies under a canopy would be most likely; this might have been placed on the north side of the choir in the place of honour usually reserved for founders. The antiquary John Leland, who wrote his 'Itineraries' in the years 1535–43, visited Hull. He recorded that 'at the late supressing of it were founde dyverse trowehes [troughs] of leade with bones in a volte under [by which he probably meant 'at a lower level than'] the high altare ther' which must have been the de la Pole tombs, although he gave no account of the form their monuments took as they had undoubtedly been demolished before his visit.[34]

A significant clue as to the identity of the civilian and wife at Hull is that he has dangling from his belt a probe, used by wool merchants for testing the quality of wool (Figure 7.7). It is highly unlikely that the upwardly mobile de la Poles would have chosen to be commemorated as wool merchants. As is often the case, anti-

---

30   I am grateful to Dr Jane Crease for this comparison.
31   Raine 1836, p. 119; Cook 1882, *passim*.
32   Raine 1836, p. 76.
33   CoA: MS L8, fol. 75.
34   Toulmin Smith 1964, vol. 1, p. 50.

Fig. 7.7. Detail of effigy to Robert de Selby (d.1390) showing wool probe. Hull (Yorkshire).

quarian notes provide the answer to the identity of the couple. Leland recorded that 'Selby is buried yn the south side of the waulle of isle by the quire: and his wife also, with very fair images.'[35] Richard de Selby was a prominent Hull merchant of the Staple of Calais, who traded, *inter alia*, with Gascony and the Low Countries and who served at least six times as mayor of Hull.[36] In 1382 he was one of the two most generous donors who contributed £4 each to the cost of making Hull's

[35] Ibid., p. 50.
[36] *VCH Yorks ER II*, p. 82.

charter. He was associated with Holy Trinity church as early as 1361, when £5 raised by Hull Corporation by means of a special duty on wool exports was placed in the keeping of him and Walter Box 'for the work of the church', perhaps the completion of the chancel. In 1375, Robert, his wife Emma and her influential brother Richard Ravenser, archdeacon of Lincoln, who died in 1386, obtained licence to grant lands in Hull worth £10 a year to the priory of Guisborough. In return the priory was to maintain a chantry priest in Holy Trinity Church, and a hospital for twelve poor men each of whom was to receive ½ d a day, which was further augmented by Selby in 1390.[37] The hospital is thought to have stood on the north side of the churchyard. The Ravenser chantry is believed to have been in a chapel off the south aisle of Holy Trinity Church behind the tomb in question.[38] Robert de Selby died in 1390, but whether the monument was commissioned soon after his death or contemporaneously with the chantry foundation is uncertain.

This leaves the monument in the canopied niche to the west of the Selby tomb as possibly commemorating members of the de la Pole family. It is very fine, but in its present state by no means original. The chapel and the tomb were badly damaged in 1651 to provide an entrance for Parliamentary soldiers to the chancel which was at that time used as a preaching house; they cut away the northern side of the tomb canopy and removed the tomb-chest.[39] Much of the carving was renewed in 1863 when Isabella Broadley restored the chapel.[40] The carved and painted heraldry is screamingly modern in appearance; in the adjacent chapel, however, two shields above the tomb have what seems to be original carving of the arms *two bars wavy*. The colours shown now are not original, but were painted in 1946, and what they were formerly is unclear. These arms, albeit with different tinctures, were borne by three members of the de la Pole family: Richard and his son William junior bore *azure two bars wavy argent*, while Richard, and Walter, the son of William de la Pole and Katherine Norwich adopted different tinctures, although his father had borne *azure, a fess between three leopards' faces or.*[41]

A date for the monument soon after the middle years of the century is indicated by the design of the canopy which, with its angels and canted shields in the cusps of the arch, is broadly influenced by the famous Percy tomb at nearby Beverley Minster, which dates from the 1340s. The Hull tomb is by no means as fine and the architectural details suggest a slightly later date, perhaps as late as the 1360s. Another comparison may be drawn between the flat tomb-chest cover on both. The Percy tomb originally had a second tomb-chest on top surmounted by a monumental brass. The top of the chest at Hull has replacement flagstones on it, but could it

[37] CPR 1377–81, p. 167 and CPR 1405–8, pp. 561–2.
[38] VCH Yorks ER I, p. 288.
[39] Ibid., p. 291; Harvey 1961, p. 472.
[40] VCH Yorks ER I, p. 292.
[41] Horrox 1983, p. 4.

too have had a brass on top? Nearby is a re-used black 'marble' slab of precisely the same dimensions as the top of the chest. In the church notes of circa 1700, the Hull historian Abraham de la Pryme recorded: 'Upon a great huge Marble Grave Stone there lyes ye Portraitures of two great men embossed in Armor formerly curiously adorn'd with inscriptions and brasses but all of them being now pluck'd of, it is not known who lies there and what they were.'[42] Although there is no proof that the slab belongs to the de la Pole tomb-chest, it is likely that it does.

This still leaves the dilemma of who is commemorated by the monument. Speculation has centred on various members of the de la Pole family (see Figure 7.4 for pedigree), but that two armoured figures were shown throws new light on the possibilities. They could represent brothers or a father and son. The other significant factor is that at least one of them must have fought in the Crécy–Calais campaign; A.S. Harvey established, through analysis of surviving shields on the tomb arch as recorded by de la Pryme in 1700 and by John Warburton, Somerset Herald, in 1724, that all the original shields are of men who served in the Crécy–Calais campaign of 1346–47.[43] Two members of the de la Pole family fit this last criterion: William junior the son of Richard, and Walter, the son of William de la Pole and Katherine Norwich. We do not know when Walter died, although it may have been soon after his return from France as nothing more is recorded of him.[44] He pre-deceased his father and thus died before the family established a mausoleum at the Charterhouse, although he was mentioned in the foundation document. A burial in Holy Trinity would be likely in his case, but the second figure could not have been his father who was definitely buried in the Charterhouse. He did have a brother, Thomas, who died in 1362, but if Walter was one of those for whom this tomb was made, there is no other obvious candidate for the second figure.[45]

This leaves Richard's son William (d.1366), who was married to Margaret Peverell.[46] A date of 1366 would fit the tomb design very well. He is a strong possibility, although there is no evidence as to his place of burial. Admittedly, William disposed of all his lands in Hull in his lifetime, his main place of residence being Castle Ashby (Northamptonshire), but it is by no means unknown for someone in his position to have chosen to be buried in the place he was born and where his parents were buried. The likelihood is that it was William who was buried here, along with his father Richard (d.1345), who, as shown above, asked in his will to be buried in Holy Trinity Church and founded a chantry there, almost certainly in the chapel into which this tomb opens. The most likely reconstruction is that either William's widow Joan or her son John, who married Joan de Cobham, chose to commemorate

---

[42] Harvey 1961, 473, n. 2.
[43] Ibid., pp. 475–7.
[44] Horrox 1983, p. 30.
[45] Ibid., pp. 29–30.
[46] Horrox 1963, p. 33.

his father and grandfather by a single monument on the north side of the chantry chapel.

The marriage between William de la Pole's eldest son Michael, 1st earl of Suffolk (d.1389), and Katherine Wingfield marked a significant stage in the shift southwards in the de la Poles' interests, but neither chose burial at Wingfield. They followed the example of Michael's parents, William de la Pole and his wife Katherine Norwich, who were buried in the priory church of the Charterhouse, which continued to be used as the family's northern mausoleum into the mid-fifteenth century. Wrythe recorded that 'Secundus fundator fuit dominus Michael de la Pole filius et heres dictorum viz Willielmi et Katherine primo comes Suffolchie qui et ipse cum uxore sua domina Katherina sepultus est in eadem dicte domus ecclesia [The second founder was Lord Michael de la Pole, son and heir of the said William and Katherine 1st earl of Suffolk who is also buried with his wife the Lady Katherine in the same church of the said house].'[47] Again we know nothing of the form of the monument, but a carved tomb with effigies under a canopy would be most likely; it might have been placed on the south side of the choir to balance the tomb of the founder.

The last known de la Pole burial recorded at the Hull Charterhouse was of William, 4th earl and later 1st duke of Suffolk, who died in 1450. In his will he directed that 'my wretched body to be buryed in my Charter-house at Hull and I will that an image of myself and another of my wife be made in stone'.[48] A high tomb with effigies was probably intended. He reached an untimely end, being beheaded in a boat off Dover while escaping to France, but his redoubtable duchess, Alice Chaucer, ensured that his wishes for burial there were in time to an extent met – although with a different type of monument. William's body was buried first at Wingfield, then in 1460 reinterred and reburied in front of the high altar in the Charterhouse church.[49] Wrythe wrote 'Huic successit dominus Willielmus de la Pole primus de ista progenie Dux Suffolchie cuius corpus quiescit honerifice ante et sub summum altare in dicte domus sancti Michaelis ecclesia [To him (his brother Michael, 3rd earl of Suffolk) succeeded the Lord William de la Pole, the first of that line to be duke of Suffolk, whose body rests honourably in front of and below the high altar in the said church of the house of St Michael].'[50] The use of the term 'honourably' is interesting in view of his dishonourable death.

Among the Ewelme muniments in the Bodleian Library, Oxford, is the receipt dated 1460 for the 1st duke's tomb monument, undoubtedly at the Hull Charter-house.[51] This records the receipt by Robert Chamberlayn pewterer and Thomas Stephenes coppersmith (both citizens of London) of a final payment of £8 13s 4d

47 CoA: MS L8, fol. 75.
48 LP: Register Stafford, fol. 189; Nicholas 1826, pp. 256–7.
49 Horrox 1983, p. 41.
50 CoA: MS L8, fol. 75.
51 Bod: Ewelme MS A40; Goodall 2001, pp. 297–8.

'pro bargania cuisdam petre marmor per Johnanem Essex marbeler [in full payment of the £35 6s 8d [owed to them] for a bargain of a certain marble stone by John Essex marbler]'. On the reverse is a note 'aquitaunce of the maromer for my lord's tomb stoon'. John Goodall assumed that what had been provided was 'a vastly expensive brass'.[52] Wrythe's use of the phrase 'in front and below the high altar' to describe his tomb might imply a floor monument, such as a brass, but not necessarily so, especially if the altar itself were on a raised platform. No known contract or testamentary provision for a monumental brass involves sums of money coming even close to such a large amount as £35 6s 8d. A comparison with amounts paid for other contemporary tomb monuments may help to throw some light on what types of tomb could be bought by such a sum at this time. The contract for making a brass closest in date to 1460 is a draft of 1466 in which James Reames, who headed the London D workshop, agreed to make the brass commemorating Richard Willoughby at Wollaton (Nottinghamshire).[53] The resultant brass is among the most accomplished of its period but it cost only 8 marks, bargained down from £5.[54] Even allowing for a smart tradesman charging a member of the nobility a higher price, there is a huge disparity between this sum and the £35 6s 8d charged for the duke of Suffolk's monument. It should be noted, however, that in 1457 the marbler John Borde of Corfe was paid £45 for the very elaborate tomb-chest on which Richard Beauchamp's cast copper-alloy effigy rested.[55] Hence a brass on a more modest tomb-chest could have cost de la Pole's executors £35 6s 8d, but this leaves other puzzling aspects of the receipt unaddressed.

John Essex was a known maker of monumental brasses, being responsible for the long-lived workshop group known as Series B.[56] This points to the monument being some sort of monumental brass. However, he is also known to have worked in collaboration with Thomas Stevyns only on two very special commissions. In 1454 they were called upon to advise Henry VI on plans for his monument at Westminster, but which however failed to materialise.[57] What we know of these discussions centred on the location of the monument in the Confessor's chapel, not what form it might take, although a tomb-chest with a cast copper-alloy must have been likely in view of the number of similar tomb monuments already in the chapel. Also in 1454, Essex and Stevyns worked together on elements of the cast gilt copper-alloy tomb to Richard Beauchamp, earl of Warwick. They contracted to provide the copper-alloy plate on which the effigy would rest and the inscription, both of which were to be gilt, as well as the hearse set over the effigy, all at a cost of £135.[58] The inscription

---

52 Goodall 2001, p. 191.
53 Saul 2006.
54 For some other comparisons, see Saul 2006, p. 178.
55 Nichols 1838, pp. 32–3.
56 Emmerson 1978, pp. 67–8.
57 Ibid., p. 67; Stanley 1868, pp. 576–7.
58 Nichols 1838, pp. 32–3.

Fig. 7.8. Tomb monument of Alice de la Pole, duchess of Suffolk (d.1475), at Ewelme (Oxfordshire).

was cast rather than engraved and Stevyns may have been involved partly for this aspect of the work. The casting of the effigy itself and the weepers of the tomb-chest were contracted to a founder, William Austen, at a cost of £18 15s 6d, excluding the cost of gilding.[59]

Brasses were made by marblers, but coppersmiths appear to have been involved when casting was required. The involvement of a pewterer is puzzling, but it may be significant that polished pewter looks very like silver. Could Alice have commissioned a cast-copper alloy tomb for her husband? This perhaps seems unlikely, even though she was lavish in her patronage. Possibly more likely is that the duke's monument was a monumental brass but with cast gilt copper-alloy elements, such as a relief inscription or perhaps copper-alloy and pewter 'weeper' figures in housings in a Purbeck marble tomb-chest. In the absence of any other evidence, we can only speculate.

It may be significant that Alice's parents, Thomas Chaucer (d.1434) and Maud (d.1436), had been commemorated by a fine brass of circa 1440 from the London B workshop on a Purbeck marble tomb-chest at Ewelme (Oxfordshire).[60] As their sole surviving issue, it is by no means improbable that it was Alice who commissioned the monument for her parents and decided upon its form, then subsequently chose a more elaborate version for her husband's tomb. The Ewelme tomb monument was extensively restored in 1843–4, when a new inscription, reproducing the old, was added to the chamfer on the tomb-chest and the inlaid enamelled shields were also entirely renewed.[61] Various heraldic errors were made in the course of the restoration, but an analysis of the original heraldry, recorded in antiquarian notes, demonstrates that the tomb was in place by 1438.[62] It is, however, almost certainly not in its original position, but was originally free-standing. One possibility is that the Chaucer brass was originally in the position of honour in the newly built St John chapel in the arch on the north side separating it from the chancel, but was moved westwards when Alice chose to be commemorated at Ewelme rather than at the Hull Charterhouse or Wingfield Church.

This position of honour near the altar of the chapel is occupied by Alice's own tomb constructed of alabaster, likely to have been made in the closing years of Alice's life (Figure 7.8).[63] She is depicted as a vowess, but her coronet underlines her exalted status. The Order of the Garter is shown around her left forearm. It is interesting that she chose to be buried and commemorated in her own foundation at Ewelme, rather than in the de la Poles' established mausolea at Hull and Wingfield. Most alabaster monuments of this time appear to have been carved in the Midlands near the alabaster outcrops, but Alice's monument is far superior to such tombs and was

59 Ibid., pp. 30–1.
60 Kent 1949, p. 95.
61 Goodall 2001, pp. 169–70.
62 Ibid., pp. 170–5.
63 Ibid., pp. 175–93. For alabaster see Ramsay 2001.

undoubtedly a special commission from top London carvers. It is what is known as a 'double-decker' tomb with an effigy showing her in life on the top of the tomb-chest and, in a stone cage beneath, as a cadaver. The latter can only be seen by crouching down and peering between the bars of the stone cage. This tomb type was introduced to England earlier in the fifteenth century; it was only ever a minority taste but was most popular with the higher clergy. Indeed, this is the only surviving example of a female shown as a cadaver on a carved tomb, although more examples of female cadavers or skeletons survive on brasses. It is interesting – and rather puzzling – to note that the nose on the cadaver has been broken, but that of Alice in life is almost faultless apart from a tiny putty patch to her nose and the loss of part of her coronet. The delicate and potentially fragile gablette above Alice's head remains in absolutely perfect undamaged condition. In fact the whole monument is utterly remarkable for the apparent lack of both wear and mutilation. It is hard to believe that we are seeing original, undamaged, fifteenth-century work and indeed close inspection reveals that the canopy and chest of the monument have been reassembled with many parts misaligned, and it has been the subject of at least one restoration with parts re-carved and replaced. Shining a light through various parts of the alabaster reveals that several different shades of stone, almost certainly from different quarries, have been used, indicating that many parts have been replaced at various times.

The tomb is known to have undergone restorations on two occasions. The large sum of £94 9s 6d was spent in 1791–2 by the foundation, but what was done by the Mr Bingley employed was not specified.[64] If only basic work was needed it might be thought that the foundation would have employed a local workman, maybe even a jobbing builder, but local trade directories list no man of this name. The workman may have been John Bingley, a London sculptor active some years either side of 1790; he signed two tablets in St Bartholomew the Less in London.[65] He went bankrupt in 1807, his address at that time being Upper John Street, St Pancras.[66] If this identification is correct, the employment of a metropolitan sculptor suggests specialist carving was required. The apparent perfection of the top effigy might lead one to believe that it was substantially re-carved or even replaced, but this seems not to have been the case. Physical examination suggests that several small breaks, including to her nose, were mended with putty and the heads of five angels were replaced – one on each side of the chest and three of the figures supporting the effigy. In addition, comparison with a drawing by Grimm made for Gough in 1782 reveals that damage to the lion's tail was repaired.[67] It may be that some re-painting was carried out, but even so it

---

[64] Goodall 2001, p. 232, n. 42.
[65] His signed and documented works are listed in Roscoe, Hardy and Sullivan 2009, p. 110.
[66] *London Gazette* issue 16004, 24 February 1807, pp. 252–3. It followed the normal course in five subsequent announcements, culminating in his discharge on 12 February 1811 (hearing announced in Gazette Issue 16444 published, 15 January 1811). Bingley's stock was auctioned in March 1807 after his bankruptcy. (*Morning Chronicle*, 23 March 1807).
[67] Bod: Gough Maps 227, fol. 245.

is difficult to see this costing nearly £95. Unless any further evidence turns up, what exactly took place at Ewelme must remain an enigma. Additional work was carried out in the nineteenth century, including the replacement of the brass inscription on the chamfer of the tomb-chest. This adheres to the original wording and reads: 'Orate pro anima Serenissimae Principessae Aliciae Ducissae Suffolchiae, huius ecclesiae patronae, & primae fundatricis huijus elemosynariae quae obiit 20 die mensis Maij; anno Di. 1475. litera Dominicali A. [Pray for the soul of the most serene princess Alice, duchess of Suffolk, patron of this church and first founder of this almshouse, who died on 20th day of May in the year of Our Lord 1475. Dominical letter A.].' At some stage the upper effigy has been scrubbed to remove all traces of polychromy. Signs of abrasion are evident on flat surfaces such as her cheeks and the upper pillow.

The most remarkable element of this tomb is the contents of the caged section of the chest. Inside is a cadaver, still retaining original polychromy. It gazes at religious images painted on the bottom of the tomb-chest above. They are not of high quality but are exceptional survivals. Alice looks directly at an image of the Annunciation. Below that is St Mary Magdelene, holding a palm and pot, and a kneeling figure of St John the Baptist, to whom the chantry chapel was dedicated, pointing to the Lamb of God with the Standard of the Resurrection. This is the most intimate part of the monument, showing Alice in death seeking the intercession of favoured saints to shorten her time in Purgatory and thus ensure her entry into Heaven.

De la Pole brasses at Wingfield

The remainder of the known de la Pole monuments are at Wingfield. The earliest is a slab of Purbeck marble with just the inscription from a monumental brass remaining, although there was originally a military figure and four shields at the corners (Figure 7.9). The inscription reads: 'Hic jacet Richardus de la Pole filius Domini Michaelis de la Pole nuper Comitis Suffolcie qui obiit xviii die Decembris Anno domini MCCCCIII cujus anime propicietur deus.' It thus commemorates Richard de la Pole (d.1403), who was a younger son of Michael, earl of Suffolk, and his wife Katherine Wingfield. The indent is now in the tower, and was seen in the south aisle, with the lower part covered, by the Suffolk antiquary David Davy of Yoxford (1769–1851) who visited in 1827 and 1838; the Chorographer, however, saw it circa 1600 in 'the north side of the church' and Edmund Gillingwater recorded it as being in the Trinity chapel in 1796.[68] In his will Richard requested burial in the collegiate church at Wingfield, and on 14 February 1405–6 Richard's brother, the earl, received a licence to establish a chantry of a priest to perform divine service

---

[68] BL: MS Add. 19092, fol. 403; Davy 1982, pp. 101, 223; MacCulloch 1976, p. 72; BL: MS Add. 19092, fol. 392; Aldwell 1925, p. 41.

Fig. 7.9. Brass to Richard de la Pole (d.1403), Wingfield (Suffolk).

at the altar of the Holy Trinity in Wingfield Church for Richard's soul.[69] This was the chapel at the east end of the north side of the church. It was named as such in wills of the early sixteenth century.[70] The chantry may have been installed in an existing part of the aisle; the remnants of glazing date to the mid fourteenth century, indicating that it formed part of the original build following Sir John Wingfield's death.[71] However, the marvellous painted woodwork, including a parclose screen of likely early fifteenth-century date, points to it having been re-fitted at the time of the establishment of the chantry.[72] It is likely that Richard de la Pole's brass was moved when the easternmost chapel became a vestry or when much of the church was tiled in the restoration of 1866–80.[73] The Chorographer observed that Richard de la Pole 'layeth in complet armour under his feete a lyon couchant, on his gravestone fower tymes the armes of De la Pole with a flowerdelis on the fesse'. The inscription on the brass shows that it was made in the London B workshop. The lost figure would have looked very much like that of Sir William Moyne (d.1404) at Sawtry (Huntingdonshire); the only significant difference is that the latter rests his head on a helm with his crest.[74]

The Chorographer went on to record 'hard by him layeth also his brother John de la Pole' with this inscription '"Hic iacet Mr. Johannes de la Pole filius D'ni Michaelis de la Pole quonda' Comitis Suffolcie bacalarius utrisqu' juris. Canonicus in ecc'lia Cathedrali Ebor' ac in eccl'ia Collegiata de Beverley qui obiit 4 die Februarij a'o D'ni' cuius p'piet'r Deus.'"[75] Master John de la Pole was a Canon of York and a Prebendary of Wistow in the York Diocese.[76] In his will, proved in February 1415, John requested burial in the collegiate church of Wingfield, near the altar of the Holy Trinity, and left lands for the support of a chaplain at that altar.[77] Unfortunately the indents from that chapel have been moved elsewhere in the church. There are three indents to members of the clergy surviving in the church. One in the tower can immediately be ruled out as it is a Norwich series 6 composition of circa 1520–30; it shows a small figure of a priest, with a disproportionately large chalice above and to the side imagery of Christ rising from the tomb.[78] The remaining two indents, one in the chancel and

---

[69] TNA: PROB 11/2a; *CPR, Ric. II*, vol. I, p. 141.
[70] Aldwell 1925, pp. 113–14.
[71] I am grateful to Richard Marks for dating the glass.
[72] I am grateful to Lucy Wrapson, Hamilton Kerr Institute, for her preliminary observations on the parclose screen. There is another part of the north aisle which has been petitioned off – that now housing the organ – but this is highly unlikely to have been the chantry chapel as it is barely big enough to hold an altar and the brasses that were recorded as being there. Moreover, it was known as St Katherine's chapel in the medieval period and housed an image of that saint, as evidenced in wills of Wingfield residents: Aldwell 1925, pp. 40, 114.
[73] Ibid., p. 41.
[74] Lack, Stuchfield and Whittemore 2012, p. 153.
[75] MacCulloch 1976, p. 72.
[76] Jones 1963, p. 93.
[77] TNA: PROB 11/2b, 245r–245v.
[78] Badham 2012. For the Norwich workshops, see Greenwood and Norris 1976, pp. 26–7.

Fig. 7.10. Indent of lost brass to Master John de la Pole (d.1415), Wingfield (Suffolk).

one in the south chapel, are of broadly the right date; they are in Purbeck marble and unquestionably from a London workshop, probably that known as London B. The correct one can be identified as a result of the Chorographer recording that John de la Pole's brass bore four shields, all with variants of the de la Pole arms. The indent in the south chapel is the better preserved but it has only two shields, so also can be ruled out. The indent in the chancel is badly worn and much of the surface broken, but if it is examined at very close quarters the traces of four shields can be detected (Figure 7.10). Parts of the outlines remain and lead plugs for fixing rivets also help to confirm positioning. Two shields are either side of the arch of the canopy and there are two more shields beneath the figure. Clerical indents are difficult to date with precision but this one is not inconsistent with a date of circa 1415.

Other members of the de la Pole family may have been commemorated by lost brasses, including one recorded by the Chorographer on the south side of the chancel with an inscription reading 'Hic jacet Margareta filia secunda Edmundi Comitis Suffolcie que obijt vicesimo secundo Januarij a'o D'ni' 1498'.[79] Blois mentioned 'a stone for D^n Margaria fil. Comit. Suff. 1481'.[80] Clearly there is some confusion as to details, but the lady in question was most likely to have been Margaret, the daughter of John de la Pole, a younger brother of the 2nd earl, who married John de la Foix, earl of Kendal, Comte de Benauges, Viscomte of Castillion and de Meille, Knight of the Garter. The Chorographer noted that this brass had shields with the arms 'Quarterly 1 and 4 de la Pole and *argent a chief gules a lyon rampant or* empaled; 2 and 3 Wingfelde'. Davy drew a rough sketch of the indent in the south chapel in the same position as described by the Chorographer.[81] The inlay had been completely lost by this time, but the indent still remains in the chapel (Figure 7.11). It shows that the lady was in widow's weeds and that the arms were on lozenges, which would have been appropriate for a high-status lady who was armigerous in her own right. It is thus virtually certain that it commemorates Margaret.

In 1796 Gillingwater noted that 'the matrices on the grave-stones now lying in that place formerly contained effigies, shields and inscriptions and other ornaments all now gone'.[82] Davy also drew many of them, although the majority had only an inscription. Only a minority now remain, the remainder doubtless having been discarded when the eastern part of the church was tiled. Several are to priests or to people of lower status than the Wingfields, but there is one in the south aisle which may have commemorated a member of the Wingfield family shown in armour.[83] Unfortunately the indent seems no longer to survive. The outline of the figure as drawn by Davy compares with the brass to William Wingfield (d.1481), at Letheringham,

[79] MacCulloch 1976, p. 73.
[80] SROI: CG17–775, fol. 75.
[81] BL: MS Add. 19092, fol. 403.
[82] Ibid., fol. 392.
[83] Ibid., fol. 404.

Fig. 7.11. Indent of lost brass to Margaret, the daughter of John de la Pole c.1487. Wingfield (Suffolk).

suggesting a date in the 1480s.[84] The most likely candidate is John de la Pole, earl of Lincoln, who died in 1487 at the battle of Stoke. Whether he was subsequently buried at Wingfield is unknown, but it seems entirely possible. He was attainted, so it is unlikely that he would have been given a lavish tomb, even though the attainder was reversed in 1493.

De la Pole high tomb monuments at Wingfield

The first of the remaining high tombs at Wingfield to members of the de la Pole family commemorates Michael de la Pole, 2nd earl of Suffolk, who died at Harfleur in 1415, and his wife Katherine, daughter of the earl of Stafford (d.1419) (Figures 7.12 and 7.13). In his will the earl gave several options regarding his burial, depending on where he died.[85] If he died in the north part of England he requested burial at the Hull Charterhouse, between the tomb of his father and mother and the high altar there, 'without any tomb to be made over me, except a flat stone', by which he almost certainly meant a brass. If he was to die elsewhere in England he requested burial 'in the Collegiate Church of Wyngfelde, in the north side of the altar of the Blessed Virgin'. Finally, if he were to die outside England, he suggested that his body or bones could be brought back for burial at Wingfield. Whether his body was ever buried at Wingfield is uncertain, as in the late fifteenth century Wrythe wrote that Michael's body was 'still not buried at Wingfield'.[86] Nonetheless his tomb monument, which may therefore be a cenotaph, is to be found in an arch between the chancel and the Lady Chapel, which was rebuilt, probably circa 1460–7, under the direction of Alice, duchess of Suffolk, by Master-mason Hawes of Occold.[87] Key parts of the contract detail that 'the Channcell of Wyngfeld to be lengthened xiij fete ... and on the southside to be made a newe arche asmoche . and of the same werkmanshyp as the arche is . of there my lordes fader and his moderes tomb is now . and the same tombe to be remeved into the seid newe arche in the same forme as it is now .'. This new arch is an accomplished imitation of the early fifteenth-century arch to the west, decorated by the heraldic devices of the Wingfield wings and Stafford knots. The effigies of the couple rest on a finely carved tomb-chest. It has generally been assumed that this chest is contemporary with the effigies, but, as John Goodall has pointed out, the plinth is too long to have fitted into the original canopy arch to the west, so the chest must be a replacement dating from the 1460s or a re-arrangement of the original chest.[88] Indeed, the arch in which it was originally positioned is 2.25

---

[84] Monumental Brass Society 1988, Figure 222.
[85] LP: Register Chichele, I, fol. 283; Nicholas 1826, vol. II, p. 189; Jacob 1938, pp. 58–60.
[86] CoA: MS L8, fol. 75.
[87] Bod: Ewelme MS Add. 37; reproduced in Goodall 2001, pp. 269–73 and Goodall 2003, pp. 164–5.
[88] Goodall 2003, p. 167.

Fig. 7.12. Tomb monument of Michael de la Pole, 2nd earl of Suffolk (d.1415), and his wife Katherine from north side. Wingfield (Suffolk).

Fig. 7.13. Tomb monument of Michael de la Pole, 2nd earl of Suffolk (d.1415), and his wife Katherine from south side Wingfield (Suffolk).

Fig. 7.14. Effigies of Michael de la Pole, 2nd earl of Suffolk (d.1415), and his wife Katherine. Wingfield (Suffolk).

metres wide, while the full length of the tomb monument including the plinth is 1.5 metres longer. Even the effigy slab is slightly longer than the original arch, though the effigies themselves would fit. If the workmanship is examined closely there seem to be two qualities of workmanship, with two different shades of stone, suggesting that tomb-chest is therefore a re-arrangement rather than a replacement of the 1460s. The sedilia on the north side would, however, have fitted under the original arch and the detailing would fit a date in the early part of the century.

The underside chamfer of the effigy slab is adorned by alternating leopards' masks, a de la Pole device, and Stafford knots. The chalk tomb-chest below has, in addition to the sedilia, a series of thirteen canopied niches which would originally have held carved figures; some of the iron cramps which acted as fixing points for the effigies can still be seen. Notes collected by William Bedford, curate of Wingfield Church from 1684, and in 1701 set up on a tablet in the church, now lost, recorded that some of the figures then still survived, but no drawings are known of it in this state.[89] Various antiquaries including the Chorographer, Blois, John Borrett who visited in 1662, Gough and Ann Mills, writing circa 1822 although probably using old sources, recorded the names as Katherina, Margareta, Thomas, Milo, Alexander, Thomas, Phillipa, Elizabeth, Isabella, Johannes, Willielmus, Michaell and Ann, albeit not consistently in the same order.[90] Of these, Katherine, the first Thomas, Miles, Philippa and Isabel do not appear in the records, so may have died as children. Now faint traces of only two of the names can be deciphered on the effigy slab above two of the niches of the southern side (Plate XVIII). The letters were first marked out with a scriber and then painted; the first letter of each name seems to have been in red paint, with black for the rest. The name on the right of the pair is 'Thomas', but although that on the left is too fragmentary for certainty, it is probably Alexander. The Chorographer also recorded that there had been a brass epitaph, presumably a marginal inscription, which was lost by his time, but there is no trace of this now.

Perhaps the most interesting aspect of this monument is that the effigies are carved from wood (Figure 7.14). Sadly they have been covered by several layers of modern paint, but would originally have been entirely covered with polychromy and surface finishes, such that it would have been impossible to tell that they were carved from wood and not stone. This is illustrated by the wooden effigy at Fersfield (Norfolk) commemorating Sir Robert du Bois circa 1340, which is the only surviving example in England to retain substantial original polychromy.[91] Although wooden effigies are now relatively uncommon, it is likely that there were once a great many more. In addition to the ninety-three known to survive, twenty-seven

[89] Page 1844, p. 436.
[90] MacCulloch 1976, p. 73; SROI: CG17–775, fol. 74; Bod: MS Suffolk 7, fol. 48; Gough 1786–96, vol. 2, p. 319; SROI: HD2418–51, fol. 296.
[91] Boldrick, Park and Williamson 2002, pp. 50–1.

are documented but lost.[92] They form a particularly vulnerable category of medieval monument, for a variety of reasons. It is entirely plausible that hundreds more could have been lost without any record. It is also worthy of note that the Wingfield pair are especially unusual for their date. An analysis of the corpus of wooden effigies by date shows a very interesting pattern. The earliest date from the last quarter of the thirteenth century and they remained comparatively numerous until the middle of the fourteenth century. The Black Death led to an inevitable dip in numbers but wooden effigies never regained the popularity they had enjoyed in the first half of the century, probably owing to the increasing preference amongst the aristocratic and knightly classes in particular for alabaster effigies with partial polychromy. No wooden effigies that we know of were produced between 1422 and 1484, so the Wingfield pair are right at the end of the main period of production. Why those who commissioned the effigies should have made this choice is puzzling, although when completely covered by polychromy no-one would have known that wood had been used in place of stone. Possibly this choice could have been connected to the downfall of their son William's fortunes.[93] After selling various manors to pay off the huge ransom of £20,000 required to free him from the French, it may be that when he came to construct a tomb for his parents he needed to economise by opting for wooden effigies.

The effigies now have a covering of thick paint, applied by Revd Dr Robert Leman, who died in 1779.[94] Ann Mills, writing circa 1822, may have seen them before the paint was applied. She recorded that the effigies were 'hollow, open at the back and single' by which she meant carved separately;[95] the open backs may have been filled with charcoal as a desiccant. She added that on the belt on the military effigy were just visible the Wingfield arms. The earliest description of this effigy was provided in 1662 by Borrett.[96] He noted that there were painted arms of de la Pole impaling Wingfield on the breast on the coat armour. This is odd since these arms were those of Michael's parents, but perhaps Borrett saw only part of the blazon.[97] His notes reveal that arms of Stafford were certainly on the tomb-chest along with de la Pole and Wingfield.

It is very likely that before the eighteenth-century covering paint was applied, the male figure at least was subject to some re-carving, or re-modelling with plaster, and that the paint was intended to hide this. Sir Michael's figure has too many sharp but slightly wobbly edges. The most doubtful areas are his head, including the deeply set face, the lack of detail on the crest beneath it, his left arm and his sword belt. His hands are suspiciously shorter than those of his lady's. There also appears to be the

---

92 Unpublished analysis of information largely taken from Fryer 1924.
93 I am grateful to Peter Bloore for this suggestion.
94 SROI: HD2418–51, fol. 296.
95 Ibid., fol. 296.
96 Bod: MS Suffolk 7, fol. 48.
97 I am grateful to Ron Fiske for this interesting observation.

ghost of the left quillon from his sword, one of the two bars forming the cross-guard, which would have been lying on the slab by his left side, and the line of one side of the scabbard, which indicates that the remains of the sword have been chiselled off. One intriguing and revealing detail is the representation of his thumbs and fingers, within his cupped hands. This survival of minor detail supports the view that his effigy was originally much more finely carved than now appears. The lady's figure looks to be in very good condition apart from active death watch beetle damage, although it has deteriorated since Fryer illustrated it in 1924.[98] It appears to be much more finely carved than the companion effigy, hinting at a metropolitan origin for the figures. It is also odd that the lady's effigy is longer than that of Sir Michael; normally ladies are shown about 6 inches shorter than their husbands. Why is uncertain; the two effigies might have been commissioned separately and a mistake made in the size of the second one, although they do not look much different in date.

Although Sir Michael did not refer to his tomb monument in his will, various features suggest that it was made in his lifetime, although still in the early fifteenth century. The couple are shown recumbent, with their hands at prayer. He is in armour and rests his head on a helm with the de la Pole crest. It is usually described as a Saracen or Wild Man's head, but in contemporary documents and as recorded by Joan Corder it is: *the head of a bearded man wearing a round cap or hat with side pieces covering the ears.*[99] On his head Sir Michael wears a great bascinet with a plain orle around it. Below the gorget is a scalloped fringe, presumably intended to be of mail. His torso and limbs are protected by plate armour, with a covering coat armour. The overall appearance of the armour has a decidedly early character to it.[100] The leg armour is simple in design, without the 'demi-cuisse' construction which quickly became dominant after circa 1410. The poleyns and couters carry only simple wings, rather than the rondels that were the pervading fashion by the time of the Agincourt campaign. The spaudlers have no besagews or frontal extensions – another feature to be expected on an armour of circa 1415 or later. The great bascinet is another key element. However, it too has an early look about it. The high-pointed skull is something associated with earlier rather than later armour, with the skulls of later great bascinets rapidly becoming lower and more rounded. All this would be consistent with a date from circa 1410 onwards. Moving on to the dress of the female figure, it may be significant that his wife Katherine is not depicted as a widow, indicating a date of design before his death. She wears a houpelande, which is gathered tightly under the bust, with wide hanging sleeves; this garment was fashionable circa 1380–1420.[101] It has a deep collar, which is folded over the mantle that covers her gown. This stands clear of the neck and opens slightly at the top, an early fifteenth century

---

98   Fryer 1925, pp. 49–50 and Plates XX and XXI.
99   Corder 1998, p. 307.
100 I am grateful to Toby Capwell for advice on the date of the armour.
101 Scott 1986, pp. 53–9.

Fig. 7.15. Detail of ceiling of canopy on tomb monument to John de la Pole, 2nd duke of Suffolk (d.1491), and his wife, Elizabeth of York (d. ?1503). Wingfield (Suffolk).

development, again a style of circa 1410. Her hair is bound in prominent cauls at either side of the head, held in place by fine nets patterned with four-leaved flowers set in squares. Over this is a deep fillet decorated by roses, enclosing the veil which falls to her neck. This again points to a date closer to circa 1410 rather than after Sir Michael's death in 1415.

The final tomb at Wingfield, and arguably the finest, commemorates John de la Pole, 2nd duke of Suffolk (d.1491), and his wife, Elizabeth of York (d.1503?), sister of Edward IV and Richard III (Plate XIX). Stothard described the effigies as 'for the time, the most interesting specimens that I could have selected; all the colours I contrived to make out with but a little difficulty'.[102] The monument is located against the north side of the chancel to the west of Sir John Wingfield's tomb and is a typical late-fifteenth-century wall tomb built on an ornamental Purbeck marble plinth. The front of the tomb-chest carved from alabaster is decorated with five shields within elaborately carved quatrefoils. The back arch is depressed with a quatrefoil frieze and cresting over. The detailed decoration of the ceiling of the canopy, carved from chalk, is puzzling. It has a double row of panels, each of which repeats north to south. There are three by two to each side of the ceiling joint line (Figure 7.15). The first group from west to east shows: a single five petal rose-en-soleil, a Yorkist symbol; a double Tudor two by five petal rose with four trefoil leaves, reflecting loyalty and royalty;

[102] Bray 1851, p. 58.

Fig. 7.16. Detail of tomb chest respond on tomb monument to John de la Pole, 2nd duke of Suffolk (d.1491), and his wife, Elizabeth of York (d. ?1503). Wingfield (Suffolk).

and a single five petal rose. The second group, from east to west, shows: a double two by five petal rose with four trefoil leaves differently arranged from those in the first group; a single five petal rose-en-soleil; and a narrower double panel of two blind tri-lobed arches. Such an uneven arrangement is inconsistent with the high standard of the rest of the monument, although the original paint might have made some sense of the design. There are various inconsistencies in the design of the canopy and chest which suggests that there might have been some conflict between the intended site and where it is now.[103] The tomb-chest with the quatrefoil panels has returns at each end. That at the east has one complete quatrefoil panel with another half-panel following, with the remainder built in (Figure 7.15). The west end is similar, but here there has been room to cut the second panel in two, with half mounted on the wall and joined to the first half. Perhaps there was some mistake with the dimensions and it had to be modified to fit or maybe the monument was modified at some un-recorded restoration; as explained below, the figures have certainly not remained untouched since the monument was first set up.

The Chorographer recorded that the brass inscription was missing even by his day, although at that time four coats of arms were displayed 'aboute the tombe', presumably on the chest.[104] They included the arms of England and France, indicating Eliza-

[103]   I am grateful to Ron Fiske for these observations.
[104]   MacCulloch 1976, p. 72.

beth's royal blood, the Mortimer earls of March and the Burgh earls of Ulster, as well as de la Pole. The shields on the front of the chest have been scrubbed clean of paint, but a red ground survives on the eastern end of the tomb. This shield has the centre raised in impalement, but there is no trace of the charges (Figure 7.16).

The effigies are carved from alabaster and are notable for the degree of fine detailing, indicating that this was an expensive commission (Figure 7.17). The duke rests his head on a helm, with the family crest of *the head of a bearded man*. The duke is bareheaded and wears a coronet. His hands are also bare, rather than being protected by gauntlets. Over his plate armour is an ermine-lined garter robe, with the cross and motto of the Order on his left shoulder. His sword has an IHS inscription on the locket. The Garter is secured below the left knee with a strap and buckle. The duchess wears a veiled head-dress surmounted by a coronet, with the pleated widow's barbe. Over a belted kirtle and a *surcoat ouverte* is a mantle fastened in front with a cord. Both effigies rest their feet on lions; these are not ordinary animals but heraldic beasts. The reverse of the early nineteenth century drawing by Revd David Powell from the Ron Fiske Collection notes that the effigies had considerable remains of original painting.[105] The duke's lion has two tails and was gold, from which Powell concluded that it was the lion of Burghersh, which Alice Chaucer took from her mother in preference to the original Chaucer arms.[106] The duchess's lion was white, which represents the lion of Mortimer, which she took from her paternal grandmother.

The fact that Elizabeth is in widow's attire demonstrates that the tomb must have been made after John's death. Elizabeth was the likely patron and chose high-quality work. The elements of the tomb may have come from more than one workshop. The effigies bear the hall-marks of the Midlands alabasterers. There is a close comparison between the male figure and those at Chilton (Suffolk) to Robert Crane (d.1500, but made in lifetime) and Wethersfield (Essex) probably commemorating Henry Wentworth (d.1484 but made c.1490).[107] These two comparators are simplified versions of the effigy at Wingfield, emphasising that the latter was an especially high-status commission. The chest almost certainly came from the same workshop, but the chalk canopy was more likely to have been commissioned from another workshop.

Alabaster effigies were more sparingly painted than those made of freestone or wood. The faces, hands and any other exposed skin were left bare to reveal the translucent beauty of the stone itself. The lips and eyes were painted and a pink

---

[105] I am grateful to Ron Fiske for allowing me access to the drawing.

[106] Martin 2013.

[107] Gardner 1940, Figures 282 and 283. The 1500 will of Robert Crane of Waldingfield (Suffolk) requested in relation to Chilton church near Sudbury 'And my body to holy sepultur that is to say in the tombe of alabaster standing in the chauncell of Chylton church' (Canterbury Sede Vacante wills, CCA-DCc-Register/F 118–19). I am grateful to Simon Cotton for this reference. See also www.churchmonumentssociety.org/Monument_of_the_Month.html, monument of the month for April 2014.

Fig. 7.17. Effigies of John de la Pole, 2nd duke of Suffolk (d. 1491), and his wife, Elizabeth of York (d. ?1503). Wingfield (Suffolk).

blush added to the cheeks. It is interesting that the female effigy is carved from an especially pure piece of alabaster, which would have allowed her to display a beautiful pale complexion. Such a large piece of very pure alabaster was probably in very short supply by this time, so would have cost a great deal. This adds to the impression that this was an expensive commission. In contrast, the military effigy, like the tomb-chest, is carved from a slightly darker, mottled piece of alabaster, similar to that deployed at Ewelme, although still lacking the dark streaks which mar most alabaster effigies of the era. For him a more weather-beaten, ruddy complexion would not have been inappropriate. The rest of the figures would have been richly painted, as Stothard's coloured study shows, although some details are not totally correct (Plate XX).

Large amounts of original paint survive even two hundred years after Stothard saw the monument. The most extensive areas of paint are on the male effigy, especially his hair and the crest at the head end and the lion at the foot (Plates XXI and XXII). Yet there are other areas of paint on protected parts of his effigy, in particular in the area between the two effigies. Traces of the blue of the garter robe can be seen, although no paint survives on the garter as such (Plate XXIII). The grip of the sword is a translucent green bound with gold and the pommel and quillons are also gold (Plate XXIV). The scabbard is patterned in red and has a gold and red chape at the end; beneath can be seen the two golden tails of the lion at his feet. The dagger grip and pommel and the underneath of the sabatons are black, although this is probably tarnished silver leaf (Plate XXV). The helmet is red; and the mail and the rowel spur on the left foot are gold. The duchess's figure is much more difficult to examine but has significantly less paint remaining. The gold of the coronet is still clear; her upper pillow was red while the bottom one was green (Plate XXVI). Part of her *surcoat ouverte* retains red colouring, while the cord fastening her mantle which ends in a tassel has traces of gold leaf (Plate XXVII). Traces also survive of the blue of her mantle.

Another significant feature of the duchess's effigy is that it is a great deal more damaged than her husband's effigy (Figure 7.17). Her hands and arms have been broken off. Her nose is damaged. One of the tassels of the cord fastening her mantle has gone, as have sections of the cords. Both angels supporting her cushions have lost their upper halves. It should also be noted that the effigy of the lady is less deep than that of her husband, raising questions as to why he was left intact while the iconoclasts reached over him to hack at his lady. It is also odd that his effigy retains far more colour than hers. In my view, the most likely conclusion is that they could not always have been arranged this way around and that the lady was originally on the outside of the tomb and thus more vulnerable to damage.[108] A corner of her

---

[108]   This is not the only possible explanation. Peter Bloore has suggested to me that the two figures might not in fact have originally been in the same place, next to one another. The evidence of the graffiti might be interpreted as meaning that was originally not just on the other side of her but somewhere else entirely, where he could be reached by graffiti perpetrators, whereas Elizabeth was

effigy slab has also been broken off, which would have been very difficult to do while she was *in situ*, but could have happened if the two figures had been removed from the tomb. When this apparent change of position took place is unrecorded. Several antiquarian drawings of the early nineteenth century show them arranged as they are now and Ann Mills, writing circa 1822, recorded that 'at his left hand lies his wife'.[109] Moving further back Richard Gough provided a full description of the figures in his *Sepulchral Monuments* published in two volumes in 1786 and 1796, but failed to note which way around they were.[110] It is worthy of note that the effigy of Sir John has a substantial amount of seventeenth- and eighteenth-century graffiti, whereas there is none whatsoever on Elizabeth. It may be that the suggested re-arrangement took place in the sixteenth or early seventeenth century.

Curiously, this was the last known de la Pole burial at Wingfield. Although John and Elizabeth had seven sons and four daughters, not one seems to have been buried there, ending the family's association with the Wingfield in a single generation.

Conclusion

In conclusion, I would like briefly to examine what can be said about the de la Pole tomb monuments as a group. Often, in the medieval period, successive generations of families chose very similar monuments, but that is not the case with the Wingfield and de la Pole families. A number of monumental brasses were commissioned, mostly, but not exclusively, to the lesser members of the family. In addition, there are four high tombs: two at Wingfield and one each at Hull and Ewelme. Only one of these appears probably not to have featured carved effigies. Of the remainder, one is of wood and two of alabaster. However, to contemporary eyes, once these carved tombs had the surface painted and embellished the differences between the core materials would not have been so apparent.

In examining the locations of burial and commemoration of the de la Pole family various interesting choices can be highlighted (Figure 7.4). First, although Richard de la Pole and his descendants chose burial in the parish church of Holy Trinity, Hull, his brother William and his family did not follow his example but instead established their own foundation of the Charterhouse, even though the de la Pole monument in the parish church was erected at the same time as the Charterhouse's foundation. There were several possible reasons for this choice. It may have been prompted by William's greater ambition socially; faced with the erection of monuments to the

---

in a safer position. Could it be that she was in what is now the vestry, and therefore more protected, and he was more accessible, perhaps in front of the altar? Or she was protected by now-lost railings? The two effigy slabs are also different lengths, and the tomb-chest in the recess seems to show signs of being altered at some stage.

[109] SROI: HD2418–51, fol. 300.

[110] Gough 1786–96, vol. 2, p. 318.

merchant classes in Holy Trinity, he may have considered that burial there lacked social cachet. It is also possible that William's branch of the family opted to be buried in a location where they had more control over the prayers for their soul, rather than risk it to a chantry in an urban church, which might be subjugated in the general scheme of activities in an urban, guild-orientated church.

There are other noteworthy aspects of the choices the family made about burial locations. In the main part wives followed the choices made by their husbands. Even the heiress of Sir John Wingfield, Katherine Wingfield, opted to be buried with her husband, Michael, 1st earl of Suffolk, in her father-in-law's foundation of the Hull Charterhouse rather than her father's collegiate church at Wingfield, where the family had established their base. The exception was Alice Chaucer, who, having buried and commemorated her husband William, 1st duke of Suffolk, followed her own private path to heavenly redemption, not just in her native church but also in her own, single tomb. Although she is shown as a vowess, the imagery of the coronet and the Order of the Garter and the inscription grandiloquently describing her as 'Serenissimae Principessae Aliciae Ducissae Suffolchiae [the most serene princess Alice duchess of Suffolk]' all make evident her exalted status. She had, of course, been much married, but she was a comparatively minor heiress and her last husband had brought her the status of a duchess. It might thus have been thought more likely that she would have been buried with him or at Wingfield. Yet Alice was famously of an independent and capable character and was an important patron in her own right, especially in her widowhood, in Wingfield and Ewelme and beyond.[III] Ewelme Manor became a significant centre of affairs for the de la Poles, but its importance did not outstrip Wingfield for the family as a whole. Alice chose to be buried in what was, to an extent, her personal foundation, which is again celebrated in the inscription, which proclaims that she was 'huius ecclesiae patronae, & primae fundatricis huijus [patron of this church and first founder of this almshouse]'. That she had founded the almshouse is significant as with this act she had provided for a group of grateful beneficiaries duty bound to offer up heartfelt prayers for her soul.

It is also interesting that quite a few of the younger members of the various generations of the de la Pole family were memorialised at Wingfield, rather than spreading their wings and acceding to manors in their own right, with burial in their own churches. Even Master John de la Pole, a canon of York, did not choose burial in York Minster or elsewhere in Yorkshire where he had spent his adult life. Instead, many of the de la Poles appear to have maintained a nuclear family approach, perhaps attracted by the collegiate atmosphere of prayer for the departed. It might also have been a choice intended to emphasise the dominance of the de la Pole family. The gradual accretion of family monuments in the church would have made a significant

---

[III]   Goodall 2001, pp. 11–13.

visual statement, dispelling any doubts as to the family's fecundity, succession and continuity of authority.

When we examine the texts and imagery of the de la Pole monuments, there is one negative point which stands out. The family established their own religious foundations at Hull, Wingfield and Ewelme to attract prayers from the living faithful to speed up their passage through Purgatory, all this being somewhat suggestive of a genuine piety. Part of the purpose of commissioning monuments was to enlist prayerful assistance from clergy, friends and onlookers.[112] Monuments were thus a vital weapon in the battle for salvation of the soul. Sir John Wingfield's tomb probably had lost sculpted and painted religious imagery, but in only one of the de la Pole monuments is there any overt religious imagery. This exception is Duchess Alice's tomb at Ewelme, but as explained earlier, the paintings of saints are only in the most intimate part of the monument and show Alice in death seeking the intercession of favoured saints. Even an examination of the known monumental inscriptions to members of the de la Pole family reveals little religious content; it is limited to the standard opening request for prayers for the person commemorated and the customary conclusion asking God to have mercy of their souls. This may be established by the fact that virtually all of the monuments examined in this chapter were located in dedicated family mausoulea, either in the Charterhouse, the collegiate church at Wingfield, or at Ewelme, where there were ready-made congregations of priests to pray for the souls of the commemorated. Perhaps in these circumstances religious imagery on monuments would have been regarded as redundant. It is tempting to speculate that saintly imagery associated with funeral monuments was focused mainly other than in dedicated chantries or collegiate churches, when prayers from passers-by, as opposed to those from permanently resident clergy, would have been facilitated, and the religious effects magnified, by the incorporation of such saints.

Instead of religious references on the monuments, texts and images concentrate on the status of those commemorated, proclaiming them to be or linking them to the de la Pole earls and dukes of Suffolk. Lineage and blood were important to the family, as demonstrated by the proud displays of heraldry that adorned their tombs. Blois recorded that the glass in the windows also included many shields with the arms of de la Pole and their connections, as well as at least one kneeling figure.[113] The de la Poles were fertile couples, virtually all producing at least an heir and a spare. The 1st duke's monument had named statues of his children adorning his tomb-chest. Although offspring were not overtly depicted on the 2nd duke's monument, he had seven sons and four daughters. His tomb monument celebrates the apogee of the

[112] This is made clear, for example, in the will of Robert Toste (d.1458), provost of the Collegiate Church of Wingham (Kent); he requested 'a marble stone be laid over me with an inscription to induce people to pray for my soul', Nicholas 1826, p. 288.
[113] SROI: CG17–775, fols 74–5.

family's climb into the highest ranks of the nobility through his marriage to the sister of two kings. He is shown as a Garter knight in all his splendour. Even though after the Yorkist defeat at Bosworth his wife remained linked by blood to the new queen, his position in the closing years of his life must have looked increasingly fragile. Alas for those who emulate Icarus, who flew too close to the sun. Within a generation the de la Pole line was effectively extinct and the Wingfield and Hull foundations were dissolved in 1542. In the circumstances we are lucky to have what remains of Wingfield College and the two families' monuments.

Acknowledgements

I owe a considerable debt of gratitude to Edward Martin and the late Peter Heseltine for assistance with manuscript sources. I am also grateful to Jennifer Alexander, Jon Bayliss, John Blatchly, Toby Capwell, David Carrington, Simon Cotton, Jane Crease, Mark Downing, Ron Fiske, Brian and Moira Gittos, Peter Martingdale, Richard Marks, Eddie Sinclair, Martin Stuchfield and Lucy Wrapson for help and advice. Paul Cockerham and Nigel Saul have read through an earlier draft of this chapter and suggested valuable improvements. C.B. Newham and my husband Tim Sutton have been generous in the provision of photographs. Finally, Peter Bloore and Edward Martin made a number of helpful comments during the editing process.

8

Chapel or Closet?
The Question of the Vestry at Wingfield

JOHN GOODALL

This is a chapter about an ostensibly unpromising subject. To a modern visitor the vestry of Wingfield Church is typical of its kind: a long, thin chamber to the north of the chancel filled with cupboards, clutter and flower-arranging paraphernalia. Only a diligent visitor, armed with a key, could penetrate this room. Yet removed and humdrum as it might seem, the vestry deserves and repays detailed attention. Since 1925 it has conventionally been identified as the former Chapel of the Holy Trinity, according to various documentary sources the burial place of several members of the de la Pole family. This identification seems to me incorrect. In fact there is clear evidence that this room was built in the 1360s as a vestry and that it was subsequently adapted and extended almost exactly a century later by Alice, duchess of Suffolk, to accommodate a family pew. In this latter form it may have incorporated an altar. As such it is a rare surviving example of a so-called closet (sometimes also termed a parclose or oratory), a type of space once universal in aristocratic residences and great churches. To understand the basis for this assertion it is necessary to try and unravel in broad outline the evolution of the church as it is presently understood.[1]

The present fabric of the aisled nave with its clerestorey and western tower were erected following the foundation of a college on the site in 1362. It should be said that the architectural details of these parts of the building are entirely characteristic of this date in this region. The arcades, for example, are set on octagonal columns – a common form in fourteenth-century parish churches in Norfolk and Suffolk – and the south aisle window tracery (the windows in the north aisle have all been replaced in later re-buildings) incorporates flower patterns, a detail popularised by the Ramsey family of masons active in Norwich Cathedral priory and the king's works during the first half of the fourteenth century. Also belonging to this early phase is the north wall of the chancel, which preserves both the monument of the

---

[1]   An overview of the development proposed here but with a different comparative emphasis is set out both in Goodall 2001, pp. 51–65 and Goodall 2003.

college founder, Sir John Wingfield, and a door to the vestry on the north side of the building. Both features appear to remain in their original position despite repeated changes to the fabric around them.

Of the liturgical plan of this fourteenth-century building we know very little. The chancel appears to have been laid out as a single, long and narrow space. Aside from a section of the north wall occupied by the vestry (incidentally, an entirely characteristic position for such a chamber), it is likely to have been lit through its full length to the sides by two-light windows and possessed a larger east window. The chancel doubtless incorporated a centrally placed high altar at its eastern extreme in the conventional manner. Whether the rood screen originally crossed the church on the line of the chancel arch or stood to the west of it and divided the architectural nave into two liturgical spaces is not now clear (the present steps to the rood loft certainly date to the fifteenth century and follow the enlargement of the chancel). A blocked squint to the south of the chancel arch presumably indicates the position of one side altar in the east end of the south aisle. Nothing is certainly known of the dedication of this altar. As will become apparent, however, there is a good circumstantial case for supposing that it was to the Virgin, a common dedication of principal southern altars.

By the terms of his will, proved in 1415, Michael de la Pole, 2nd earl of Suffolk, requested burial to the north side of the altar of the Blessed Virgin at Wingfield.[2] This direction proves that by the date of his death there had been completed a new Lady Chapel to the south side of the chancel. If the original Lady Altar did lie at the east end of the south aisle, this was effectively an architectural aggrandisement of it, a point that will be returned to. The new chapel communicated with the main volume of the chancel through two unequally proportioned arcade arches ornamented with carving. The larger of the pair, to the west, was presumably filled with choir stalls for the college canons. That to the east formed the canopy of the tomb of the 2nd earl and his countess. With one of the arches blocked by the tomb and the other by choir stalls, access to the chapel was probably from the west through the east end of the south nave aisle.

It is around the time of the creation of the new Lady Chapel that another chapel in the church is first documented. On 14 February1405/6 the earl of Suffolk received a licence to establish a chantry at the altar of the Holy Trinity in Wingfield Church. We know from the antiquarian known as the Chorographer, who visited Wingfield in around 1600, that three de la Pole brasses lay in or around this chapel. All have disappeared or been moved during the nineteenth-century restoration of the interior.[3] Nevertheless, the Chorographer identifies the position of the brasses 'In the north side of the churche.' He then goes on to describe the extant tombs to Sir John Wingfield and John de la Pole, duke of Suffolk, 'On the north side of the chauncell.'

2   Transcribed in Aldwell 1925, pp. 26–7.
3   See Badham in this volume for these monuments.

This distinction drawn between the 'church' and the 'chancel' has been understood to locate the brasses and the Holy Trinity Chapel in the modern vestry, a discrete space to the north of the building. Yet there is a perfectly good alternative reading: it would be logical and conventional, if – just like its counterpart to the south – the north nave aisle had been erected in the 1360s with an altar at its eastern end. Moreover, such an altar, dedicated to the Trinity, could reasonably be described as standing to the north of the 'church' rather than to the north of the 'chancel'. As will become apparent, the cumulative weight of evidence from what we know of later changes to the building strongly supports this supposition.

The next series of changes to the church can only be fully understood through the chance survival of a draft builder's estimate in the Ewelme muniments, which can be dated 1460–7.[4] This outlines a series of proposed alterations to Wingfield that were to be undertaken at the behest of Alice de la Pole, then the dowager duchess of Suffolk, by a certain Hawes, a mason of Occold. Hawes is a figure otherwise unknown in the documentary record, though attempts have been made – in my opinion both methodologically and circumstantially misconceived – to create an architectural oeuvre for him.[5]

The works proposed in the estimate are broadly legible in the surviving fabric. It explains that the chancel and Lady Chapel should both be extended eastwards and made level with each other. Meanwhile, that the two spaces should be interconnected with a third new arch of 'the same sort and form' as the existing tomb canopy completed by 1415. This arch was to form the new canopy for the second earl and countess's monument, which was to be translated into it. The estimate also makes complex stipulations about adaptations to the fenestration of the extended chancel and Lady Chapel. A new five-light east window was to be inserted above the high altar and a clerestory added to the structure. By contrast, the east window of the Lady Chapel was to be reused in the enlarged interior and a new aisle window created in imitation of the form of its existing counterparts.

While all these adaptations can be traced in the fabric of the building, the estimate nevertheless fails to describe in full the changes that must have actually attended upon the work. The explanation for this is not clear but perhaps it was only a draft document. The clerestory, for example, incorporates seven windows on each side rather than the six stipulated in the estimate and the roof must have been rebuilt though no explicit mention is made of this undertaking. Similarly, in its present form the monument of the second earl and countess of Suffolk would not physically fit under its original canopy arch, proof that it was reworked in the 1460s. Lastly, in many physical details the magnificent fifteenth-century stalls and associated rood screen are accommodated to the form of the extended building and can therefore be reasonably associated with Hawes's work.

---

4 Goodall 2001, pp. 269–70.
5 Haward 1993, pp. 147–8 and *passim*.

In relation to this work it is interesting to note that the present east window of the Lady Chapel appears by its detailing to belong to the 1360s church. This could conceivably be the original chancel east window, though it is rather small for such a position. Much more likely is that it originally came from the east end of the south aisle, as a straight-forward reading of Hawes' estimate would imply. If so the window must have been recycled once already in the works to the Lady Chapel completed by 1415. One possible reason for such reuse is that the iconography of the lost glass formed an appropriate backdrop to the altar it lit. In other words, the survival of this window further implies that the present Lady Chapel is the enlarged setting for an altar that stood in the 1360s at the east end of the south aisle.

In various points the fabric of the chancel, however, also proves that the 1460s changes to the church went much further than the estimate proposed. Hawes makes it clear that minimal changes were intended to the north wall of the chancel. According to the estimate, a new window was to be created in the extended lateral north wall of the chancel after the fashion of the existing south chancel window (though, confusingly, the latter was presumably about to be subsumed within the extended Lady Chapel). Meanwhile, 'the vestry that is there shall stand as it doth'. This last reference is very important because it clearly identifies the room to the north of the chancel as a vestry (not the chapel of the Holy Trinity).

In fact the vestry manifestly did undergo important changes. That it did so furthermore implicitly suggests that the room was altered to accommodate some new and additional function. What Hawes evidently undertook was the eastward extension of the vestry and the reorganisation of both its fenestration and interior. As in the Lady Chapel, an earlier window, complete with its late fourteenth-century stained glass (which partially still survives), was reset in the new east wall of the vestry. At the same time a new external door with identical mouldings to the 1460s east window was punched through the north wall. External entrances to medieval vestries are extremely unusual. Because these rooms housed valuables and were used by priests robing for the celebration of Mass it made sense for both security and prac-tical reasons for the vestry door to open off the chancel. This external door is the first of several signs that the Wingfield vestry was being adapted for an unusual purpose.

The interior of the vestry was ornamented to an unusual degree. Its roof was decorated, apparently with Marian imagery (the initials AM – presumably for *Ave Maria* – and roses).[6] While the main medieval ceiling panels have sadly been lost, the purlins and wall plate timbers preserve clear evidence of colouring with abstract patterns, florettes and architectural details in green, black, white and red. In the east window, meanwhile, there remains a collage of medieval glass fragments. These include the remains of two substantial fourteenth-century canopies, evidence perhaps that the main lights presented freestanding figures of saints. Such devotional imagery

---

[6] See transcriptions in Aldwell 1925, p. 51.

would have been appropriate over an altar. In the north and south walls to either side of the east window are small niches of uncertain function.

Internally the vestry is divided for two-thirds of its lengths by a wooden gallery, the upper floor of which is lit by two small windows punched through the north wall. A screen with dado panels closes off the gallery floor at the eastern end. Its panels were painted alternately red and green and one is cut through with a small opening to look down at the east end of the vestry. A section of the balcony screen has been cut away to accommodate the ladder that today gives access to the gallery; originally there must have been a stair to the upper floor though there is no clear evidence for its position or arrangement. From the upper floor two slits or squints overlook the chancel. These are low-set in the wall and carefully raked so as to give a view of the High Altar. It seems reasonable to assume from this pair of niches that the gallery accommodated more than one person at a time. Since it would have been necessary to sit or kneel to use the squints, the low position of the niches further implies the existence of furniture in this space.

The most obvious interpretation of this space is as a closet or parclose, a privileged space reserved for private devotion and the observation of the Elevation during Mass. Little is securely known about the early development of the closet in English architecture but from at least the thirteenth century they are known to have taken one of two forms. The first was of fabric. An early example of such a structure was the 1230s bed erected by Henry III in the Painted Chamber at Westminster (indeed, it is probably from beds that the tradition of fabric closets developed. As did the connected tradition of canopies of estate, fabric cloths that dignified and overhung thrones).[7] Around the bed at Westminster was a tent-like enclosure of posts and rails dressed in curtains for the king's privacy. From within this was an angled squint into the adjacent chapel.[8]

Images of tent-like closets are a commonplace of donor portraits in stained glass, manuscripts and paintings from the fourteenth to the sixteenth century. To judge from such depictions, by about 1500 these tents might be either round (as on the panel of *The Family of Henry VII with St George and the Dragon*, Anon, 1505–9, Royal Collection), polygonal (as seen above the royal portraits of the family of Henry VII in the stained glass of Great Malvern Priory), or rectangular in plan (as depicted in the frontispiece illustration of a Flemish manuscript of *Grace entiere sur le fait du gouvernement d'un Prince* produced around 1500 for the English market, British Library MSS Royal 16 f ii, fol. 210v). Almost invariably the donor is shown as kneeling on a predieu with a manuscript – presumably a psalter – open in front of them. Such furnishings would suit the low squints at Wingfield. There may possibly

---

[7] Goodall 2011, pp. 29–30.
[8] Binski 1986, pp. 13–15.

survive two predieus from lost fifteenth-century tent closets on the altar steps of the Beauchamp Chapel at Warwick.[9]

There are besides many donor portraits that show praying figures against the background of fabric hangings. A good case in point would be the images of the Roos family from the William Window in York Minster, probably of 1414, which are shown against paled hangings of white and blue. These could be intended to represent tent closets or simply the rich fabric decoration of the alternative form of closet: chambers overlooking or attached to chapels or churches. The earliest surviving securely identified chambers of this kind in Britain are to be found in the North Welsh castles of Edward I. Conwy Castle, begun in 1283, for example, has a pair of closets overlooking the chapel altar. These are accessed from outside the chapel and were presumably intended for the respective use of the king and queen. There are comparable arrangements in much more modest buildings of the same date, as for example the arched squints from the great chamber to the chapel of Little Wenham in Suffolk, or in the early fourteenth-century design of the chapel at Broughton, Oxfordshire.

By the mid fourteenth century – doubtless in imitation of such royal creations as the king's closet of St Stephen's Chapel – such rooms were beginning to appear in collegiate churches as well as domestic chapels. The outstanding early example of a closet of this type is to be found in the chancel of the collegiate church of St Mary's, Warwick, rebuilt 1367–97. Within the depth of the wall to the south of the high altar is a narrow and exquisitely vaulted chamber. It is panelled internally and at one extreme preserves a keyhole squint looking towards the high altar above a surviving wooden shelf. From this vantage point it is also possible today to look down at two fifteenth-century altars: that of a sumptuous smaller chapel and then beyond that of the great Lady Chapel (familiar today as the Beauchamp Chapel). In the fifteenth century a secondary closet was also created beside that of the earl and overlooked the Beauchamp Chapel. It preserves two benches. Presumably when the earl used the closet at Warwick his immediate followers or family used this subsidiary room and left him to his devotions in the closet proper.

The explanation for such use probably lies in the occasions at which the earl of Warwick came to his collegiate church. As has been alluded to, there are countless examples of chapel closets in residences. Indeed, in royal palaces from the fourteenth century onwards there might often be closets both to a private and a household chapel.[10] These are the spaces that would have been used for the devotions of the great on a day-to-day basis. But major feasts demanded greater ceremony and – certainly in the royal household – were used for carefully choreographed public

9 There is no obvious liturgical explanation for this remarkable pair of surviving predieus. They are shaped to fit the altar steps, which demonstrates that they have not been moved.
10 Wilson 2002, pp. 37–40.

display.[11] Where the king led the nobility are likely to have followed. While there is no documentation to prove the fact, therefore, the earl of Warwick presumably came to St Mary's Church on great feasts. And his closet needed an overflow chamber because he came accompanied either with his family or entourage. At Wingfield the closet was presumably accessed from the external north door to the vestry and its pair of squints perhaps suggest a similar formal use.

It should finally be said that certainly by the close of the Middle Ages closets could actually contain their own altars. One of the best examples of this is to be found in the probable royal closets that flank the High Altar of the Lady Chapel of Westminster Abbey.[12] As has been said, the physical evidence of the vestry at Wingfield does not clearly prove the existence of an altar but it strongly suggests it. There is devotional glass in the east window and also a squint cut through the timber panels of the balcony that could convincingly have overlooked an altar. Whether or not one existed, however, this was not the same as the altar dedicated to the Trinity. And it is to the question of where this altar stood that this account should finally turn.

Immediately to the west of the vestry, in what is now the organ chamber, there clearly once existed a side chapel that is awkwardly intruded into the original church plan of the 1360s. The date of this intrusion can be reasonably inferred from detailing of the arch of the chapel that opens into the chancel. It differs slightly in both moulding and treatment from the arches of the Lady Chapel opposite, proof that it was not created in the changes to the church completed by 1415. The decoration of the arch is, however, tailored to respect the existing choir stalls of the 1460s, powerful evidence that the two are contemporary.

This dating may seem to preclude a dedication to the Holy Trinity: the altar is first described in 1406 so it cannot possibly have occupied a space that was only created sixty years later. One way out of this problem, however, is to propose an evolution of space almost identical to that proposed for the Lady altar in the south aisle. That is to say that an altar dedicated to the Trinity stood at the extreme east end of the north nave aisle in the 1360s. There it attracted the three burials described in the Chorographer as being to the north of the church. But then, as part the work undertaken by Alice de la Pole, the setting for the altar was transposed eastwards. As with the changes to the Lady Chapel, this preserved but aggrandised the inherited liturgical geography of the building and the setting for her family tombs (which was evidently a matter of deep concern to the duchess in the 1460s).[13] Incidentally, if this analysis is correct, the present north window of the chapel almost certainly belongs to a programme of repair documented in three wills of 1504.[14]

---

[11] Hayward 2007, pp. 129–42 presents a fascinating analysis of chapel ceremonial in the reign of Henry VIII.

[12] Wilson 2003, pp. 167–73.

[13] Much of the Ewelme documentation relating to the reordering of family chantries and tombs dates to this decade. See Goodall 2001, p. 270.

[14] Aldwell 1925, pp. 113–14.

Any attempt to reconstruct the functional and liturgical topography of a medieval parish church is fraught with difficulties. Besides the simple destruction of altars and fittings, the evolution of their interiors was both complex and intense. It was, moreover, shaped by inherited patterns. If the analysis presented in this chapter is correct, the chamber to the north of the chancel at Wingfield was created as vestry, a function that might reasonably been inferred from its original form and position in the church plan. It was, however, adapted to serve additionally as a closet, perhaps with an altar. Meanwhile, the principal north and south nave altars, retained consistent dedications but moved over time. Without good documentary evidence, a well-preserved set of furnishings and the close scrutiny of the fabric, such an evolution would be impossible to postulate. St Andrew's Wingfield is – in short – a chastening reminder of how incredibly challenging parish churches are to interpret.

THE LATER HISTORY

9

Alice Chaucer, Duchess of Suffolk (d.1475), and her East Anglian Estates

Rowena E. Archer

Nothing captures the life of Alice Chaucer more effectively than the image of her in death – on her tomb in St Mary's Church in Ewelme in Oxfordshire, the probable place of her birth, the caput of her Chaucer inheritance and the likely place of her death. The 7 foot alabaster effigy betokens a woman of self-importance and confidence who had succeeded in life and wished to be remembered thus in death. The commoner at birth is declared on the inscription to have become a 'serene princess' and the angels around the chest tomb present the coats of arms of her more distinguished ancestry – that of Roet and Burghersh – and of her greatest marriages – Montague and de la Pole. Her mortality is acknowledged but hidden away at the base of the tomb behind a stone cage, via her sculpted cadaver where humility is tinged with more than a little pride by being, uniquely among such sculptures, in expensive alabaster; it can only properly be seen by the visitor ready to prostrate themselves on the floor. There is no doubt that this was her home but wherever there was land there was a strong and abiding attachment and in eastern England this derived both from her parents and her first and third husbands. What distinguished her landholding here, as opposed to that which she held in other parts of England, was its much more troubled history, in which ancient dormant claims as well as newer ones, made her ever vigilant and demanded a firm hand as local and national politics slowly descended into the chaos of civil war.

Indeed, Alice was born into a world in chaos. Her father had survived the deposition of Richard II and his strong Lancastrian connections brought him to a new height with the usurpation of his cousin Henry Bolingbroke. Thomas Chaucer's aunt had borne Henry Bolingbroke's father, John of Gaunt, four offspring – the Beaufort children – who had been legitimised when Katherine Roet/Swynford finally married Gaunt in 1397.[1] Rebellion was the order of the day when Alice made her first

---

[1] My greatest debt is to Professor Colin Richmond who has long encouraged me to write about Alice and who has generously shared at every turn his own thoughts and insights into this extraordinary woman. He has prevented me from glossing her faults, ever the danger that faces the

appearance, in 1404 or 1405. Ricardian supporters, the Percies and Owain Glyndŵr, were threatening the new regime. Alice's grandfather Geoffrey was dead; her parents had been married some seven years and if there had been other children they had not survived. Thomas was thirty-seven or thirty-eight and Alice became in many ways the son he never had and the focus of his attention.[2] The bond between them was a close one and he taught her what he could about being a landowner and surviving in the maelstrom of politics. No-one has described Thomas better than K.B. McFarlane: 'a self-made man of great wealth, acquisitive yet circumspect, politic and *affairé*, well-versed in all branches of administration and diplomacy, a practised chairman and envoy, influential and respected'.[3] His daughter, however, was a woman of great wealth but made largely by marriage, acquisitive but unrestrained; political rather than politic, well versed in many branches of administration but not in diplomacy, an interfering chairman, influential and, in many quarters, detested. It should not have been so. Thomas showed her how to advance through marriage alliances and taught her the importance of retaining land. His own marriage to the heiress Maud Burghersh had played a major part in his rise while many were the childless couples and vulnerable widows who succumbed to his charms and sold him the interest in their lands as he grew richer on the profits of his service to the early Lancastrian governments. His daughter was not always charming.

Alice's meteoric social rise began early. The uncanonical union with Sir John Phelip for which no dispensation was sought, though one was needed since she was only nine or ten, did not last long. When barely thirty Sir John succumbed to dysentery contracted at the siege of Harfleur in 1415 and Lady Alice Phelip returned to the care of her parents. Sometime between 1421 and 1424 Thomas contracted her in marriage to Thomas Montague, earl of Salisbury. It was an immense social coup, doubtless made possible by a combination of Chaucer's close proximity to his second cousin, Henry V, and the fact that it was now clear to all that Alice would be her father's sole heiress. First and foremost a soldier, Montague was frequently captaining English forces in the Hundred Years War and Alice on occasions travelled with him, quite undaunted by the danger of a war zone. At a Paris wedding in 1424 the English ally, Philip, duke of Burgundy, attempted to seduce her, to the immense fury of Salisbury.[4] This second marriage did not last long either, for Thomas was killed by shrapnel raised by a cannon shot at the siege of Orleans in 1428 but the real gain was that Alice was now countess of Salisbury.[5] Her third marriage followed very swiftly – to a man in his early thirties who had, surprisingly, never been married

biographer. I am also indebted to Professor Ralph Griffiths for commenting on an earlier draft of this chapter. See the Chaucer pedigree.

[2]   For Alice's early life and biographies of Thomas Chaucer see Roskell, Clark and Rawcliffe 1992, vol. II, pp. 524–32; Ruud 1926 *passim*.

[3]   McFarlane 1945, p. 337.

[4]   Dupont 1837, p. 225.

[5]   See Warner 1998, pp. 146–73, for the life of Salisbury.

and whom she had almost certainly known for sometime. William de la Pole had survived an attack of dysentery at Harfleur and missed the battle of Agincourt but in the following years was often to be found in the company of Salisbury and in 1428 he replaced the latter as commander at Orleans, eventually fleeing the city and taking refuge further up the Loire at Jargeau where he was captured by the forces of Joan of Arc and had to be ransomed.[6] A licence for the marriage to Alice was issued on 11 November 1430.[7] In 1432 Alice received robes of the Order of the Garter, her husband having been made a Garter knight in 1421 and on her tomb she displays her garter on her left forearm.[8] In 1444 she became marchioness of Suffolk; countess of Pembroke in 1447; and, finally, duchess of Suffolk in 1448. She had been made by marriage more spectacularly than most.

At every marital stage land had been an equally important factor in her rise and every new acre was subject to close scrutiny both at the time of the grant and ever after. The first marriage had been made conditional upon her having a jointure in all the Phelip properties and, at the same time, her father had added a group of lands centred upon Donnington Castle in Berkshire which he had almost certainly bought for that purpose. For sixty years Lady Alice Phelip held the entire estate, preventing Sir John's heir, his brother William, from ever holding it, or indeed the latter's daughter, or eldest grandson. In the end William's second grandson, William Beaumont, who remained a loyal Lancastrian, recovered the lands in 1485, a decade after Alice's death. On Salisbury's demise more land and money accrued to Alice under the English common law which assigned to widows one-third of their deceased husband's estates; her jointure this time was a relatively modest eight manors.[9] The negotiations for her jointure in de la Pole lands were to rumble on for several years but eventually she got a huge proportion of these.[10] In 1434 and 1437 respectively, Alice lost both parents and the, by now substantial, Chaucer inheritance was hers. That her father had taught her well is perhaps best seen from evidence given by her de la Pole son after her death, that she had gone on buying up land throughout her last widowhood.[11] The legal records are littered with suits brought by Alice chasing claims, unpaid rents, missing goods and residual rights in every corner of the realm.[12]

---

[6] See Watts 2004.

[7] CPR 1429–36, p. 86.

[8] Cokayne 1911, Appendix B, p. 596. Alice received robes from 1434 to 1436, 1439 to 1446 and in 1448 and 1449.

[9] Alice had some difficulty securing this jointure as Thomas had failed to secure the proper licence for it and Alice was challenged later by her step-daughter Alice Montague. Hicks 1991, p. 356.

[10] There are ten documents relating to the settlement in the BL Harleian manuscripts. BL Add. Charter 2016, dated 1435, represents a late attempt to make a change to the settlement. Alice's accounts for 1453–4 in BL, Egerton Roll 8779 list sixty manors or parts thereof though some are not de la Pole properties.

[11] CCR 1476–85, p. 29.

[12] The story of this will have to wait upon my publication of a full account of Alice's life.

Fig. 9a. Chaucer/De la Pole pedigree

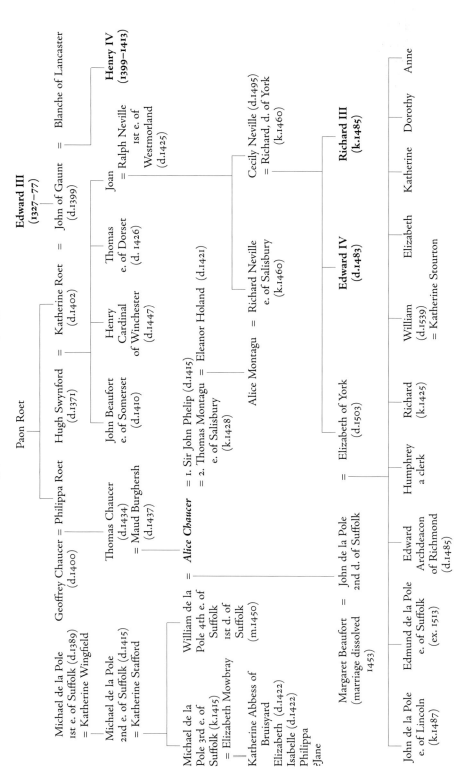

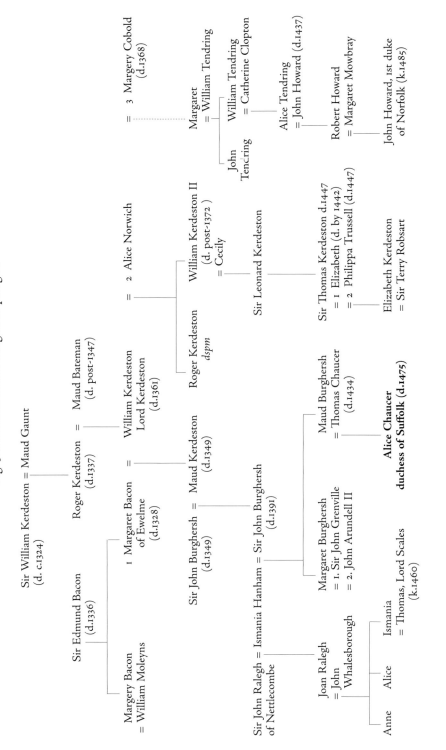

Fig. 9b. Kerdeston and Burghersh pedigree

What was Alice Chaucer worth? This is one of the most vexed questions faced by the historian of the aristocracy, given the patchy nature of surviving financial records both in terms of their number and because any one account was almost always only telling part of the story. In addition total income could vary substantially from one year to the next for a whole variety of reasons, not least because of temporary gains or grants. Then there is the impossible task of putting a value on the total goods and chattels, gold and silver plate, jewellery, tapestries and furnishings that adorned noble houses.[13] Here one can only speculate but it seems clear that much of the wealth of the aristocracy was in this form, making a total monetary calculation impossible. Phelip had left Alice the furnishings of one room in his house together with a covered cup of gold and a gold ewer.[14] What was this worth? In his will Salisbury had, among other things, bequeathed to Alice the colossal sum of 4,000 marks, of which 1,000 was to be in gold and the rest in jewellery and other goods.[15] What was the value of the cloth of gold that Alice wore to the christening of her goddaughter, Eleanor Moleyns, in 1426, or of the goblet with a gold cover that was her gift to the infant?[16] Occasional references suggest a capacity to deal in huge sums, such as the grant by Edward IV to Alice in 1467 of the manor of Grovebury (Bedfordshire) in recompense for 2,800 marks owing to her by the Crown.[17] In her final long widowhood her lands comprised 130 manors scattered through twenty-two shires, 144 parcels of land, some of them of thousands of acres, two London residences, five castles,[18] several country manor houses, hundreds of bailiwicks and rights of advowson, one almshouse and one school. There is but one imperfect set of accounts remaining, for Norfolk, Suffolk and Essex, for the year 1453–4, recording an income of just over £1,300.[19] The Phelip lands in 1414 were worth some £460. Thomas Montague for all his fame was not notably well endowed, his total income being given at his death as only £725, but he had received huge sums at various stages in his life for his services to the Crown.[20] Presumably some of this was what made the cash bequests possible under the terms of his will.[21] There is no surviving inquisition post-mortem for Alice from which to make at least some kind of overall assessment but her annual income can scarcely have been less than £2,000, making her by the standards of the day one of the wealthiest inhabitants of England.

---

[13] Bod MS DD. Ewelme, EM A 47 comprises inventories of Alice's goods of eye-watering richness. See Goodall 2001, pp. 282–91. See also Cleland 2007, pp. 48–56.

[14] TNA Prob11/2B/203. Phelip left his Chaucer in-laws £40 and his other bequests amounted to nearly £250.

[15] Jacob 1937, 392–3.

[16] *CIPM*, vol. XXV, p. 455. See p. 195 for the significance of her god-daughter Eleanor.

[17] CPR 1467–77, p. 362.

[18] Wingfield and Eye (Suffolk), Claxton (Norfolk), Ewelme Palace (Oxfordshire); Donnington (Berkshire).

[19] BL Egerton Roll, 8779.

[20] Hicks 1991, p. 356 for Montague's lands; Warner 1998, pp. 149–51, for grants.

[21] Over £1,400 was bequeathed in this way. Jacob 1937, pp. 390–8.

In 1430, when she married William, Alice was something of a new comer to East Anglia, certainly to Wingfield, where the castle was, at least in theory, the caput of the de la Pole lands. The surviving south façade points, of course, to William's fourteenth-century progenitors and behind, the much later work, to the de la Pole successors.[22] There is not much evidence of fifteenth-century building. William was often on the move, either in France or, once his career in the king's household took off, up and down to London. For him, Ewelme, so convenient for Windsor and the capital, was far more useful as a residence. There is limited surviving record of Alice being at the castle, but the transfer to Oxfordshire in 1466 of such luxury goods as those inventoried in the Ewelme papers is highly suggestive of the importance of Wingfield as a place in regular use. Nonetheless it is evident that she also resided in the county at Westhorpe and Eye.[23] In her 1453 accounts there are two entries relating to income from Wingfield. The bailiff, John Edward, paid over the not very impressive sum of £11 3s some of which he had passed to the treasurer of Alice's household while Old Wingfield and Fressingfield were in the hands of a farmer who accounted for £36 19s 4d, more than half of which was arrears and who had paid out, in addition, the annuity of 20 marks owing to the abbess of Bruisyard. These accounts do also show that she was at Wingfield for at least some of that year with administrators bringing her both information and cash. In practice, given the large number of residences at her disposal, Alice was often moving from one property to another.[24]

Even before 1430 East Anglia was not, however, completely unknown to Alice, for there was a long family history in this area, one that she evidently knew well and she leapt to protect claims to ancestral lands in the 1440s and 1450s when they seemed to be under threat. Her mother's Burghersh family looked to Sir Edmund Bacon, Alice's great-great-great-grandfather, for the claim to Ewelme but, from the Kerdeston family, into which Sir Edmund's daughter Margaret had married, had come a group of lands which included the castle of Claxton in Norfolk where Alice was also wont to reside. In 1453 it was undergoing repairs.[25] In the 1450s Alice was in dispute about ownership of these manors with the descendants of other branches of the Kerdeston family, including John Howard, the future duke of Norfolk. Any thought that these were minor outlying properties of little importance is banished by a reading of the record of her suit which rehearses in extraordinary detail the

[22] Aldwell 1925, pp. 31–4. The licence to crenellate is dated 1385.
[23] See note 13 above. Aldwell 1925 conjures up a romantic image of Alice 'for ten lonely years' living out her widowhood at Wingfield based on the Paston Letters though these actually never mention her being in residence there. *CAD*, vol. V, p. 96. Flenley 1911, p. 129 states that Suffolk was at 'Est horp be side Bury' following his release from the Tower in March 1450. Virgoe 1997 quotes Flenley but this must be an error on the part of the chronicler as there was no East Thorp near Bury.
[24] BL Egerton Roll, 8779. For the payments to the Abbess of Bruisyard, see Archer 2003, pp. 12–26. For the manor of Old Wingfield see Aldwell 1925, p. 3, who identifies four manors in Wingfield at different periods.
[25] See the Burghersh pedigree fig. 9b, p. 191. Gairdner 1904, iv, p. 163; BL Egerton 8779.

tortuous history of their descent from Bacon and Willliam Kerdeston, the latter's three marriages offering endless scope for counterclaims, not that Alice was in any doubt about her rights.[26] Maud Burghersh's inheritance also included lands in Stratford (Suffolk), Hatfield Peverel (Essex) and Bourn (Cambridgeshire).[27] To these must be added the manors of Nedging and Kettlebaston (Suffolk) which had been granted to Sir John Phelip following the execution for treason of their owner, Henry, Lord Scrope, in 1415. While there is no evidence of Alice visiting these, the confirmation of the grant of them to her and William in 1440 shows that they were at least under some sort of control.[28]

So far as social contacts with East Anglian society go, Alice's links were fragile before 1430 but some seeds were already sown for later expansion of these connections. Through her first brother-in-law, Sir William Phelip, she was at least indirectly involved in the region. The latter had inherited Dennington in Suffolk from his father in 1407, and in 1415, as executor of the will of his younger brother John, he surely had some contact with Alice. At the same time Sir William became closely involved with the succession to the de la Pole estates after the death of the second earl of Suffolk and he became a trusted and close servant of both Henry V and his successor. There is nothing to indicate tension over the Phelip lands, so many of which were in Alice's hands but it seems reasonable to suppose that Sir William was anxious to observe how she was managing estates that he hoped would eventually return to him or his heirs. After 1430 the two Williams who might have been rivals in the household of the young Henry VI seem to have cooperated fully with each other, notably over Chaucer interests and property.[29] More interesting is the Paston family, like Alice also *nouveau riche*, to whom she was connected through her parents. This went back at least to 1427 when Thomas Chaucer sold the manor of Gresham (Norfolk) to his friend Judge William Paston, son of the foresighted but very lowly Clement who had sent his boy to school.[30] The story here is a tangle of disinheritance, family quarrels, debts, defaulters, divided loyalties and dubious marriages that trumps any modern-day soap opera. The politic and circumspect Thomas had balanced the competing elements of this saga with consummate skill, remaining 'influential and respected' by all the parties concerned.[31] The heir to the fourteenth-century owners of Gresham, William Moleyns (d.1425), was also a friend of Thomas so it was no mean feat to bring a resolution to the problem of this manor's future. In addition Thomas was

---

[26] There were nine manors in dispute and whatever the nature of Howard's claim they were all under Alice's control in 1453: BL Egerton Roll, 8779. Some details of this dispute are to be found in Cokayne 1929, pp. 195–9. The full story will appear in my forthcoming biography of Alice.

[27] Ruud 1926, pp. 109–11.

[28] CCR 1413–19, p. 236; CPR 1436–41, p. 400.

[29] Roskell, Clark and Rawcliffe 1992, vol. IV, pp. 68–74 on the Phelip brothers; Watts 1996, pp. 158–62, on Suffolk and Phelip's cooperation.

[30] Richmond 1990, pp. 2–3 on the origins of the Pastons.

[31] McFarlane 1945, p. 337.

an interested party himself for the descent of this manor which went all the way back, yet again, to Sir Edmund Bacon and but for the survival of the Moleyns line it would have belonged to Chaucer's wife.[32] It was surely a symptom of that keen eye for land acquisition that led Thomas Chaucer to involve himself in the marriage of his friend's son, another William Moleyns, and to ensure that Alice should be the godmother to their only child Eleanor.[33] When in 1448, twenty-one years after the legitimate sale of Gresham to Paston, Robert, Lord Moleyns launched a full-scale attack on the property, the carefully nurtured Chaucer–Paston–Moleyns relationship fared less well in the hands of Alice. Though she seems to have played no direct part in events it cannot have helped that the local lawyer John Heydon, associate of both Sir William Phelip and William de la Pole and, by this stage directly linked to Alice herself, had been the chief supporter of this aggression.[34]

With a few scattered lands in East Anglia, a few skeletons in the landed wardrobe and a potential network of East Anglian associates, the de la Pole marriage gave Alice a chance to involve herself rather more on her own account in the region. It is possible that the couple spent the early years together here, most probably at Wingfield itself, for Thomas and Maud Chaucer were at Ewelme but the remodelling of the church there, the foundation of the almshouse and the building of a palace in the Thames Valley in the years immediately after Maud died in 1437 suggest a kind of reorientation. Nevertheless, by the early 1440s, there are signs of Alice's growing influence in the east. In January 1444 James Gresham, legal clerk to Judge William Paston, reported, among much other business, that he had conversed with Drew Barentine who had been sent with one of Paston's bills to Alice. Barentine had told Gresham 'she was weel remembred of þe matier' adding 'ye shulde not need to drede yow, for she seid al shuld be weel'. This was all that Barentine could or would tell him but he advised Gresham to go and see Alice and remind her of the bill. Gresham had replied that he would not be 'admytted' to the countess's presence but Barentine had then told him he would just have to find the means. Gresham expressed huge reservations to the judge. He explained that he would only be able to see Alice if he went via some of her men and if that were the case he would have to tell them Paston's business in full. He could not, however, distinguish those men well disposed to the judge from those who 'wolde yow not weel'. He reported that Alice was now gone to London and asked for advice on what action he should take next.[35] What the bill contained and what the upshot was of the letter is unknown but what is not in doubt is the influence that Alice evidently had quite independently of her husband. Who were the men whom she had about her who so filled Gresham with anxiety?

<hr />

[32] For this tortuous story see Richmond 1990, pp. 47–53; see also Castor 2000, pp. 135–9.
[33] See above note 16.
[34] I am grateful to Dr Charles Moreton and the History of Parliament Trust, London, for permission to consult Dr Moreton's unpublished article on John Heydon for the 1422–1509 section of the History. See p. 196 for the history of Alice's link to Heydon.
[35] Davis 1976, vol. ii, p. 13; Richmond 1990, p. 5, for discussion of the bill.

Some answer may be found in a bizarre incident reported by the corporation of Norwich in the autumn of 1450 as part of the history of events linked to 'Gladman's Insurrection' in 1443, named after John Gladman who had evidently cut a rather striking figure riding about the city wearing a paper crown, inciting riots and in particular an attack on the cathedral. With William de la Pole dead, the city was bent on making trenchant allegations against the duke and his cronies, in particular Sir Thomas Tuddenham and John Heydon. They recounted how sometime before 2 June 1448[36] Countess Alice had visited the city in the company of Tuddenham and two others unnamed. All four were in disguise, Alice like 'an huswyf of the cuntre'. Was this in some imitation of Gladman's disguising or was all of this pure invention by the corporation? As Colin Richmond has put it, 'the mind, *my mind*, does boggle; other minds should too'.[37] Towards nightfall the four headed out of the city towards Lakenham Woods,'to tak the ayr and disport theym self'. They did not get far, for Thomas Aylmer, keeper of the city ditches, stood in their path whereupon a fight ensued and the countess allegedly was 'sore afrayd'. Once again there are many unanswered questions, not least what William might have thought of his wife planning disports with one of his closest associates. The city of Norwich complained that although the mayor arrested Aylmer and imprisoned him for thirty weeks, Alice and Tuddenham bore the city a great hatred. The corporation went on to link the two directly, and indeed they clearly were linked, with John Heydon, who had briefly served as the city's recorder before being dismissed. The city complained that along with Alice the two had 'spirited up the duke of Suffolk' in order to get the city's privileges confiscated.[38] In its effort to defend itself the city resorted to arguing that Gladman's disguising with his crown was a harmless portrayal of the celebrations of the end of Christmas. Alice's disguising was presented in far more malevolent terms and the juxtaposition of the two raises the question of how much in the story of Alice was also manufactured. Nevertheless the episode suggests that Alice Chaucer was regarded as a figure capable of independently playing a significant role in the murky story of East Anglian politics.[39]

This then is the figure who faced her *annus horribilis* in 1450. Whilst the marriage of Alice to William de la Pole cemented her social standing, for William it advanced his political standing through Alice's powerful familial connections. His career at home follows the marriage; it does not precede it. Architect of the peace policy with France, William proved a poor manager of its execution and when the Norman capital fell in November 1449 a scapegoat was needed. Unwisely offering to answer his critics in January 1450, William was incarcerated in the Tower. Alice did what she could, not least for the sake of her only child, John, aged seven. In imitation

---

[36] The date on which Alice became duchess of Suffolk
[37] In a lecture given on 28 June 2010.
[38] Hudson and Tingey 1906, pp. 344–5.
[39] Blomefield 1806, vol. III, p. 154 for further details.

perhaps of her father's opportunism, she it was who arranged speedily the boy's marriage to Margaret Beaufort while William was a prisoner. No matter that the marriage required not one but two dispensations, the couple being both underage and related within prohibited degrees of consanguinity; time was of the essence and did not allow for such formalities.[40] Alice knew as much as anyone what a good marriage could achieve. Outside the immediate royal circle Alice's nearest most powerful relatives were the Beauforts and she had kept her links to members of the family alive.[41] As is clear, she knew her family history and genealogy. All that stood between the Beaufort heiress and the crown of England, given that Henry VI had no heir, was a parliamentary statute that barred the Beaufort line from the succession. What had been done by one parliament could easily be undone by another, and the well-informed Commons in the parliament of 1450 interpreted the marriage as an attempt by William to secure the crown of England for his heir.[42] They may have been right and it was certainly an extremely serious charge, implying treason. It is notable that the only article to which he responded in detail from the many in the two sets of charges levelled against him was that concerning the marriage. However, claiming that he had originally intended his son to marry Anne Beauchamp, the daughter of the duke of Warwick, was hardly a satisfactory answer to a charge that related to the very changed circumstances following Anne's early death.[43] William's fall from grace was swift. Released from the Tower at night on 17 March, he was chased by a London mob as he headed for Suffolk to prepare for his five-year exile, the sentence that had been imposed to spare him full-scale parliamentary impeachment and possible execution.

Over the following weeks William seems to have resided at Westhorpe rather than Wingfield.[44] On 30 April, the night before his departure, Suffolk wrote a remarkable letter of advice to Young John, commending him to his God and to his king and then more immediately instructing him 'to love, to worshepe youre lady and moder, and also that ye obey alwey hyr commaundements, and to beleve hyr councelles and

---

[40] The dispensation was finally granted on 18 August 1450: *CPapR 1447–55*, pp. 472–3.

[41] Cardinal Beaufort had assisted her over claims for her Montague jointure and he was a feoffee for the lands settled on Alice and William at the time of their marriage: BL Harleian Charter 43. E.19; Add. Charter 2016; Northamptonshire County Record Office, Fitzwilliam (Milton) MS 2046; *CPR 1429–36*, p. 36.

[42] *PROME*, vol. V, p. 177.

[43] Griffiths 1979, pp. 19–23, for details of the Beaufort claim. Cokayne 1959, pp. 384–5. In May 1444 William had been given the wardship and marriage of Margaret Beaufort but she was a minor if well-connected heiress at that time. Anne Beauchamp was born in February 1444 when John de la Pole was not yet two. She had died at Ewelme on 3 January 1449, a clear sign that she had been snapped up as a future bride for William's heir because of her great wealth, but her demise opened up the opportunity for a new alliance for the de la Poles. The Beaufort family was not wealthy but it had a vastly greater political significance by 1449 given the absence of a direct heir to the throne. See Jones and Underwood 1992, pp. 26, 35–7, though they accept Suffolk's claims and assert that there was never any real prospect of a Beaufort claim to the Crown.

[44] See footnote 23 above.

advises in alle your werks'.[45] Two days later, Alice was left to face the world and bring up her son alone. William's seizure at sea by pirates who scoffed at the king's safe conduct was followed by his savage murder at the hands of a blundering headsman who finally severed the ducal head with his rusty sword at the sixth attempt. The mutilated body was laid up on Dover sands and the news was already spreading by 5 May.[46] The death unleashed a battery of problems that were especially acute in East Anglia where the intense dislike of the dead duke rapidly became apparent. Enemies, old and new, pounced on his property and his family. Alice's survival now depended upon her political wit and skills and it was immediately clear that the way ahead was not going to be straightforward. Her earliest assailants were John Mowbray, duke of Norfolk, and his men. Norfolk, not for the first time, seized the manor of Stockton (Norfolk); the parks at Wingfield and Eye were ravaged several times, the earliest invasion in fact occurring even before Suffolk was dead, the marauders helping themselves to deer; and further afield even as late as August defeated soldiers returning from France tore down the Suffolk arms wherever they found them.[47] If this reaction against Suffolk is unsurprising the same cannot be said for the more direct targeting of his widow. A plan was hatched to put Alice on trial for high treason. At the autumn parliament the Commons brought a petition for the removal of twenty-nine traitors about the king with a prohibition on them coming within 12 miles of the monarch; it named her second after the duke of Somerset.[48] Such extreme measures against a mere widow reinforce the impression that even after William's death Alice was seen to pose some kind of threat in her own right. That she was by no means a spent force, however, was quickly made plain, though it was to take nearly a decade of careful manoeuvring before her position was completely secure.

Whatever her shock and grief at her husband's fate, Alice had made her first defensive moves within a week, securing a grant of the keeping of all the de la Pole property during John's minority; then she got the duke of Norfolk out of Stockton, at least for the time being; the treason trial was abandoned; and the king rejected the petition for the removal of his favourites.[49] All of this suggests that she continued to be able to call upon support in high places. Her 1453 accounts make it clear that the key members of the de la Pole affinity had coalesced around her, including Thomas Tuddenham and John Heydon, Edward Grimston, who had also been threatened

---

[45] Gairdner 1904, vol. II, pp. 142–3.

[46] Ibid., pp. 146–7. The gruesome tale is told by William Lomnor writing from London to John Paston in Norfolk.

[47] TNA Early Chancery Proceedings, C1/25/77; 26/164; BL Egerton Roll, 8779; Flenley 1911, p. 134. TNA King's Bench, KB9/118/1, mm 22, 28–9; 118/2, mm 16–17; 270A; 27/778; 27/766 Coram Rege roti. 71v, 76. I am indebted to Miss Margaret Condon for advice on this material.

[48] *PROME*, vol. V, p. 217. Castor 2000, pp. 110–11 on Norfolk's coveting of Stockton in the 1440s.

[49] *CFR*, 1445–52, p. 154. As early as 1444, as a precaution against William's early death, Alice had been promised the guardianship of their son: *CPR 1441–6*, p. 319; *CFR 1445–52*, pp. 181, 217 and 263; Stevenson 1861–4, II, ii, p. 770.

with a treason trial and named in the Commons' petition, John Ulveston and Philip Wentworth.[50] They had probably done so from the start of the crisis. These and others, in receipt of annuities and fees, were travelling the countryside, frequently on the road from Wingfield to London, collecting revenues, holding local courts, delivering cash to her and settling her debts, purchasing animals, clothing and building materials. There was also the important project of managing the building of the church tower at Eye in memory of the dead duke. Not everything had gone smoothly. Some entries go beyond routine administrative tasks and are more clearly suggestive of a continuous concern for the security of her position. No fewer than ten former sheriffs of Norfolk and Suffolk had dealings with the duchess that year; time and again in her life Alice was to take some trouble over local appointments. Besides Norfolk, others were jostling for the rule of the shire in the vacuum created by William's death, notably Thomas, Lord Scales. In June 1451 Alice had seen the de la Pole lands placed in the custody of Scales and Miles Stapleton.[51] It was in February 1453 that the duchess had made her complaints against Norfolk and his followers listing the many attacks that had been made, and though she had the satisfaction of seeing Norfolk bound over to keep the peace with her in the huge sum of £10,000, in December 1453 the duke had to be bound again this time in a recognisance of £12,000.[52]

Vigilance was still required. The 1453 accounts recorded no revenues from Stockton that year as it had been taken again by Norfolk though the escheator and 'divers attorneys' had been paid for support to get it back and Philip Wentworth had ridden over there from London to take possession. No wonder that a deputy of her receiver-general was paid in February 1454 to discover how many men were riding to London with the duke of Norfolk and to report back directly to Alice.[53] How far she played a wider and more direct role in bringing complaints against Norfolk and in sustaining the rule of Tuddenham and Heydon is not clear but both were in her pay. It has been argued that Scales was the political heir to Suffolk in East Anglia, but Scales was closely connected to Alice. He had been at the Paris wedding in 1424 when Burgundy had been overfamiliar with Alice; he was married to Alice's cousin, Ismania Whalesborough; and he and Alice were jointly the godparents of Eleanor Moleyns. Scales holding the de la Pole lands may not have been as unnerving as it perhaps seems but even if it was, by act of the parliament of 1453–4, probably in the second session, the duchess recovered control of the de la Pole lands from Scales. How far she was helped in this move by her close servant Philip Wentworth and by Gilbert Debenham, both elected to the parliament in defiance of Norfolk's effort to

---

[50] BL Egerton Roll, 8779. *CPR, 1446–52*, p. 444. For Ulveston and Wentworth see Richmond 1990, pp. 240–1; Castor 2000, pp. 98, 157, 159, 162 and 176n; Smith 1984, pp. 61–4.

[51] *CFR, 1445–52*, pp. 220–1.

[52] TNA KB27/766, Coram Rege roti, 71v, 76; *CCR, 1447–54*, p. 476.

[53] BL Egerton Roll, 8779.

get his own men returned, can only be surmised,[54] but all of this adds up to someone who was politically very astute. If Norfolk thought that the rule of the shire would neatly pass to him with Suffolk gone he had not reckoned on the duke's widow and was rapidly disabused of the notion. His proclamation in 1451 that everyone should know that 'we woll have the princypall rewle and governance throwh all this schir, of whiche we ber our name' was largely bluster.[55]

It was not, however, merely in East Anglia that tensions were rising, and Alice Chaucer, already fully aware of the national political scene and mindful of the future of her son, appears to have been rethinking what might have seemed the unthinkable, namely her Lancastrian loyalties. The sailors who had murdered her husband had obliquely referred to Richard, duke of York, an absentee lord over seas and a man whom they threatened to make king. In September 1450 he had returned from Ireland and added his own criticisms of the failures in government to those of Cade's rebels. Alice's relationship with York is interesting but elusive. Due largely to his absence, he had played no part in the crisis that had brought William to his death. York was her cousin and she evidently saw any of these highly placed cousins as potential allies. His coat of arms had been placed on her father's tomb in Ewelme to signify the family connections. Roger Virgoe has suggested that it was Norfolk who was behind the petition for the removal of those about the king and the Pastons were enthusiastic that York had 'putte a bille to the Kynge and desyryd meche thynge qwych is meche after the Comouns desire, and all is up on justice, and to putte all thos that ben indyted under arest', though the precise contents of this bill are not known.[56] York's attack on her Beaufort cousin, Edmund, duke of Somerset, may have increased her doubts about him, and his close relationship with the duke of Norfolk might have complicated Alice's views, but she seems to have appreciated that on the national scale he was now a major player and she was nothing if not a survivor. She was surely sufficiently shrewd to see that the House of Lancaster was in deep trouble.

In the end, her opportunity to ally with York came in an unexpected guise. In February 1453, apparently by Henry VI's own intervention, a 'divorce' was allowed

---

[54] Virgoe 1997, pp. 54–7 for the disputed election. There is no evidence of direct interference on Alice's part but the dispute appears in the record of sessions at which Alice had pleaded her case of Norfolk's trespass.

[55] Smith 1984, pp. 68–9 and *passim*, made much of Scales's role in keeping the affinity together but made no reference to Suffolk's widow. Castor 2000, pp. 161, 164 and 171; Watts 1996, p. 239n, give credit to both Scales and Alice for keeping the affinity together. Gairdner 1904, vol. II, p. 259; Richmond 1990, pp. 135–47, discusses the complex story of the descent of Stockton and of how Duke William acquired it in the first place; Castor 2000, pp. 110–11 and 179.

[56] Virgoe 1997, p. 54, offers no supporting evidence for the assertion that it was undoubtedly Norfolk who was behind the petition. Gairdner 1904, vol. II, p. 174. William Wayte's comments about York's bill come one month before the parliament opened and there is nothing to reveal what the 'bill' in question contained in detail but since in general he was calling for Somerset's removal it may possibly have referred to other undesirables in the court as well.

between John de la Pole and Margaret Beaufort and shortly afterwards Margaret was married to the king's eldest half brother, Edmund Tudor, in a move that looks very much as if the king was anxious to strengthen the royal family as the crisis over the lack of an heir deepened.[57] There is no evidence of a dispensation, which would have been required for this from the relevant ecclesiastical authorities, and it was certainly not for the king to permit such things to happen. Indeed, this action would have required a dispensation from the original dispensation to marry, which had been granted on the grounds that John and Margaret had not known that they were related within prohibited degrees; a faintly absurd statement given that, at the time, they had been seven and six, respectively. Of course in February 1453 the couple were still underage, a matter that seems to have been ignored, if indeed it was known in Rome, in the 1450 dispensation, for it had in fact described Margaret as John's wife. Did some loyal bishop consider it within his remit to allow the separation? If Alice regarded this uncoupling as some kind of slur on her good name she soon came to regard it as another opportunity for a fresh alliance and she entered negotiations with York. In a series of bonds made in February 1458 an instalment plan was made for payments to be handed over to Alice in respect of the marriage of John to York's daughter, Elizabeth.[58] Given that York had proved himself a rebel in 1455 and had lost his position as protector in 1456 this was something of a gamble. Any reassurance provided by the Loveday ceremony of reconciliation between York and the Lancastrian government in March 1458 was surely shattered by the events of 1459–60 with York first an exile in Ireland and then being killed at Wakefield, his severed head displayed at York, mocked with a paper crown. If these events left Alice feeling that she had been unwise, the feeling was not to last and besides she seems to have been skilled enough to have retained a foot in both camps, for in October 1460 at one and the same time she was using her links with York to influence the choice of sheriffs in the Thames Valley and yet was, according to one Paston correspondent, in 'great favour' with Queen Margaret and Prince Edward. Trimming paid off and in 1461 it was reported that the duchess, in the glow of the victory of Edward IV at Towton, was heading to the coronation at London.[59]

Alice was in her late fifties; Norfolk had died soon after the battle of Towton and been succeeded by a minor whose ability to act was severely curtailed by the survival of his grandmother and mother who were holding the greater portion of his lands; her son's future seemed assured and he had proved his Yorkist loyalties fighting with Warwick the Kingmaker at St Albans in February and then at Towton. She had safely steered a course into the new Yorkist world; she might have rested on these laurels. Instead she turned her attention to an old set of goals, largely driven by

[57] Jones and Underwood 1992, p. 38; Harriss 1972, p. 209. Queen Margaret's pregnancy may still not have been known.
[58] *CAD*, vol. IV, p. 26.
[59] Gairdner 1904, vol. III, pp. 226, 228 and 278.

the dead William's unfinished business, which she evidently now thought she could achieve through her new political networks. Her reputation with the Pastons was such that by 1462 Margaret Paston was writing to her husband that the disordered state of the shire was the result of the Suffolks' maintenance of traitors and extortioners. The people 'love not in no wyse the Dwke of Sowthfolk nor hys modyr', she declared. Four years later it was with the voice of experience that she advised her son, newly come into his inheritance, that he should be wary of her 'for she is sotill and hath sotill councell'.[60] Margaret Paston's bitter resentment of Alice was sometimes expressed in evidently derogatory descriptions of her as 'myn olde Lady' though this was perhaps also to distinguish her from the young Duchess Elizabeth, Alice's daughter-in-law.[61] It is once again a story of property.

On 5 November 1459 the old soldier Sir John Fastolf had died in the great brick castle that he had built for himself at Caister. He was a former enemy of William. John Paston was at his bedside and at once began the interminable dispute about Fastolf's will, Paston under suspicion of having forged it, making himself the heir. The Pastons, however, now found themselves in equal measure the heirs not just to the lands but to old disputes concerning those lands. If Alice had stood on the sidelines with regard to the Moleyns property at Gresham, which she did not own, she was not prepared to do the same with four manors which her dead husband had convinced himself that he did own.[62] The first of these was Dedham, in Essex, a property comprising the two manors of Overhall and Netherhall that had been held by the de la Poles in the fourteenth century but been legitimately bought by Fastolf. Faced with Suffolk's covetise and anxious to prevent the duke's ambition to take the even more valuable estate at Hellesden, Fastolf had made several generous offers to Suffolk, not least, that he would give Overhall to Young John and sell Netherhall to Suffolk at a reasonable rate, all for the sake of peace. The duke swept all offers aside and simply seized Dedham but Fastolf got redress when the duke was murdered. Notwithstanding, Alice's accountant listed Dedham in her 1453 accounts as though she owned it, with a note about Fastolf's illegal occupancy. By August 1461 Dedham appears to have been lost to Alice forever; John Paston's son reported how he had daily asked Henry Bourgchier, earl of Essex to approach the king on Paston's behalf for the manor of Dedham but all he got was the king's promise that he would be as good a lord to Paston as he would to the poorest man in England. It was assuredly the issue of Young John's inheritance that drove Alice to get the property back once the knight was dead and pointedly she ensured that it was immediately transferred to her son to whom it had been offered by Fastolf.[63]

---

[60] Gairdner 1904, vol. IV, p. 221.

[61] Ibid., pp. 163, 205; Gairdner 1898, p. 4, gives her birthday as 22 September 1444.

[62] What follows is much indebted to Colin Richmond's trilogy; the full story from Alice's perspective will have to wait for my forthcoming biography of her.

[63] Gairdner 1904, vol. III, pp. 301–2; Richmond 1990, p. 238, suggests that he had Dedham by 1461; Gairdner 1904, vol. IV, p. 158.

Next, but rather less cleanly executed, was her assault on Cotton in Suffolk, the birthplace that William had sold to Sir John in order to raise his ransom following capture at Jargeau in 1429. In 1441 Suffolk had accused Fastolf of non-payment and there had followed a lengthy dispute but one that in 1453 showed Alice in possession, the manor being recorded as in the hands of her farmer, James Blondell, not a local yeoman like many of the others on her properties but a Norman who had probably first encountered Suffolk in France and who had been in the service of Queen Margaret of Anjou.[64] He was presumably not a man to be trifled with. Fastolf appears, nevertheless, to have recovered the property and there the story rested until he died when Alice Chaucer once again entered the fray. The charge had actually been led by those executors of Fastolf's will who had turned against Paston but when they rode to Cotton on Friday, 3 September 1462 to tell the tenants not to pay their rents to Paston they had in their company John Andrew, a servant of Duchess Alice. It was a man of Andrew's who was left behind to keep the place.[65] While the two camps fought out the legalities of the case and Cotton itself fell into decay, Alice kept a watching brief. On 28 October 1468 an unknown correspondent warned John Paston that 'my Lady Suffolk would enter, and when she shulde enter few men shulde knowe, it shulde be do so sodenly'. He went on to say that the duchess was going to have her way over the choice of sheriff in the forthcoming round of appointments. Early the following year the executors opposed to Paston confirmed the grant to Alice. Cotton was not transferred to John. Whether she paid for it or not is unknown but so diminished was the manor by 1471 that the house was beyond full repair and the roof tiles were removed to be re-used at Westhorpe.[66] It may have been with a bit of a sneer that Alice assigned the revenues of Cotton for the fulfilment of her will.[67]

By the late 1460s, however, the fate of two other manors, Hellesdon and Drayton (Norfolk), had cast that of Cotton somewhat into the shade. Alice's determination to have them contrary to every rule of law was of an altogether different order. William had hoped to have them, so conveniently were they situated across the river Yare from his own manor of Costessey but he had never managed to achieve his end. The first sign of trouble came in April 1465 when Margaret Paston began to relay to her husband the news of claims being made to them both.[68] Her increasingly anxious letters in May, June and July were full of foreboding while John endeavoured to reassure her on the legal front, namely that the de la Poles had no legal case for having

[64] Smith 1984, p. 66. Napier 1858, p. 64, recites the proof of age of William de la Pole; Morgan 1973, p. 14, for Blondell. Richmond 1990, pp. 236–41.

[65] Gairdner 1904, vol. III, pp. 308–9, gives the date as 1461 but Richmond 2000, pp. 199–200, has given the correct dating of these events. John Andrew was one of those de la Pole servants who had remained about her after Duke William's death and is to be found in her 1453–4 accounts: BL Egerton Roll, 8779.

[66] Gairdner 1904, vol. IV, pp. 303–4, and vol. V, p. 5; Richmond 1990, p. 237.

[67] CCR 1476–85, p. 29.

[68] Gairdner 1904, vol. IV, p. 129.

them. He rehearsed their ancestry for her and said that they had no claim and he had told Henry Boteler, one of Alice's counsellors, that he should tell that to 'my old Lady of Suffolk'.[69] He failed after all this time to recognise that Alice Chaucer did not play by the rules, least of all the legal rules; his wife Margaret was not so naïve. Nor was John's bailiff, Richard Calle, and both offered their warnings through the late summer and autumn but John Paston continued to place his hopes in rational legal arguments. In the end, Alice simply sent in her men on 15 October 1465. As adroit at collecting information as her opponent, Margaret Paston reported not just the appalling destruction of Hellesdon and Drayton but the names of those involved and their mistress. For all that the letters spoke more often of the duke of Suffolk, Margaret knew that behind the 23-year-old was his mother and 'her doggeboltes'.[70] She identified the chief dog's bodies as Sir John Heveningham and Sir John Wyndfeld, the former was there in the 1453 accounts along with William Harleston, at that time her surveyor of Westhorpe, and a man whose name is mentioned more often in connection with the attacks over the summer than any other and with whom Margaret had had direct and unpleasant dealings on 1 August.[71] Margaret identified Harleston, John Andrew, evidently a busy man who was dividing his time between taking Cotton and ransacking Hellesdon, the bailiff of Costessey (this had been John Palmer in 1453–4), and John Dogett, the son of the bailiff of Drayton, as among the 'fals shrewys' who had informed her that 'the old Lady and the Duke is set fervently ageyn us'.[72] She wrote in some detail of the bailiff of Eye, John Bottisford, who had been Alice's bailiff there, where she now resided, at least since 1453, for he had not only taken some of Paston's men as prisoners to Eye but had been one of the great thieves who had used a cart to remove Paston's goods. Then there was the bailiff of Alice's manor of Stradbroke, Thomas Slyford, and a companion, Porter,[73] who had desecrated the church. Margaret's report suggested that it had become a tourist attraction: 'in gode feith there wyll no cryatur think how fowle and orubelly it ys arrayed but yf they sey it. Ther comyth much pepyll dayly to wonder ther upon, both of Norwych and of other placys, and they speke shamfully therof.'[74]

In the months and years that followed, the Pastons tried in vain to recover their costs and hold on to the manors. They importuned George Neville, archbishop of York and chancellor, and when he fell from grace they placed their hopes in the king himself. Sir John Paston had evidently forgotten the sophistries of Edward IV that he had heard in good faith over the seizure of Dedham, when he had taken at face

[69] Ibid., p. 165.
[70] Ibid., p. 205.
[71] Ibid., p. 170.
[72] Ibid., p. 148, p. 170, for Dogett. Richmond 1990, p. 240 fn. 144, for the 'Dogett dynasty' of de la Pole servants, and Gairdner 1904, vol. IV, p. 205 for the same and the others.
[73] Gairdner 1904, vol. IV, pp. 206–7. This might conceivably have been the Simon Portell alias Barker who was Alice's bailiff there in 1453: BL Egerton Roll, 8779.
[74] Gairdner 1904, vol. IV, p. 206.

value the monarch's declaration that he would hold with Paston's right in the matter and would not show favour 'mor to one man then to anothyr'.[75] This is not the place to discuss at length the genuineness of Edward IV's concern for justice but there is plenty of evidence that more important matters, or issues of patronage, overrode the niceties of justice when it suited him.[76] In fact, Alice had, long before the assault, been trying to persuade the Fastolf executors to let her buy the property. Quite why she assaulted it under such circumstances is unclear – impatience perhaps? What is absolutely clear is that Alice was confident of the outcome. Just as Edward had not lifted a finger over Dedham he was not prepared to help out over Hellesden and Drayton. When he eventually visited the site in June 1469 he got away with the stupidest of remarks, that the lodge could as easily have fallen down as been pulled down. So stupid that the Pastons' uncle could only say, presumably with great irony, that his nephews trusted the king's good grace.[77] Even Margaret had placed her hopes in Edward and remarked that Alice had more or less run away to Ewelme in case she was called to account. But Alice had not run away; she surely knew that the king would not back the Pastons against 'hys welle be lovyd broder the Duke of Suffolk'.[78] In 1472 Margaret Paston reported to her son 'the Duchesse of Suffolkis men sey that she will not depart from Heylesdon ner Drayton, – she would rather departe from money'.[79]

Alice Chaucer had lived a long life through the endless political upheavals that so characterised the fifteenth century. Some she had experienced directly; some had surely caused her enormous grief and fear; and some she had at times probably enjoyed. She had basked in the glory of both the houses of Lancaster and of York, and she had played her part on both the local and national scale. In the localities her priorities were her lands and after 1442 the future of her son. These proved to be more challenging in East Anglia than in other regions. She kept her eye, directly, or indirectly through carefully constructed networks, on the activities of all those who were players on the political scene of the region, and like her or loathe her none could discount her or her views and none defeated her when faced with her ambitions. She demonstrated all her life a political agility that exceeded that of many of her contemporaries, for she died in her bed, most likely at Ewelme, in the quieter times of Edward IV's second reign.

---

[75] See above; Gairdner 1904, vol. III, p. 302.
[76] See in general, Ross 1974, pp. 388–413.
[77] Gairdner 1904, vol. V, p. 32.
[78] Gairdner 1904, vol. IV, p. 66 and vol. V, p. 15.
[79] Gairdner 1904, vol. V, p. 155.

10

The Wars of the Roses, the Downfall of the de la Poles and the Dissolution of Wingfield College

Diarmaid MacCulloch

Should we be talking of the Wars of the Roses at all? Not long ago it was fashionable to play down the concept of 'Wars of the Roses': they were something that the Victorians had thought up and labelled, and they ought to be left behind after junior school history. This would be a mistake. First, it is a fact that contemporaries and near-contemporaries really did think of the troubles of fifteenth-century England as a series of civil wars, even before the Tudors made the idea one of the reasons why their own dynasty was a good thing. In fact, Edward IV's propaganda for his government anticipated what the Tudors would later say. Even the symbolism of roses was around in the fifteenth century, although it was not always used in the Victorian manner.

The fighting did disrupt a country which otherwise would have been unusually prosperous, centralised and powerful in Europe. It was also more extensive than some historians have allowed. The lowest figure ever was put forward by J.R. Lander in 1965: twelve to thirteen weeks of active campaigning between 1455 and 1487. This figure gained a lot of currency in the debunking of the Wars of the Roses, but in the late 1980s, A.J. Pollard was prepared to try a very different figure: for the first phase of the war from 1459 to 1471, five out of twelve years.[1] From 1483 to 1487 the campaigns were shorter and more interrupted, but they still have to be added to the total. And then there is the war which carried on in the troubled imaginations of Henry VII and Henry VIII. One could say that that war lasted until the 1540s.

There is also the question of how many were actually involved in fighting. Again, historians of a generation ago were inclined to play this down: a healthy reaction against wild medieval statistics. But the largest armies genuinely were large. The biggest confrontation was probably the battle of Towton which put Edward IV on the throne in 1461; this may have involved up to 45,000 men between the two sides. Compare this with the 23,000 men who fought the most vicious and destructive

---

[1]   Pollard 1988, pp. 74–6.

battle of the seventeenth-century English Civil War, the battle of Naseby (1645); only Marston Moor (1644) saw as many troops as Towton (roughly about the same number). The battles of Barnet and Tewkesbury (both 1471), Bosworth (1485) and Stoke (1487) may have involved ten or twelve thousand; and one has to realise what this means in fifteenth-century terms. At the time, the population of London was about 50,000; the population of the second largest city in England, Norwich, was less than 10,000. So in fifteenth-century terms, the battle of Towton was like uprooting all the inhabitants of London, putting them in a field and then asking them to kill each other. The lesser battles were like uprooting Norwich, and doing the same thing. All involved heavy casualties.

Having established that there is something serious to talk about, the next problem is to make sense of the whole process. Coming from the study of later periods, this is especially baffling, because there seem to be so few markers around; especially there is no ideology apparent in the struggles. In the first half of the war there was at least a dynastic dimension, but after 1471 even this disappeared, for the House of Lancaster was effectively destroyed. Further conflicts were primarily within the House of York, and were about power. Dynastic legitimacy became a fig-leaf for faction, greed and an obstinate determination to hang on to past gains.

A first stage is to establish a chronology, and see what phases are detectable; there is a sequence of at least six. One should begin at the end of the fourteenth century, with the failure of government of Richard II, and the breakdown of relations with his chief noblemen. It was sheer folly on Richard's part to exclude one nobleman, Henry of Lancaster, from the greatest private estate in the land, and it was a wave of outrage against the attempt which brought Henry to the point of invasion. But then it was very strange for Henry to change tack, claim the throne and eventually murder Richard. The result was that Henry was never entirely secure on the throne. The problem, haunting him and successive rulers, was one of genealogy (if genealogy bores you, then you are lost in the fifteenth century). It was not clear on what principle the Crown of England passed from one candidate to another. Did it descend to the heir male, like a piece of land? If so, Henry had a good claim, apart from the fact that he had murdered the previous heir male. But it was possible that the Crown did not descend like a piece of land; it might pass to the heir general, in other words the claimant through the senior female, who was nearer to Edward III's line than Henry was as the heir male.

So Phase One of the sequence, although not Phase One of the war, was the uncertain establishment of the Lancastrian dynasty. Because of its shaky claim by heredity, the only secure way for it to become permanent was to show results: long-term success. Henry IV never really did this; he died (1413) a troubled and insecure man. His son Henry V turned to the formula which had served Edward III well: fighting France. Luckily for him, France was in a state of chaos at the time, and in any case, Henry V was a good general. If there is any date when the Lancastrian dynasty can be said to have won respectability, it is 1415, with the battle of Agincourt, a very risky gamble which paid off. Thereafter the English built up a highly impressive French territory, and also (at least to start with) built up a good deal of local goodwill in it.

Phase Two, then, began in 1415: the secure establishment of the dynasty, with the prospect of a joint Anglo-French monarchy. It was the golden age of the de la Poles, in the time of William, first marquis and first duke of Suffolk, but the marriage which his son and heir made in mid-century carried with it seeds of disaster. Up to the first duke's time, his family might be said to have not enough genealogy; they were just Hull merchants made good. Henceforth, their problem was to have too much genealogy.

A tribute to the security which Henry V had now created was the fact that his baby son, another Henry, succeeded to the throne without challenge in 1422. More impressive still is that government in Henry VI's minority worked remarkably well, despite the fact that many of the leading participants detested each other. Things began to go wrong as soon as Henry VI reached his majority in 1436. Henry was simply incompetent: probably the most incompetent and talentless king in English history. He had no idea how to make a decision, or how to balance efforts to make friends through gifts and the need to preserve royal revenue, royal lands.

The lack of direction at the top soon brought trouble at home and overseas. At home, magnate quarrels became ever more bitter. In France, the English ceased to invest money and effort into their territories after the Truce of Tours in 1444, just at the time when the French were getting their act together and thinking about long-term revenge. The English lost local goodwill in Normandy; their commanders quarrelled, and in 1449 the French struck. Within two years they had conquered everything, and Henry VI hardly seemed to care; he may have been an outright pacifist.

The effect on home government was devastating. William duke of Suffolk took most of the blame as head of the government, and in 1450, in the middle of the French disaster, he was lynched on board ship in the middle of the Channel; his body now lies at Hull after a temporary interment at Wingfield. It was clear now that since the king was incapable of taking a lead, powerful noblemen must do so in his place; but there was nothing of the earlier sense of responsibility to a boy king. The two leading contenders, Edmund Beaufort, duke of Somerset and Richard, duke of York, were both vain, ambitious and not too bright. What was worse, York was the clearest representative of the heirs general of Edward III (we must remember that the Lancastrians were the representatives of the heirs male).

The next ten years were dominated by the quarrel between York and Somerset and their families, and by York's repeated attempts to seize power for himself. It was also the time when the de la Poles fatally acquired too much genealogy. One of the last moves of the duke of Suffolk to save himself from his enemies before his death in 1450 was to marry his heir John de la Pole to an important Lancastrian heiress, Margaret Beaufort. The boy was seven and she was six; this was not about their marital happiness. And it was destined not to last. In a rare personal intervention in politics, Henry VI around 1453 forced the de la Pole and Beaufort families to repudiate this marriage, and instead he had little Margaret Beaufort married to the king's half-brother Edmund Tudor. Margaret was nine, and she always remembered the night that she was supposedly given the choice about her future; she said that she prayed to St Nicholas about it, and that he approved of Edmund Tudor.[2]

John de la Pole was now to marry elsewhere. In 1458, his family married the boy to Elizabeth, daughter of Richard duke of York. Now de la Pole was firmly locked into the ambit of a man who was already scheming to seize the throne for his own family, tearing it away from the dynasty which had ruled for the previous half-century. So much hinged for the de la Pole family on that switch of marriage alliances. If the de la Pole marriage to Lady Margaret had lasted, that tough little lady would not have become the mother of Henry VII, the man who destroyed the de la Poles. Instead, the de la Poles were leaving behind their Lancastrian loyalties and embarking on a dynastic venture which, over the next half century, resulted in their systematic annihilation.

All was not lost for the Lancastrian monarchy in the 1450s. There was still an astonishing sense of responsibility towards the House of Lancaster among the nobility, and the first round of conflict between the duke of Somerset and York ended in 1452, with York effectively being forced to promise to behave himself. In 1453, it looked as if the sort of broad consensus which had created the government of the Minority Council might re-emerge. Now followed a wholly unpredictable disaster. In 1453, soon after his fateful decision about Lady Margaret's marriage, Henry VI went mad: it is not quite clear what a modern psychiatrist would call his condition, but in anyone's terms, it was madness, and it was a catastrophe for England's government. Who would take on the functions of kingship in the king's name? Which big male beast? Or would it not be a man after all? At the end of the year a further complication made trouble certain. Queen Margaret of Anjou gave birth to a son. This seems to have suddenly brought out maternal energy in her, and she subsequently devoted all her considerable energy to preserve her son's interests and fight off all rivals. This brought her into direct conflict with the duke of York, whose prospects of succeeding Henry VI without fuss were now dashed.

The result of all these accidents was predictable: a full-scale battle between an army of York and an army of Somerset at St Albans in 1455. Somerset was killed. Henry VI was present at the battle, and may have been wounded; certainly from now on, he was even more of a blank on the political map than ever. From now we can date the collapse in credibility of the House of Lancaster, and it is significant that the de la Poles chose this juncture, in 1458, to ally with the family of the duke of York. All the restraint which had somehow kept the aristocracy passive through the Minority Council and had prevented national political breakdown after the losses in

[2] Jones and Underwood 1992, pp. 37–8.

France was now ended. From this first battle of St Albans, we can date Phase Four: the first War of the Roses.

The details of the conflict as it broke out are not important for our current purpose, but it is worth noting yet another unexpected change of direction: in 1460 the duke of York tried to claim the throne for himself, actually within the parliament house in Westminster. There was enough remaining loyalty to the Lancastrians for this absurdity to cause general astonishment, and he had to withdraw. Although York was killed in battle a few months later, his son Edward of March came out victorious in the family feud against Queen Margaret. Now it was his turn to face an unstable decade of kingship, with Margaret stirring up trouble for him abroad, while Henry VI was a helpless prisoner in London. John de la Pole was King Edward's brother-in-law. His fortunes were locked in with the Yorkists.

Two sorts of intrigue for power and influence now characterised the events of the 1460s leading up to the restoration or Readeption of Henry VI in 1470: at home, personal struggles among Edward IV's supporters, interacting with Margaret's dynastic plots abroad. The final phase of the trouble was brought to an end with the sort of high drama that modern historiography finds slightly embarrassing: having fled the country, Edward IV returned to fight a whirlwind campaign against great odds, to defeat his opponents and to murder both Henry VI and his son. Now there was no House of Lancaster left. From then on the House of York seemed secure, despite venomous side-shows like the murder of the king's brother the duke of Clarence for plotting rebellion. From 1471 we have entered Phase Five.

Edward IV's second reign represented the sort of strong government that had not been seen in England since the reign of Henry V: there was even a success against France, and a good deal more profitable one than anything of Henry V's triumphs, in the shape of the Anglo-French Treaty of Picquigny of 1475, bringing a steady revenue stream from France to the English Crown. What went wrong was once more an accident: a king dying in his forties, leaving infant sons. Even so, this need not have been disastrous. After all, even a human disaster like Henry VI had reached adulthood with a reasonably stable government on a very similar basis. A further accident made things go wrong: the unexpected transformation of loyal, efficient brother Duke Richard of Gloucester into a power-crazy, murderous wicked uncle. We may not be able to explain his change of character very easily, but it is difficult to argue convincingly against the proposition that Richard murdered the princes in the Tower, in the course of murdering some of his more convincing rivals for power; and certainly few contemporaries made any effort to contest that likelihood.[3] By his actions, Richard gave a dramatic boost to the previously almost laughable claim to the throne of Henry Tudor, earl of Richmond, son of Lady Margaret Beaufort, that one-time de la Pole bride.

---

[3] The most balanced assessment of his reign, exploring the creditable aspects of his rule as well as the darker, is Ross 1981; see especially Chapter 5.

From 1483, Henry became the focus of all opposition to Richard both from the remnants of the old Lancastrian party and from dissident Yorkists. A second war of the Roses (which we can call Phase Six) had begun, but it was now a different sort of war of the Roses from the first; it was summed up by the Crowland Chronicler, a contemporary commentator on the battle of Bosworth, who said of Henry's victory 'the red rose, the avenger of the white, shines upon us'.[4] In other words, no longer was York fighting Lancaster: instead, a new family of the most dubious royal credentials possible, the Tudors, was posing as the righter of wrongs committed by King Richard against his own Yorkist family. Henry promised as part of his programme to marry Edward IV's eldest daughter Elizabeth of York and rule jointly with her; he conveniently forgot the latter half of that promise later on. But he had his royal bride, and out of that marital alliance, he also gained a permanent worry about any other close relative of Edward IV.

Henry's first attempt at invasion, combined with internal rebellion in 1483, did not work. Over the next two years, however, Richard alienated more and more powerful people, and one can only think that they really believed that he had murdered two children, which even by the standards of fifteenth-century England was beyond the moral norm. Consequently, King Richard relied more and more on the northern following which had built up during his brother's reign; it was a vicious circle, causing more bitter resentment in the south – and among ordinary people, not just among the nobility. This meant that when Henry tried again in 1485, he had a far better chance. He was helped as so often in medieval battles by luck: the way events went on the ground, and who had turned up in time to fight on both sides; but there are indications that by 1485 a lot of the aristocracy were simply not prepared to fight for Richard unless he showed that he could gain an overwhelming victory.

Over his entire reign, Henry remained a man who acted as if he was insecure. This was hardly surprising; he was in much the same position as Henry IV after 1399 and as Edward IV in his first reign, although Henry VII did not throw away prospective support quite as recklessly as Richard III after 1483. In fact, his power base was much narrower than any of those previous kings. He simply did not know the English nobility; all his knowledge of royal courts had been picked up in his brief exile years in France from 1483, and there was hardly anyone whom he could trust implicitly, apart from a few fellow exiles like John de Vere, thirteenth earl of Oxford and Bishop John Morton (neither of whom, significantly, had a legitimate son to stimulate their dynastic instincts; similarly Henry's own adored and politically powerful mother had only borne one child, himself). When his shaky genealogical claims to the throne were scrutinised with an indifferent eye, they would be found lamentably wanting: Henry was only a posthumous son-in-law of Edward IV. The family of a sister of the dead king, in other words, the de la Poles, or the children of

4 Pronay and Cox 1986, p. 185.

Edward's other daughter, in other words the Courtenay family, might seem to have just as good if not better claim on the throne.

Yet Henry was forced to employ noblemen who had given him no support before 1485 or even fought against him. They were never admitted into his confidence, and he clearly did not feel at ease in their company. His regime's work was done by a few handpicked bureaucrats, and he tried to keep the nobility who mattered in a perpetual state of nerves. The battle of Stoke in 1487, when John de la Pole earl of Lincoln died, is often said to be the last battle of the Wars of the Roses, but there was more trouble to come. There were invasions from pretenders, one of whom, Perkin Warbeck, may well have been an illegitimate son of Edward IV; certainly he seems to have captivated yet another sister of Edward IV, Margaret duchess of Burgundy.[5] In 1497 Henry faced an armed insurrection in the south-west which brought a real danger to the regime. It was a combination of popular fury with aristocratic leadership (even if in this case the aristocrat was not from the top rank), the most dangerous variety of rebellion possible in that age.[6]

When members of the Calais garrison were gossiping about who should succeed Henry VII on the throne at the beginning of the sixteenth century, they talked about the duke of Buckingham and Edmund de la Pole, two aristocrats who had a good share of old royal blood, but there was no mention of the son of Henry VII. The date of this report is uncertain, but it is no earlier than 1502, and it may well be as late as 1506, only three years before Henry VIII came to the throne.[7] It is not surprising that even up to his last years Henry acted as a man haunted by the prospect of disaster, and played up the prospect of renewed civil war in his propaganda for all it was worth.

Given that, the fate of the de la Poles in Henry VII's reign was almost inevitable. They had more Plantagenet blood than almost anyone else alive, but their fortunes were already in decline. In East Anglia, they had not enjoyed as much power as the Mowbray family since the lynching of the first duke of Suffolk in 1450, and it is noticeable that when in 1487 John de la Pole earl of Lincoln was attainted after his death at the battle of Stoke, no East Anglian gentleman was attainted alongside him; evidently they had all kept their distance from him. His father, John duke of Suffolk, for all the splendour of his tomb at Wingfield, was living in discreet obscurity when he died in May 1492. The widow of the earl of Lincoln lived on as late as 1532, maintaining her due place in East Anglian society, but an elderly dowager was rarely to be seen as an independent political force; so it proved with her.[8]

Then came the gradual beating-down of the last male generation, the earl of Lincoln's brother Edmund, and the other brothers, Richard and William de la Pole.

5   A fine study of Warbeck's relationship with the Duchess of Burgundy is Wroe 2003.
6   Fletcher and MacCulloch 2008, pp. 21–3, 132–4.
7   Chrimes 1972, pp. 308–9.
8   Gunn 1988, pp. 42, 45.

The crunch came in 1501: an anxious year for Henry VII in all sorts of ways. He was under pressure, and he transferred that pressure on to all potential rivals: principally the de la Poles. That brought Edmund's second flight abroad: the issue here was an obvious piece of Crown harassment designed to destroy de la Pole morale. Edmund became entangled in a lawsuit with a wealthy yeoman of Rishangles called William Rivet; Edmund claimed that Rivet was his villein. The case reached the King's Council, very unusually in a claim of villeinage, and in 1501, Edmund was humiliatingly defeated in the Court of King's Bench and heavy damages were awarded against him. That must have shattered his nerve; hence the flight abroad.[9]

Flight did Edmund no good. For a while, rulers in mainland Europe played around with him as a bargaining card with Henry VII, but in 1506, Henry did a deal with the Archduke Philip to surrender Edmund to England. Henry VIII executed him in 1513. Brother William died in the Tower. Brother Richard died fighting for the king of France against the holy Roman emperor at the battle of Pavia in 1525; he had proved useless to the French as a dynastic pawn. Now there were no male de la Poles alive, and only one senior Courtenay, who after a life warped by imprisonment in the Tower of London, was to die abroad mysteriously in 1556. The Tudors' dynastic nightmare of rival Yorkist claimants was over.

In the middle of this fall of a great noble house, the college which had become its mausoleum and spiritual home was not likely to prosper, but in fact Wingfield College's years without a protector after Edmund de la Pole's flight were short-lived. A year after Edmund's execution, in 1514, Henry VIII's favourite and jousting companion Charles Brandon was created duke of Suffolk, at the same time that the Howard family had their dukedom of Norfolk restored to them: that was a careful balancing-act by the king, who might put to good use the distinct lack of goodwill between the Brandons and the Howards, and it was also an effective means of crushing any hopes that the remaining de la Poles might have of regaining their titles and estates.[10] Brandon's marriage in February 1515 to Henry's sister Mary, so recently the widow of King Louis XII of France, tested the king's patience severely, but ultimately that rash act did not affect the new duke of Suffolk's usefulness in occupying the former place of the de la Poles in East Anglian society, with a steady series of royal grants of their former estates to him.

The parvenu duke was not likely to neglect the college which could provide him with the symbols of ducal power, and which might be expected to become the family mausoleum of the Brandons when the time came. Wingfield Castle was about the one stable home base for him and his French queen, in a life which was notably peripatetic, to judge by his surviving correspondence.[11] There are a few fragments of

---

[9] MacCulloch 1986, p. 54.
[10] On the Brandons and the Howards, see MacCulloch 1986, pp. 56–9, and on Brandon's gradual consolidation of the de la Pole inheritance, Gunn 1988, pp. 40–3.
[11] MacCulloch 1986, pp. 59–60.

evidence for this relationship: for instance, the duke presented one of the brethren of the college to one of his East Anglian livings in 1524.[12] The most satisfying surviving symbol of his interest is the early sixteenth-century panelling so recently discovered in the college building and now displayed in the remaining fragment of its hall, with its fashionable portrait medallions of a man and wife who are undoubtedly representations of the duke and the French queen: these are images of honour due to frequent visitors to social occasions in the college. The most likely commissioner for the panelling was the last master of the college, Robert Budde, who was appointed master in 1531; Budde was Brandon's chaplain. The comptroller of the duke's household, Richard Freston, was also the college's steward.[13]

The college's position abruptly changed in the late 1530s because the duke of Suffolk himself was dramatically moved like a chess-piece across the map of England: from 1537 he was uprooted from life in Suffolk by the king and set up with new estates, new stately homes and new responsibilities in Lincolnshire.[14] The motive was to see to the settling of the county which had been the spark for violent resistance to the Crown's religious plans in 1536, but it also addressed the problem which had been recurrent in East Anglia for more than a century: two powerful magnates contending for local supremacy, one with the Suffolk title as earl, marquis or duke, the other with the title of Norfolk. Suffolk's preferred residence in Lincolnshire became Tattershall Castle, which had its own fine collegiate church standing beside it, but in any case, in his last years, the duke was increasingly influenced by his characterful young fourth wife, Catherine Willoughby, who emerged as one of the most convinced and energetic Protestants among the mid-Tudor political elite. Chantry colleges were no longer to be among the priorities of the Brandons.[15]

It was therefore not surprising that Wingfield College became one of the first major chantry colleges in Suffolk to be dissolved by Henry VIII's commissioners, in 1542 (Tattershall College was to survive up to 1545, a few months before the duke of Suffolk's death). Richard Freston, so intimately involved in the affairs of both duke and college, was one of the main winners from the end of the college. On 17 December 1541, he had secured a 99-year lease of its rectory of Stradbroke for 8 pounds per annum: in effect an alienation by the master and brethren of this major property to an old friend who could stand them in good stead.[16] Freston's will made in 1558 also reveals that he bought 'the camping close' in Wingfield from the Master Robert Budd, though it is not clear whether or not that transaction happened before

[12] Gunn 1988, p. 105.
[13] Gunn 1988, p. 164. Freston is identified as 'capitalis Seneschallus et Supervisor' of the college in TNA: E164/31, fol. 14v.
[14] On what follows, see Gunn 1988, Chapter 5, and MacCulloch 1986, pp. 67–71.
[15] For her career, see Read 1963.
[16] Bodleian Library, Oxford, MS Tanner 137, fol. 46.

or after the surrender of the college.[17] It may also be significant that the college owed the duke of Suffolk 30 pounds at the day of its dissolution, which may indicate some further private sweetener to make sure that the master and brethren would be treated well. This detail forms part of a rare survival: a private memorandum from Sir Richard Rich, chancellor of the Court of Augmentations, to his subordinate the Suffolk man Nicholas Bacon, on arrangements for taking the surrender of the college. Rich's memorandum can be dated to mid-May 1542 by the surviving formal commission to take the surrender which was issued on 12 May; the surrender itself followed on 2 June and the commissioners made their certificate in Augmentations on 17 June 1542.[18] Rich instructed Bacon to appoint one of the brethren to serve the parish cure of Wingfield, with the incentive of an annual stipend of £6 13s 4d, larger than the annual 5 pounds assigned to his colleagues. With a certain predictability, Rich also directed Bacon to lease the building of the college itself to its late steward Richard Freston.

Four brethren beside the master signed the deed of surrender on 2 June: Peter Brinkley, John Stanard, Thomas Campyon and Edmund Harcocke. It is noticeable that none of them had been recorded as among the brethren at the episcopal visitation in 1532, and it is possible that the family surnames of the latter three conceal individuals who are otherwise known to us by place-name surnames in religion when they had been members of one or other East Anglian monastic house.[19] Certainly Peter Brinkley was a refugee trying to preserve something of his previous regular life: a genuine scholar with a DD degree, who had been a Franciscan and warden of Babwell Friary just outside Bury St Edmunds when Babwell surrendered in 1539. Brinkley had nevertheless become a pluralist, and in 1542 he was probably non-resident at Wingfield, still living in Bury.[20] When the exchequer carried out a nationwide survey of monastic and collegiate pensioners for Cardinal Pole in 1556, all former members of the college except John Stanard were still drawing their pensions (20 pounds per annum for Budde, 5 pounds for the others and a further 2 pounds for Edward Reve, who had probably been a junior chaplain, not one of the brethren). Stanard was not included in the list probably because he was the priest on whom Nicholas Bacon had prevailed to serve the parish in 1542; he was certainly serving Wingfield around 1555, and when on 8 January 1558 Sir Richard Freston made his

[17] Freston's will is TNA (PRO), PROB 11/42A/61 (Prerogative Court of Canterbury wills 13 Welles).
[18] The certificates are pr. in *Appendix to the Seventh Report of the Deputy Keeper of the Public Records*, Appendix II, p. 49. The memorandum is among the Bacon family papers, Chicago University Library MS Bacon no. 4487, pr. MacCulloch 2007, no. 7.
[19] Jessopp 1888, p. 296.
[20] Chambers 1966, p. 180. Brinkley may have gone on living at Fornham while a brother of Wingfield, and was serving as parish priest at St James Bury St Edmunds in 1543, among much other preferment (Peet 1980, p. 316; Baskerville 1933, pp. 57, 215).

will at his home which was the former priory of Mendham 4 miles from Wingfield, Stanard was among the witnesses.[21]

Thus there was considerable continuity at Wingfield through the Dissolution: the church building continued as the parish church of the large parish, and to judge by the unusual survival of its medieval organ *in situ* into the eighteenth century, its interior was initially little disturbed. That included the de la Pole tombs, still so remarkably well preserved, but there was very little likelihood that Brandon would follow the fifteenth-century de la Poles by using this shrine to the ducal Suffolk title as his mausoleum when he died in 1545. Instead, he lies buried in St George's Chapel, Windsor, at the initiative and expense of his royal master and old friend. There was no incentive for the duke's Protestant widow to bring the bodies of her two young sons back to a defunct chantry college when the little duke of Suffolk and his younger brother were carried off by the sweating sickness in 1551; they were buried where they had died, in the country house of the bishop of Lincoln at Buckden in Huntingdonshire.[22]

Through the story of the interplay between the fate of the de la Poles and the fate of the realm, we have seen a recurrent cycle of instability. A regime seized power, spent several years in insecurity, then established itself on a fairly permanent basis as the result of a major success – in Henry V's case, victory in France, in Edward IV's case, the final destruction of the rival royal house. Twice the success was then broken by accidents: first the breakdown of Henry VI and then the early death of Edward IV. What stopped the cycle of instability, success and disaster in the case of the Tudors? Quite simply, the lack of accidents, and the fact that by 1509 there was a convincing male heir to keep the de la Poles and Courtenays at bay. Even so, it was a close-run thing, for the overthrow of five kings in a century had severely damaged national confidence in the Crown.

Surveying the sorry decline of the de la Poles, it is easy to feel that the fault did not lie in them alone: they lived in an accident-prone political system. It is possible to go beyond my six-phase structure to detect a three-stage pattern in the century of events; they were remarkably cyclical. Some other patterns seem sheer accidents: for instance, two strong kings died young. One pattern is less accidental, though still puzzling: five times, leading noblemen turned a real or imagined grievance into a claim for the throne, quite out of the blue, and to general astonishment – Henry of Lancaster, Richard of York, Edward IV on his return in 1471, Richard of Gloucester and finally Henry Tudor. One might even add the events of the Readeption of Henry VI to make a sixth example of this pattern. Here the Earl of Warwick ('Warwick the King-maker') moved from demanding influence for himself from Edward IV to actually deposing the king and replacing him with the puppet Henry VI: in effect trying to

---

[21] Pole's survey is TNA: E164/31, fol. 14v; on Stanard/Stannerd, see Freeman Bullen 1936, p. 315, and Freston's will, TNA: PROB 11/42A/61.
[22] Cokayne 1953, pp. 460–1.

become king himself, with a frontman who was imbecile and incapable of governing. Six times in a century, a nobleman's fury suddenly tipped over into king-making. We have to remember again in considering Henry VII's conduct towards the de la Poles that they had as good if not a better claim to the throne than any of the above, once Richard III was dead. Certainly better than the claim of Henry VII.

Here we see a clash between the ideal of central government and recurrent behaviour patterns within the higher aristocracy; but we should also note the form that these repeated aristocratic coups took. Noblemen like the Lancastrians or Yorkists did not rebel to carve out their own duchy or mini-kingdom; they tried to take the whole kingdom. Contrast this with France, equally torn apart by civil war in the fifteenth century, but where regional magnates were virtually independent; dukes really were dukes in France. One of them, the duke of Burgundy, actually founded one of the most significant states in fifteenth-century Europe, partly out of territory which belonged in theory to his lord the king of France. England remained faithful to the centralised realm which had already been well established when the Normans arrived, at a time when troubles in France and the Holy Roman Empire led to long-term political disintegration.

Historians used to single out one factor in particular as being part of the weakness of England's late medieval government, and have made it a traditional scapegoat for the Wars of the Roses: bastard feudalism. How do we define this? It is the system in which the relationship between lord and subordinate revolves around money payment expressed in a contract rather than a gift of land. Aristocrats retain men in their household by these contracts, technically known as indentures, and the relationship is expressed by the wearing of livery by the subordinate. The de la Poles were fully conversant with this system. Victorian and early twentieth-century historians tended to deplore the institution of bastard feudalism, and blame it for the breakdown of order in fifteenth-century England. They said that it cut across loyalties to central government and distorted the working of royal justice; it created temporary relationships based on financial self-interest and put power in the hands of the most wealthy and acquisitive noblemen.

In reality, there was nothing new about bastard feudalism in the fifteenth century. The debates about it in the learned journals in the last few decades leave the reader floundering around in the twelfth and even the eleventh century.[23] Bastard feudalism was thus already a quaint old English custom in the fifteenth century. It had been subverting royal justice for almost as long as there had been royal justice. Nor did it end then, though the Crown did its best to hedge it around with restrictions, such as curbs on the wearing of livery. One might say that as long as there were great landed magnates around in British politics, which really means down to 1914, there were forms of bastard feudalism around in the British political system. In any case,

---

[23] From a vast literature, a helpful set of discussions is Coss 1989, together with the debate between D. Crouch and D.A. Carpenter in *Past and Present*, vol. CXXXI (May 1991), pp. 165–203.

there was always variety within bastard feudalism; it did not only exist on the level of magnate and subordinate.

And below the nobility were the people who were beginning to be called gentlemen in the fourteenth century. Their interests might be very different from those of a great magnate; in fact they might be far more inclined to seek partnership with central government against local magnates than to become their willing instruments: to seek good government against arbitrary aristocratic power. They would seek to create local communities to avoid the effects of the irresponsible aristocratic feuding which we have glimpsed in this survey. Even in fourteenth- and fifteenth-century England, there were shires where there was no great aristocratic power to stand in the way of gentry communities running their own affairs as they wished. That much developed in the next two centuries.[24]

Of course there were bastard feudal affinities in the English civil wars; there are now plenty of detailed studies of examples. But like regionalism, we are really discussing effect rather than cause when we look at bastard feudalism. Bastard feudalism was part of a well-established system which could be used for good or for ill. When the political atmosphere was healthy, it was part of everyday healthy politics; when things were bad, it was poisoned. We fall back, boringly, on the inability of the medieval English political system to control the behaviour of its nobility without a really strong king in charge; and strong kingship was as much the exception as the rule right from the late twelfth-century creation of the centralised royal state in England. If things were to change, if the violent cycles of the fifteenth century were to stop, the system itself must change; but it took two centuries to achieve that, and we would have to extend this micro-study way beyond the fifteenth century, perhaps to the Glorious Revolution of 1688 and the establishment of the Bank of England in 1694. And by then, the de la Poles were long dead and gone.

[24] For further discussion, see MacCulloch 1996.

Appendix
Historical Timeline for Wingfield College

Peter Bloore and Edward Martin

Lords of Wingfield manor before the foundation of the college

1113–25: Ernald fitz Roger alias Ruffus of Clopton, Hasketon, Akenham and Whittingham in Fressingfield in Suffolk was granted the manor Stradbroke with Wingfield by Stephen, count of Blois and lord of Eye, in fee-farm. He died in the 1160s.

1160s: Ernald (II) Ruffus. Dead by 1187.

By 1187: Ernald (III) Ruffus. Founded Woodbridge Priory c.1193. Died c.1209–12.

1209–12: Hugh (I) Ruffus. Sheriff of Norfolk and Suffolk 1225–7. Granted markets in his manors of Stradbroke and Woodbridge (for the benefit of the priory there) 1227.

1230: Hugh (II) Ruffus (le Rus). Died a minor.

1232: William le Rus. Dead by 1253.

1253: Alice le Rus. Born 1246/7, died 1300/1. Married firstly, Richard Lungespye (died 1261). She married secondly, by 1265, Sir Richard (I) de Brewse of Stinton Hall in Salle, Norfolk (*jure uxore*).

1296/7: Sir Richard (II) de Brewse, a younger son, given the manors of Stradbroke and Wingfield by his mother Alice. He married in 1296, Eleanor, widow of John de Verdon (d.1295) and daughter of Sir Thomas de Furnivall.

The Wingfield family and the foundation of Wingfield College

1270s: John de Wingfield acquired 69 acres of land in Wingfield formerly held by Frombald Flemyng. This would eventually become the site of Wingfield Castle.

1314: Death of John's son, Roger de Wingfield, a king's clerk who in 1312 had been entrusted with the custody of the town and castle of Orford in Suffolk.

1326: John de Wingfield, Roger's nephew, confirmed in the possession of the 69 acres acquired by his grandfather.

By 1330: Marriage of John de Wingfield to Eleanor, probably the daughter of Thomas de Verlay of Saxmundham and Sternfield in Suffolk, a royal servant.

1333: John de Wingfield took part in the siege of Berwick with King Edward III.

1336: John de Wingfield, as a servant of John de Warenne, earl of Surrey, applied his seal to a receipt (see plate xxx).

1340: Sir John de Wingfield recorded as a knight.

1346: Sir John de Wingfield was in the company of knights around King Edward III in the third division at the battle of Crécy on the 26 August; his brother, Sir Thomas, was in the second division with the earls of Northampton and Arundel.

1347: Sir John de Wingfield was part of the English army that captured Calais. In reward, King Edward III granted him the right to have a fair in Saxmundham (Suffolk) on the eve and day of St John the Baptist's Nativity (23–24 June) and he was exempted from service on assizes etc. 'for good service in the war on this side the seas and elsewhere'.

1356, 19 September: Sir John de Wingfield fought at the battle of Poitiers alongside Edward, the Black Prince. Sir John captured Louis, Sire D'Aubigny and Edward III later purchased this hostage from him for 2,500 marks (£1,666).

1357: Sir John acquired the manor of Wingfield from Sir Richard (II) de Brewse (see above). This manor house would eventually be the site of the college.

1358–59: Marriage of Katherine Wingfield, Sir John's daughter and heiress, to Sir Michael de la Pole, the son of Sir William de la Pole, a wealthy Hull wool merchant

1361: Sir John Wingfield died, possibly of the plague.

1362: 8 June: The foundation of Wingfield College. Sir Thomas Sket (Skeet or Skayt) was appointed its first master. He had been rector of Wingfield from 1329, but had transferred to Hasketon (Suffolk) in 1361. He was succeeded by Sir Peter Broun.

The college history

1362–c.1370: First main building phase at the college.

1361–75: Michael de la Pole fought in France, under the Black Prince and John of Gaunt.

1371: Sir Peter Broun resigned as master and was appointed rector of Stradbroke (Suffolk).

1372, 23 October: Stephen Coppelowe (Coplowe) appointed master by Dame Eleanor de Wingfield after the resignation of Peter Broun. He was buried in the south part of Wingfield Church in 1375.

1375: Death of Dame Eleanor de Wingfield, Sir John's widow. The formal patronage of the college now passed to Sir Michael de la Pole.

1375, 12 October: John Lef (Leef) appointed master.

1379, spring: Felling date for the north arcade plate timber of the hall in the college; the upper tie beam was felled in the early summer of 1383.

1383, January: The marriage of King Richard II and Anne of Bohemia, following negotiations in part by Sir Michael de la Pole. On 13 March 1383 Michael was appointed as lord chancellor of England.

1382–5: A larger hall added to the college, and presumably new eastern sides of the quadrangle.

1383, April: Sir Michael's eldest son, Sir Michael (II) de la Pole, married Katherine Stafford, daughter of Hugh, 2nd earl of Stafford and Philippa, daughter of Thomas Beauchamp, 11th earl of Warwick. The first de la Pole marriage into the higher aristocracy.

1385, 27 April: Michael de la Pole granted a royal licence to crenellate his Suffolk mansion houses at Wingfield, Sternfield and Huntingfield. Three months later, on 6 August, he was created earl of Suffolk, and King Richard II granted him most of the lands that had belonged to the previous earl, William de Ufford.

1386: Katherine de la Pole (née Wingfield) died.

1387, December: Michael de la Pole, an unpopular favourite of King Richard II, fled the country to escape trial for treason. His son Michael (II) de la Pole remained at Wingfield. The title of earl of Suffolk, together with the de la Pole family estates, was forfeited to the Crown.

1389: Michael (I) de la Pole died in Paris. Buried next to Katherine in the Charterhouse monastery in Hull.

1391: Michael (II) de la Pole set out in 1391 with Thomas of Woodstock, duke of Gloucester on an attempted crusade to Lithuania.

1396, 23 December: Robert de Bolton appointed master of the college.

1398: Michael de a Pole restored as earl of Suffolk and regained most of his father's estates. Briefly lost his earldom on the accession of King Henry IV, but was again restored in 1399.

1401: Michael de la Pole granted land and rent in Stradbroke, Wingfield, Syleham and Earsham Street to the master and chaplains of the college.

1406: Michael de la Pole grants the manor of Benhall to the college to maintain a priest to perform divine service at the altar of the Holy Trinity in Wingfield Church for the soul of his brother Richard.

1414: Michael's brother John de la Pole, a canon of York, died and was buried in Wingfield Church next to the altar of the Holy Trinity. John also left money to the college.

1415: A disastrous year for the de la Poles. Michael de la Pole, earl of Suffolk, died of dysentery at the siege of Harfleur. His body was shipped home to Wingfield. His eldest son Michael (III) de la Pole died at Agincourt only five weeks later. His brother, William de la Pole (1396–1450), succeeded him as the fourth earl.

1428, 18 June: John Burthan(m) appointed master of the college.

1429: William de la Pole, earl of Suffolk, was captured by the French at Jargeau, having been forced to lift the siege of Orleans by Joan of Arc. His brothers, Sir Alexander and Sir John, died there, but William was ransomed for £20,000, which damaged the family's finances.

1430: Licence was granted for Alice Chaucer to marry William de la Pole.

1433, 2 April: Master Henry Trevilian appointed master of the college.

1434: William de la Pole appointed joint constable, with his wife and infant son, of Wallingford Castle – a post formerly held by Alice's father, Sir Thomas Chaucer, who died that year.

1437: Alice Chaucer inherited Ewelme and other lands in Oxfordshire and a considerable fortune from her mother, Maud Chaucer, the heiress of the de Burghersh family of Ewelme.

1438: William de la Pole endowed the college with lands and rents in memory of his mother and his uncle Richard. He built the tomb to his parents in the church, and extended the chancel to accommodate it.

1442, 27 September: Alice de la Pole gave birth to her only certain child, John de la Pole.

1444: William de la Pole created marquess of Suffolk.

1445, March: William de la Pole stood proxy for King Henry VI in his marriage to Margaret of Anjou at Nancy Cathedral. Alice was also present. William and Mary escorted Margaret to England, where she married the king on 23 April, and was crowned at Westminster on 30 May. Alice was made a lady-in-waiting.

1447: William and Alice de la Pole became earl and countess of Pembroke on the death of Humphrey, duke of Gloucester.

1448: William de la Pole created duke of Suffolk.

1450, 2 May: William de la Pole murdered on the boat, the *Nicholas of the Tower*, belonging to the duke of Exeter, constable of the Tower of London. His son John was only eight, and was for many years under the tutelage of Alice. On 8 May Alice de la Pole secured the keeping of all the de la Pole lands, including Wingfield Castle.

1455: Alice de la Pole made custodian of the duke of Exeter at the castle at Wallingford. She was a joint constable of Wallingford until at least 1471 and possibly until her death.

1458: Marriage of Alice's son, John de la Pole, to Elizabeth Plantagenet, daughter of Richard, duke of York and a sister of the future King Edward IV.

1460s: Alice de la Pole's extension to the east end of the church and redevelopment of the vestry/chapel.

1463: John de la Pole was acknowledged as being of age and was confirmed as 2nd duke of Suffolk.

1466: Alice de la Pole moved her belongings from Wingfield to Ewelme. Her son John now used Wingfield as his main residence.

1467: John and Elizabeth's infant son, John, is created earl of Lincoln.

1471, 14 March: Appointment of Master William Baynard (Bagerd) as master of the college.

1472–5: Alice de la Pole became the custodian of Queen Margaret of Anjou, her former friend and patron, keeping her prisoner possibly sometimes at Wingfield Castle as well as Wallingford.

1472: John de la Pole was made a Knight of the Garter and was appointed high steward of Oxford University. He was also lieutenant of Ireland for a short time in 1478.

1475: Alice de la Pole died between 20 May and 9 June 1475 and was buried at Ewelme.

1475, July: King Edward IV invaded France, hoping to reclaim English possessions such as Gascony. He was accompanied by his brother-in-law John de la Pole, duke of Suffolk.

1484: John de la Pole, earl of Lincoln, was appointed as the king's lieutenant in Ireland by his uncle Richard III and appears to have been recognised as Richard's heir apparent.

1485: Richard III defeated by Henry Tudor at the battle of Bosworth. Although John de la Pole, earl of Lincoln, fought for his uncle, he escaped attainder and his father, Duke John, was in the procession, carrying the queen's sceptre, at Henry VII's coronation.

1487: Duchess Elizabeth's sister, Margaret of York, dowager duchess of Burgundy plotted against Henry VII. The earl of Lincoln travelled to his aunt in Flanders and joined the cause of the pretender Lambert Simnel – possibly using him as a stalking horse for his own regal ambitions. The earl crossed to England leading a Burgundian-financed army of German mercenaries, but was killed at the battle of Stoke near Newark on the 16 June 1487.

1492: Death of John de la Pole, 2nd duke of Suffolk. His son Edmund only succeeded briefly to the dukedom, but agreed in 1493 to being demoted to an earl.

1499: Suspected of treason, Edmund de la Pole and his brother Richard fled to France. Over the next few years they both schemed to raise armies to invade

England. Their brother William was arrested at Wingfield Castle and spent the rest of his life in the Tower of London (thirty-eight years).

1503: Death of the dowager duchess of Suffolk, Elizabeth Plantagenet, possibly still living in the castle at Wingfield. Buried with her husband in Wingfield Church.

1506: Edmund de la Pole captured in France by Henry VII's agents and taken to the Tower of London.

1509: Henry VIII appointed William Stafford as the keeper of the castle and park at Wingfield, followed shortly afterwards by John Sharpe.

1510: Henry VIII granted Wingfield and other manors to Sir Thomas Howard (later 3rd duke of Norfolk) and Anne his wife, the daughter of King Edward IV. Although Anne died soon afterwards, Howard retained a life interest in the properties until his death in 1554.

1513: Edmund de la Pole executed by Henry VIII as 'a turbulent man and too close to the throne'.

1514: Henry VIII had made his jousting partner and court favourite, Charles Brandon, his master of horse and marshal of his army in France in 1513, and in February 1514 he made him the duke of Suffolk. A year later, 'for the support of his title', Brandon was granted virtually all the lands formerly held by the previous dukes of Suffolk, the disgraced de la Poles – including the reversion of the manor of Wingfield and the patronage of the college.

1515: At the Abbey of Cluny Charles Brandon secretly married Mary Tudor, dowager queen of France and sister of Henry VIII. On their return to England, and after being pardoned and fined by the king, they were openly married at Greenwich Hall on 13 May 1515 with Henry VIII and Katherine of Aragon in attendance. The wealth of the new patrons may have resulted in the Tudor building work in the hall of Wingfield College.

1516: Brandon obtains 'an almost ruinous lease' of Wingfield Castle from Sir Thomas Howard.

1520: Visitation of the college by the bishop of Norwich; Master Thomas Dey was then the master.

1520s: Charles and Mary moved their Suffolk base to their newly built mansion at Westhorpe Hall.

1525: Richard de la Pole, who styled himself duke of Suffolk and nicknamed 'the White Rose', was killed at battle of Pavia in Italy, fighting for the French king

1531, 14 December: Following the death of Thomas Dey, Charles Brandon installed his own chaplain, Sir Robert Budde, as master of the college.

1532, 4 or 6 July: the last visitation of this college by Richard Nix, bishop of Norwich.

1533, 25 June: Mary Tudor died at Westhorpe Hall, Suffolk, and was buried at the abbey in Bury St Edmunds.

1534: Act of Parliament passed declaring the king supreme head of the Church of England. Sir Robert Budde, master of the college, and four of the fellows signed the acknowledgement of the royal supremacy on 17 October 1534.

1538/9: Death of Sir William de la Pole in the Tower of London, the last of the male line of the de la Poles.

1538: Charles Brandon forced by Henry VIII to exchange Wingfield Castle and other estates in Suffolk for lands in Lincolnshire.

1544: Sir Henry Jernegan (Jerningham) purchased Wingfield Castle from Henry VIII. A lawyer, he was marshal of the Inner Temple 1549–50. In 1553 he was among the first to join the Princess Mary at Kenninghall and it was he who raised Suffolk on her behalf. Vice-chamberlain of the household and captain of the guard to Queen Mary 1553–57; master of the horse 1557–8. In 1547 he obtained Costessey in Norfolk and went to live there (rebuilding the house there in 1564).

1542, 2 June: The college was voluntarily surrendered. The instrument of surrender was signed by Robert Budde, master, and by four fellows. The collegiate church was taken over by the parish.

1543: The college buildings were leased to Richard Freston of Mendham Priory (formerly the comptroller of Brandon's Suffolk estates and a friend of Master Budde) for twenty-one years. A religious conservative who was knighted by Queen Mary at her coronation in 1553 and was cofferer of the household to her 1553–7. He died in 1558.

1545: Chickering Chapel (owned by the college) granted to William Boldero and Robert Parker.

Post-dissolution occupants of the college building

1547: King Edward VI granted the college to the bishopric of Norwich in exchange for some other property. The bishops made various long leases of the property over the next several centuries, and from then on it was a purely secular dwelling house. The main families living in the house include:

1558: Richard Hopton esq., a relative of Dr John Hopton, bishop of Norwich.

1642–54: Robert Edgar esq. (c.1560–1654) from a family seated at Great Glemham Hall in Suffolk.

1654–1700s: John Cornwallis esq., married, as his second wife, Frances Edgar, a great-niece of Robert Edgar. He was sheriff of Suffolk in 1698, but died the same year. His fourth wife, Grace Bishop, continued to live in the house after his death.

1743 onwards: Atkinson family.

1747–60: Gooch family.

1760–c.1790: Samuel Jessup, formerly of Mendham. His wife Mary was buried in Wingfield Church in 1770.

1790–c.1798: John Rix Birch (1769–1811). Born at Redgrave, he was the grandson of Samuel Jessup. He added the Palladian front and many Georgian features to the college, turning it into an 'elegant modern built house'. A lieutenant in the Cambridgeshire Militia, living in Norwich, 1798. His stock and household effects at Wingfield sold in 1808. Died in the West Indies 1811.

1801: Butcher family. From the 1830s George Fenn Pretty is the tenant farmer.

1853–61: Thomas Collingwood Hughes and his wife Elizabeth (nee Butcher) own the freehold, but the tenant farmers are still the Pretty family.

1861–1927: The Gowing family (the Gowing occupancy started with a lease to Robert Gowing in 1861. In 1862 the freehold of the house and estate was sold at auction on behalf of the Butcher/Collingwood families to the Church Commissioners, but the Gowings retained the lease).

1927–73: The Edwards family (initially leaseholders, but in 1951 Frederick Edwards bought the freehold from the Church Commissioners).

1973–2004: The Chance family. Ian Chance restored the house and ran an arts charity from it called Wingfield Arts and Music.

2004: Peter Bloore and Jane Greenwood and family.

2012: The 650th anniversary of the founding of the college in 1362.

Bibliography

Printed Sources

Aitkens, P., 1997. 'Wingfield College, Suffolk: An Appraisal of the Medieval Site and Buildings 1362–1550', unpublished report, copies at Suffolk County Council Archaeological Service and Wingfield College

—— 1998. 'Wingfield College, Suffolk: A Survey of the Timber-Framed Medieval Structures', unpublished report, copies at English Heritage and Wingfield College

—— 2009. 'Wingfield College: North Elevation – A Reconstruction, December, 2009', unpublished report produced for UEA as part of the 2009–11 Wingfield Research Project

Aitkens, P., T. Easton and E. Martin, 1999. 'Wingfield', *Proceedings of the Suffolk Institute of Archaeology and History*, vol. XXXIX, part 3, pp. 392–7

Alcock, N.W., P.A. Faulkner and S.R. Jones, 1978. 'Maxstoke Castle, Warwickshire', *Archaeological Journal*, vol. CXXXIV, pp. 195–233

Aldwell, S.H.W., 1925. *Wingfield: Its Church, Castle and College* (Ipswich)

Anon. (probably F. Haslewood), 1891. 'Wingfield Church' [excursion report of a visit in 1888], *Proceedings of the Suffolk Institute of Archaeology*, vol. VII, pp. xxxiv–xxxvi

Archer, R.E., 2003. 'Jane with the Blemyssh: A Skeleton in the de la Pole Closet?' in Livia Visser-Fuchs, *Tant d'emprises – So Many Undertakings: Essays in Honour of Anne F. Sutton*, *The Ricardian*, vol. xiii (Bury St Edmunds)

Arthurson, I., 2009. *The Perkin Warbeck Conspiracy* (Stroud, Gloucester)

Badham, S., 2012. 'An Unusual Clerical Indent at Wingfield, Suffolk', *Monumental Brass Society Bulletin*, vol. 115 (October), pp. 418–19

Bailey, M., 2007. *Medieval Suffolk: An Economic and Social History 1200–1500* (Woodbridge)

Barber, R., 1978. *Edward, Prince of Wales and Aquitaine: A Biography of the Black Prince* (London)

—— (ed.), 1979. *The Life and Campaigns of the Black Prince* (London)

Barceló, J.A., M. Forte and D.H. Sanders (eds), 2000. *Virtual Reality in Archaeology*, BAR, International Series 843 (Oxford)

Barker, J., 2010. *Conquest: The English Kingdom of France in the Hundred Years War* (London)

Barron, W.R.J. (ed.), 1974. *Sir Gawain and the Green Knight* (Manchester)

Baskerville, G., 1933. 'Married Clergy and Pensioned Religious in Norwich Diocese, 1555', *English Historical Review*, vol. XLVIII, no. 43–64, pp. 199–228

Baxendall, M., 1999. 'The Perception of Riemenschneider', in J. Chapuis (ed.), *Tilman Riemenschneider: Master Sculptor of the Late Middle Ages* (New Haven and New York)

Bettley, J., forthcoming. *Buildings of England, Suffolk* (new edition of the Pevsner guide)

Binski, P., 1986. 'The Painted Chamber at Westminster', Occasional Paper, New Series IX, The Society of Antiquaries of London

Blackwood, G., 2001. *Tudor and Stuart Suffolk* (Lancaster)

Blair, J., 2001. 'Purbeck Marble', in J. Blair and N. Ramsay (eds), *English Medieval Industries: Craftsmen, Techniques, Products* (London), pp. 41–56

Blatchly, J., 1974. 'The Lost and Mutilated Monuments of the Bovile and Wingfield Families at Letheringham', *Proceedings of the Suffolk Institute of Archaeology and History*, vol. XXXIII, pp. 168–94

Blomefield, F., 1739–75. *An Essay Towards a Topographical History of Norfolk*, 5 vols (London)

—— 1806. *An Essay Towards a Topographical History of the County of Norfolk*, vol. III (London)

Bloore, P., 2014. 'The Screenplay Business: Managing Creativity in Script Development in the Contemporary British Independent Film Industry', unpublished PhD dissertation, University of East Anglia

Boden, M., 2004. *Creative Mind: Myths and Mechanisms*, 2nd edn (London)

Boldrick, S., D. Park and D. Williamson, 2002. *Wonder: Painted Sculpture from Medieval England* (exhibition catalogue) (Leeds)

Booth, P.H.W., 1971. 'Taxation and Public Order: Cheshire in 1353', *Northern History*, vol. 12

—— 1981. *The Financial Administration of the Lordship and County of Cheshire, 1272–1377*, Chetham Society, third series, vol. 18

Bourdieu, P., 1977. *Outline of a Theory of Practice* (Cambridge)

—— 1984. *Distinction: A Social Critique of the Judgment of Taste* (Oxford)

—— 1993. *The Field of Cultural Production* (Columbia)

—— 1996. *The Rules of Art* (Stanford)

Bray, A.E., 1851. *Life of Thomas Stothard, R.A., with Personal Reminiscence* (London)

Bridge, M.C., 1999a. 'Ancient Monuments Laboratory Report 7/99 Tree-Ring Analysis of Timbers from Wingfield College, Wingfield, Suffolk', Historic Buildings and Monuments Commission and English Heritage (London)

—— 1999b. 'Tree-Ring Analysis of the Timbers from Wingfield Great Barn, Wingfield, Suffolk', Ancient Monuments Laboratory Report

Brown, V. (ed.), 1992. *Eye Priory Cartulary and Charters, Part One*, Suffolk Records Society Charters Series XII (Woodbridge)

—— (ed.), 1994. *Eye Priory Cartulary and Charters, Part Two*, Suffolk Records Society Charters Series XIII (Woodbridge)

Burgess, C., 2005. 'St George's College, Windsor: Context and Consequence', in N. Saul (ed.), *St George's Chapel Windsor* (Woodbridge)

Burgess, C. and M. Heale, 2008. *The Late Medieval English College and its Context* (York).

Cammidge, J., 1943. *The Black Prince: An Historical Pageant* (London)

Castor, H., 2000. *The King, the Crown, and the Duchy of Lancaster: Public Authority and Private Power, 1399–1461* (Oxford)

Cautley, H.M., 1954. *Suffolk Churches and their Treasures* (Ipswich)

Chambers, D.S. (ed.), 1966. *Faculty Office Registers 1534–1549* (Oxford)

Chance, I., 1985. *Guide to Wingfield College, Suffolk AD 1362* (Wingfield)

Chrimes, S.B., 1972. *Henry VII* (London)

Cleland, E., 2007. 'An *exemplum justitae* and the Price of Treason: How the Legend of Herkinbald Reached Henry VIII's Tapestry Collection', in R. Marks (ed.) *Late Gothic England: Art and Display* (Donnington)

Cobban, A., 1988. *Medieval English Universities* (Berkeley)

Cockerham, P., 2010. 'Lineage, Liturgy and Locus: The Changing Role of English Funeral Monuments', in S. Badham (ed.), *One Thousand Years of English Church Monuments, Ecclesiology Today*, vol. 43, pp. 7–28

Cokayne, G.E.C. (V. Gibbs, ed.) 1912. *The Complete Peerage*, vol. II (London)

—— (V. Gibbs, H.A. Doubleday and Lord Howard de Walden, eds) 1929. *The Complete Peerage*, vol. VII (London)

—— (G.H. White, ed.) 1953. *The Complete Peerage*, vol. XII pt I (London)

—— (G.H. White and R.S. Lea, eds) 1959. *The Complete Peerage*, vol. XII pt ii (London)

Cook, G.H., 1959. *English Collegiate Churches* (London)

—— 1963. *Mediaeval Chantries and Chantry Chapels* (London)

Cook, J., 1882. *The History of God's House, Hull, commonly called the Charterhouse* (Hull)

Copinger, W., 1904. *Suffolk Records*, 5 vols (London)

Copinger, W.A., 1905–11. *The Manors of Suffolk*, 7 vols (Manchester)

Corder, J., 1965. *A Dictionary of Suffolk Arms*, Suffolk Record Society, vol. VII (Ipswich)

—— (ed.) 1984. *The Visitation of Suffolk 1561*, pt II, Harleian Society New Series vol. III (London)

—— 1998. *A Dictionary of Suffolk Crests: Heraldic Crests of Suffolk Families*, Suffolk Record Society, vol. XL (Woodbridge)

Coss, P.R., 1989. 'Bastard Feudalism Revised', *Past and Present*, vol. CXXV, pp. 27–64

—— 2003. *The Origins of the English Gentry* (Cambridge)

Coulson, C., 2000. 'Fourteenth-Century Castles in Context: Apotheosis or Decline?' *Fourteenth-Century England*, vol. I, pp. 133–51

Creighton, O., 2002. *Castles and Landscapes: Power, Community and Fortification in Medieval* (Sheffield).

Creighton, O.H., 2009. *Designs Upon the Land: Elite Landscapes of the Middle Ages* (Woodbridge)

Cromwell, T.K., 1819. *Excursions in the County of Suffolk* (London)

Cunliffe, B., 1981. 'Foreword', in M. Sorrell (ed.), *Alan Sorrell: Reconstructing the Past* (London)

Curran, S., 2011. *The English Friend: A Life of William de la Pole First Duke of Suffolk* (Norwich)

Dallas, C. and D. Sherlock, 2002. 'Baconsthorpe Castle, Excavation and Finds, 1951–1972', East Anglian Archaeology Reports, no. 102 (Dereham)

Davis, N. (ed.), 1971, 1976. *Paston Letters and Papers of the Fifteenth Century*, 2 vols (Oxford)

Davy, D.E. (J. Blatchly, ed.) 1982. *A Journal of Excursions through the County of Suffolk 1823–1844*, Suffolk Records Society, vol. XXIV (Woodbridge)

De la Bédoyère, G., 1991. *The Buildings of Roman Britain* (London)

Deacon, R. and P. Lindley, 2001. *Image and Idol: Medieval Sculpture* (London)

Delumeau, J., 1990. *Sin and Fear: The Emergence of a Western Guilt Culture, 13th–18th Centuries* (London)

Department of the Environment, 1990. *This Common Inheritance: Britain's Environmental Strategy* (London)

Dewing, E.M., 1889. 'Pedigree of Wingfield of Wingfield, Letheringham, Easton', *Proceedings of the Suffolk Institute of Archaeology and History*, vol. VII

Duffy, E., 1992. *The Stripping of the Altars: Traditional Religion in England 1440–1580* (New Haven and London)

Dupont, Mlle (ed.), 1837. *Mémoires de Pierre Fenin* (Paris)

Dyer, C., 1989. *Standards of Living in the Later Middle Ages: Social Change in England c.1200–1520* (Cambridge)

Dymond, D., 1998. 'Five Building Contracts from Fifteenth-Century Suffolk', *The Antiquaries Journal*, vol. 78

Dymond, D. and E. Martin (eds), 1999. *An Historical Atlas of Suffolk* (3rd edn, Ipswich)

Earl, G. and D.W. Wheatley, 2002. 'Virtual Reconstruction and the Interpretative Process: A Case-Study from Avebury', in D.W. Wheatley, G. Earl and S. Poppy (eds), *Contemporary Themes in Archaeological Computing* (Oxford), pp. 5–15

East of England Regional Assembly, 2004. *East of England Plan: Draft Revision of the Regional Spatial Strategy for the East of England* (Bury St Edmunds)

Emery, A., 2000. *Greater Medieval Houses of England and Wales Vol II: East Anglia, Central England and Wales* (Cambridge)

Emmerson, R., 1978. 'Monumental Brasses – London Design c.1420–85', *Journal of the British Archaeological Association*, vol. CXXXI, pp. 50–78

Farrer, W., 1923. *Honors and Knights' Fees*, vol. I (Manchester)

—— 1925. *Honors and Knights' Fees*, vol. III (Manchester)

Faulkner, P.A., 1963. 'A Model of Castle Acre Priory', *Medieval Archaeology*, vol. VII, pp. 300–3

Flenley, R. (ed.), 1931. *Six Town Chronicles of England* (London)

Fletcher, A. and D. MacCulloch, 2008. *Tudor Rebellions*, 5th revised edn (Harlow)

Forte, M. and A. Siliotti, 1997. *Virtual Archaeology: Great Discoveries brought to Life through Virtual Reality* (London)

Fox, C., 1932. *The Personality of Britain* (Cardiff)

Freeman Bullen, R., 1936. 'Catalogue of Beneficed Clergy of Suffolk, 1551–1631(with a few of earlier date)', *Proceedings of the Suffolk Institute of Archaeology*, vol. XXII, pp. 294–333

Fripp, S.S., 1896. *Memoirs of the De La Poles, Dukes of Suffolk*, BL Add. MS 348960

Fryde, E.B., 1988. *William de la Pole: Merchant and King's Banker* (London)

Fryer, A.C., 1924. *Wooden Monumental Effigies in England and Wales* (London)

Gairdner, J., 1898. *History of the Life and Reign of Richard the Third* (Cambridge)

—— (ed.) 1904. *The Paston Letters and Papers, 1422–1509*, 6 vols (London)

Gallagher, E.J., 2009. *The Civil Pleas of the Suffolk Eyre of 1240*, Suffolk Record Society, vol. 52 (Woodbridge)

Gardener, A., 1940. *Alabaster Tombs of the Pre-Reformation Period in England* (Cambridge)

Gilchrist, R. and M. Olivia, 1993. *Religious Women in Medieval East Anglia: History and Archaeology c.1100–1540: Studies in East Anglian History Vol 1, Centre for East Anglian Studies* (Norwich)

Gillings, M., 2002. 'Virtual Archaeologies and the Hyper-Real: Or, What Does it Mean to Describe Something as *Virtually*-Real', in P. Fisher and D. Unwin (eds), *Virtual Reality in Geography* (London), pp. 17–34

—— 2005. 'The Real, the Virtually Real, and the Hyperreal: The Role of VR in Archaeology', in S. Smiles and S. Moser (eds), *Envisioning the Past* (Oxford), pp. 223–39

Gonner, E.C.K., 1912. *Common Land and Inclosure* (London)

Goodall, J.A., 2001. *God's House at Ewelme: Life, Devotion and Architecture in a Fifteenth-Century Almshouse* (Aldershot)

Goodall, J.A.A., 2003. 'The Architecture of Ancestry at the Collegiate Church of St Andrew, Wingfield, Suffolk', in R. Eeles and S. Tyas (eds), *Family and Dynasty in Late Medieval England*, Harlaxton Medieval Studies, vol. XI (Donington), pp. 156–72

—— 2011. *The English Castle* (New Haven and London)

Goodrick, G. and M. Gillings, 2000. 'Constructs, Simulations and Hyperreal Worlds: The Role of Virtual Reality (VR) in Archaeological Research', in G. Lock and K. Brown (eds), *On the Theory and Practice of Archaeological Computing* (Oxford), pp. 41–58

Gough, R., 1786–96. *Sepulchral Monuments in Great Britain*, 2 vols. in 5 or 8 (London)

Graham, C., 2009. 'Geophysical Survey Report, Wingfield, Suffolk', Geoscan (Upton upon Severn)

Gray, A., 1996. 'Syleham – A History to 1605', unpublished MA dissertation; copy available at Wingfield College.

Gray, H.L., 1915. *English Field Systems* (Cambridge, Mass.)

Green, D., 2001. *The Black Prince* (Stroud)

—— 2004. 'Edward the Black Prince and East Anglia: An Unlikely Association', in W.M. Ormrod (ed.), *Fourteenth-Century England, III* (Woodbridge)

—— 2007. *Edward the Black Prince: Power in Medieval Europe* (Harlow)

Greenwood, R. and M. Norris, 1976. *The Brasses of Norfolk Churches* (Norwich)

Grenfell, M., 2008. *Pierre Bourdieu* (Durham)

Gristwood, S., 2013. *Blood Sisters: The Women behind the Wars of the Roses* (London)

Gunn, S.J., 1988. *Charles Brandon, Duke of Suffolk, c.1484–1545* (Oxford)

Harper-Bill, C., 1996. 'English Religion after the Black Death', in W.M. Ormrod and P. Lindley (eds), *The Black Death in England* (Stamford)

Harrison, W., 1587. *Description of England* (Edelen ed. 1994)

Harriss, G.L. and M.A. Harriss (eds), 1972. 'John Benet's Chronicle for the Years 1400–1462', *Camden Miscellany*, vol. xxiv, Camden Society, 4th series, ix (London)

Hart, C.R., 1966. *Early Charters of Eastern England* (Leicester)

Hartley, L.P., 1953. *The Go-Between* (London)

Harvey, A.S., 1961. 'Notes on Two Heraldic Tombs', *Yorkshire Archaeological Journal*, vol. LX part 3, pp. 462–77

Harwood, W., 2008. 'The College as School: The Case of Winchester College', in Burgess and Heale (*idem*)

Haslam, R., 1982. 'Wingfield College, Suffolk', *Country Life* (7 January), 4pp.

Hatcher, J., 1970. *Rural Economy and Society in the Duchy of Cornwall 1300–1500* (Cambridge)

Haward, B., 1993. *Suffolk Medieval Church Arcades* (Ipswich)

Hayward, M., 2007. *Dress at the Court of Henry VIII* (Leeds)

Hervey, F. (ed.), 1925. *The Pinchbeck Register*, 2 vols (Brighton)

Hervey, S.H.A., 1906. *Suffolk in 1327*, Suffolk Green Books IX, vol. II (Woodbridge)

Hicks, M.A., 1991. 'The Neville Earldom of Salisbury, 1429–71', in M. Hicks, *Richard III and his Rivals* (London)

Higgins, T., P. Main and L. Lang (eds), 1996. 'Imaging the Past: Electronic Imaging and Computer Graphics in Museums and Archaeology', *British Museum Occasional Paper*, no.114 (London)

Hoppitt, R., 1989. 'A Relative Relief Map of Suffolk', *Transactions of the Suffolk Naturalist's Society*, vol. 25, pp. 80–5

Horrox, R., 1983. *The de la Poles of Hull*, East Yorkshire Local History Society (Beverley)

—— (ed.), 1994. *The Black Death* (Manchester)

Hudson, W. and J.C. Tingey (eds), 1906. *The Records of the City of Norwich*, 2 vols (Norwich)

Hutton, L.P.S., 1908. 'Schools in Suffolk', in V. Redstone, *Memorials of Old Suffolk* (London)

Jacob, E.F. (ed.), 1938. *The Register of Henry Chichele, Archbishop of Canterbury 1414–1443* (Oxford)

Jacob, E.F. and H.C. Johnson, (eds), 1937. *The Register of Henry Chichele, Archbishop of Canterbury, 1414–1443*, 2 vols, Canterbury and York Society (London)

Jenkins, S., 1999. *England's Thousand Best Churches* (London)

—— 2003. *England's Thousand Best Houses* (London)

Jessopp, A. (ed.), 1888. *Visitations of the Diocese of Norwich AD 1492–1532*, Camden Society New Series, vol. XLIII (London)

Jones, B. (ed.), 1963. *John le Neve Fasti Ecclesiae Anglicanae 1300–1541, VI Northern Province* (London)

Jones, M.K. and M.G. Underwood (eds), 1992. *The King's Mother: Lady Margaret Beaufort, Countess of Richmond and Derby* (Cambridge)

Keen, M.H., 2003. *England in the Later Middle Ages*, 2nd edn (London)

Kennett, D., 1973. 'The Bricks of Wingfield College', *Proceedings of the Suffolk Institute of Archaeology and History*, vol. XXXIII, pt 1, pp. 86–8

Kent, J.P.C., 1949. 'Monumental Brasses – A New Classification of Military Effigies c.1360–1485', *Journal of the British Archaeological Association*, 3rd series XII, pp. 70–97

Knowles, D. and R.N. Haddock, 1953. *Medieval Religious Houses* (London)

Lack, W., H.M. Stuchfield and P. Whittemore, 2003. *The Monumental Brasses of Essex*, 2 vols (London)

—— 2012. *The Monumental Brasses of Huntingdonshire* (London)

Leslie, C.R., 1845. *Memoirs of the Life of John Constable, Esq. R.A.* (London, reprinted Chicheley)

Liddiard, R., 2005. *Castles in Context: Power, Symbolism and Landscape, 1066 to 1500* (Oxford)

—— 2008. 'Living on the Edge: Commons, Castles and Regional Settlement Patterns in Medieval East Anglia', *Proceedings of the Cambridge Antiquarian Society*, vol. XLVII, pp. 169–78

Lock, G., 2003. *Using Computers in Archaeology: Towards Virtual Pasts* (London)

London Gazette, issue 16004, 24 February 1807

MacCulloch, D. (ed.), 1976. *The Chorography of Suffolk*, Suffolk Record Society, vol. XIX (Woodbridge)

—— 1986. *Suffolk and the Tudors: Politics and Religion in an English County, 1500–1600* (Oxford)

—— 1996. 'The Consolidation of England, 1485–1603', in J. Morrill (ed.), *The Oxford Illustrated History of Tudor and Stuart Britain* (Oxford), pp. 35–52

—— (ed.), 2007. *Letters from Redgrave Hall: The Bacon Family 1340–1744*, Suffolk Records Society, vol. L (Woodbridge)

Maitland, F.W., 1897. *Domesday Book and Beyond* (Cambridge)

Marks, R., 2004. *Image and Devotion in Late Medieval England* (Stroud)

Martin, E., 1990. 'Mettingham Castle: An Interpretation of a Survey of 1562', *Proceedings of the Suffolk Institute of Archaeology and History*, vol. XXXVII, pt 2, pp. 115–23

—— 1999. 'Place-Name Patterns', in D. Dymond and E. Martin (eds), *An Historical Atlas of Suffolk* (Ipswich), pp. 50–1

—— 2008. 'Not So Common Fields: The Making of the East Anglian Landscape', in A.M. Chadwick (ed.), *Recent Approaches to the Archaeology of Land Allotment*, British Archaeological Reports International Series, no. S1875 (Oxford), pp. 342–71

—— 2012. 'Norfolk, Suffolk and Essex: Medieval Rural Settlement in "Greater East Anglia"', in N. Christie and P. Stamper (eds), *Medieval Rural Settlement: Britain and Ireland, AD 800–1600* (Oxford), pp. 225–48

—— 2013. 'Heraldic Notes (and Some Signed Flushwork) around Eye Church', *Proceedings of the Suffolk Institute of Archaeology and History*, vol. 43, pt 1, pp. 132–7

Martin, E. and Satchell, M., 2008. *Wheare most Inclosures be. East Anglian Fields: History, Morphology and Management*, East Anglian Archaeology, no. 124 (Ipswich)

McFarlane, K.B., 1945. 'Henry V, Bishop Beaufort and the Red Hat, 1417–1421', *English Historical Review*, vol. lx

Meiss, M., 1951. *Painting in Florence and Siena after the Black Death* (Princeton)

Monumental Brass Society, 1988. *Monumental Brasses: The Portfolio Plates of the Monumental Brass Society 1894–1984* (London)

Moor, C., 1929. *Knights of Edward I*, vol. I, Harleian Society, vol. LXXX (London)

Morgan, D.A.L., 1973. 'The King's Affinity in the Polity of Yorkist England', *Transactions of the Royal Historical Society*, 5th series, vol. xxiii

Morning Chronicle, 23 March 1807

Mortimer, R., 1981. 'The Family of Rannulf de Glanville', *Bulletin of the Institute of Historical Research*, vol. LIV, no. 129 (May), pp. 1–16

Munby, J., 2005. 'Carpentry Works at Windsor Castle', in N. Saul (ed.), *St George's Chapel Windsor* (Woodbridge)

Munday, J.T., 1973. *A Feudal Roll for Suffolk 1302–3* (Lakenheath)

Munro, J., 2012. 'The Late Medieval Decline of English Demesne Agriculture: Demographic, Monetary, and Political–Fiscal Factors', in M. Bailey and S.H. Rigby (eds), *Town and Countryside in the Age of the Black Death: Essays in Honour of John Hatcher* (Turnhout)

Napier, H.A., 1858. *Historical Notices of the Parishes of Swyncombe and Ewelme in the County of Oxford* (Oxford)

Nicholas, N.H., 1826. *Testmenta Vetusta being Illustrations from Wills of Manners, Customs, etc as well as of the Descents and Possessions of many Distinguished Families from the Reign of Henry the Second to the Accession of Queen Elizabeth*, 2 vols (London)

Nichols, J.G., 1838. *Description of the Church of St Mary, Warwick and of the Beauchamp Chapel* (London)

Northeast, P. (ed.), 2001. *Wills of the Archdeaconry of Sudbury, 1439–1474: Part I*, Suffolk Records Society, vol. XLIV (Woodbridge)

Northeast, P. and H. Falvey (eds), 2010. *Wills of the Archdeaconry of Sudbury, 1439–1474: Part II*, Suffolk Records Society, vol. LIII (Woodbridge)

O'Sullivan, D., 2006. 'The "Little Dissolution" of the 1520s', *Post-Medieval Archaeology*, vol. 40/2, pp. 227–58

Orme, N., 2006. *Medieval Schools: From Roman Britain to Renaissance England* (New Haven and London)

Ormrod, W.M., 1990. *The Reign of Edward III: Crown and Political Society in England 1327–1377* (New Haven)

Page, A., 1844. *A Supplement to the Suffolk Traveller* (Ipswich and London)

Page, W. (ed.), 1907. *Victoria County History of Suffolk*, vol. II (London)

Peet, D.J., 1980. 'The Mid-Sixteenth-Century Parish Clergy, with Particular Consideration of the Dioceses of Norwich and York', Cambridge University PhD dissertation

Penn, T., 2011. *Winter King: The Dawn of Tudor England* (London)

Platt, C., 2007. 'Revisionism in Castle Studies: A Caution', *Medieval Archaeology*, vol. LI, pp. 83–102

Pollard, A.F., 1988. *The Wars of the Roses* (Houndmills)

Pounds, N.J.G., 1990. *The Medieval Castle in England and Wales: A Social and Political History* (Cambridge)

Powerscourt, Viscount, 1894. *Muniments of the Ancient Saxon Family of Wingfield* (privately printed)

Pronay, N. and J. Cox (eds), 1986. *The Crowland Chronicle Continuations: 1459–1486* (London)

Quiney, A., 2003. *Town Houses of Medieval Britain* (New Haven and London)

Rackham, O., 1980. *Ancient Woodland: Its History, Vegetation and Uses in England* (London)

—— 1986. *The History of the Countryside* (London)

Raine, J., 1836. *Testamenta Eboracensia* I. Surtees Society 4 (London)

Ramsay, N., 2001. 'Alabaster', in J. Blair and N. Ramsay (eds), *English Medieval Industries: Craftsmen, Techniques, Products* (London), pp. 29–40

Raven, J.J., 1895. 'Remarks on the History of Education in East Anglia', *Proceedings of the Suffolk Institute of Archaeology and Natural History*, vol. 9 (1895/7)

Read, E., 1963. *My Lady Suffolk* (New York)

Record Commission, 1783. *Rotuli Parliamentorum; ut et Petitiones, et Placita in Parliamento*, vol. II

Reilly, P., 1990. 'Towards a Virtual Archaeology', in K. Lockyear and S. Rahtz (eds), *Computer Applications and Quantitative Methods in Archaeology*, BAR, Supplementary Series 565 (Oxford), pp. 133–40

Reyce, R., 1902. *Suffolk in the XVIIth Century: The Breviary of Suffolk* (London)

Richmond, C., 1990. *The Paston Family in the Fifteenth Century: The First Phase* (Cambridge)

—— 1996. *The Paston Family in the Fifteenth Century: Fastolf's Will* (Cambridge)

—— 2000. *The Paston Family in the Fifteenth Century: Endings* (Manchester)

Ridgard, J., 1989. 'The Uprising of 1381', in D. Dymond and E. Martin (eds), *An Historical Atlas of Suffolk*, 3rd edn (Ipswich)

—— 2009. 'Mettingham, Suffolk: The Building of a Religious College with Particular Reference to the Acquisition of Books for its Library', *Proceedings of the Institute of Archaeology and History*, vol. XLII, pt 1, pp. 21–31

Rippon, S., 1996. 'Essex c.700–1066', in O. Bedwin (ed.), *The Archaeology of Essex: Proceedings of the Writtle Conference* (Chelmsford)

Roberts, B.K. and S. Wrathmell, 2000. *An Atlas of Rural Settlement in England* (London)

—— 2002. *Region and Place: A Study of English Rural Settlement* (London)

Roberts, E., 1974. 'Totternhoe Stone and Flint in Hertfordshire Churches', *Medieval Archaeology*, vol. XVIII, pp. 66–89

—— 1996. 'Edward III's Lodge at Odiham, Hampshire', *Medieval Archaeology*, vol. XXXIX, pp. 91–106

Roffey, S., 2007. *Medieval Chantry Chapels* (Woodbridge)

Roscoe, I., E. Hardy and M.G. Sullivan, 2009. *A Biographical Dictionary of Sculptors in Britain, 1660–1851* (London)

Roskell, J.S., 1984. *The Impeachment of Michael de la Pole Earl of Suffolk in 1386 in the Context of the Reign of Richard II* (Manchester)

Roskell, J.S, L. Clark and C. Rawcliffe (eds), 1992. *The History of Parliament: The House of Commons, 1386–1421*, 4 vols (Stroud)

Ross, C.D., 1974. *Edward IV* (London)

—— 1981. *Richard III* (London)

Ross, W.O. (ed.), 1940. *Middle English Sermons*, Early English Text Society, Original Series, vol. CCIX (London)

Rumble, A. (ed.), 1986. *Domesday Book: Suffolk* (Chichester)

Ruud, M., 1926. *Thomas Chaucer*, Research Publications of the University of Minnesota, Studies in Language and Literature, vol. ix (Minneapolis)

Rye, W., 1900. *Calendar of the Feet of Fines for Suffolk* (Ipswich)

—— 1901. *The Visitation of Norfolk 1563, 1589 and 1613*, Harleian Society, vol. XXXII (London)

Salt, W. (ed.), 1897. *Wrottesley, Crecy and Calais* (London)

Saul, N., 2003. *Death, Art and Memory in Medieval England: The Cobham Family and their Monuments* (Oxford)

—— 2005. 'Servants of God and the Crown: The Canons of St George's Chapel, 1348–1420', in N. Saul (ed.), *St George's Chapel Windsor* (Woodbridge)

—— 2006. 'The Contract for the Brass of Richard Willughby (d.1471) at Wollaton (Notts.)', *Nottingham Medieval Studies*, vol. L, pp. 166–93

Scarfe, N., 1986. *Suffolk in the Middle Ages* (Woodbridge)

Scott, M., 1986. *A Visual History of Costume: The Fourteenth and Fifteenth Centuries* (London)

Shaw, W.A., 1906. *The Knights of England*, vol. I (London)

Skinner, D., 2008. 'Music and reformation in the Collegiate Church of St Mary and All Saints, Fotheringay', in C. Burgess and M. Heale (eds), *The Late Medieval English College and its Context* (York)

Slater, G., 1907. *The English Peasantry and the Enclosure of Common Fields* (London)

Smith, A., 1984. 'Litigation and Politics: Sir John Fastolf's Defence of his English Property', in T. Pollard (ed.), *Property and Politics: Essays in Later Medieval English History* (Gloucester)

Soil Survey of England and Wales, 1983. *1:250,000 Soil Map of England and Wales* (Harpenden)

Sorrell, A., 1972. 'The Artist and Reconstruction', *Current Archaeology*, no. 41, vol. IV, no. 6; reprinted in M. Sorrell (ed.), 1981. *Alan Sorrell: Reconstructing the Past* (London)

Sorrell, M. (ed.), 1981. *Alan Sorrell, Reconstructing the Past* (London)

Stanley, A.P., 1868. *Historical Memorials of Westminster Abbey* (London)

Stevenson, J. (ed.), 1861–4. *Letters and Papers Illustrative of the Wars of the English in France during the Reign of Henry VI*, 2 vols in 3, Rolls Series (London)

Stothard, C.A., 1832. *The Monumental Effigies of Great Britain: Selected from our Cathedrals and Churches for the Purpose of Bringing Together and Preserving Correct Representations of the Best Historical Illustrations Extant, from the Norman Conquest to the Reign of Henry the Eighth* (London)

Taylor, J., W. Childs and L. Watkiss (eds), 2003. *The St Albans Chronicle, The Chronica maiora of Thomas Walsingham I 1376–1394* (Oxford)

Tout, T.F., 1920. *Chapters in the Administrative History of Medieval England*, vol. II (Manchester)

—— 1930. *Chapters in the Administrative History of Medieval England*, vol. V (Manchester)

—— 1933. *Chapters in the Administrative History of Medieval England*, vol. VI (Manchester)

Tracy, C., 2007. 'Master William Pykenham, Scholar, Churchman, Lawyer, and Gatehouse Builder', *Proceedings of the Suffolk Institute of Archaeology and History*, vol. XLI, pt 3, pp. 289–322

VCH Chester, vol. 2 (London, 1979)

VCH Hampshire, vol. 4 (London, 1973)

VCH Suffolk, vol. 2 (London, 1907)

VCH Yorkshire, 1969. *East Riding I* (London)

VCH Yorkshire, 1972. *East Riding 2* (London)

Vinogradoff, P., 1892. *Villainage in England* (Oxford)

Virgoe, R., 1997. *East Anglian Society and the Political Community of Late Medieval England* (Norwich)

Wagner, J., 2001. *Encyclopedia of the Wars of the Roses* (Santa Barbara)

Walker, S., 2012. 'Pole, Michael de la, Second Earl of Suffolk (1367/8–1415)', *Oxford Dictionary of National Biography*, online edn, (www.oxforddnb.com/view/article/22453)

Warner, M., 1998. 'Chivalry in Action: Thomas Montagu and the War in France, 1417–28', *Nottingham Medieval Studies*, vol. xlii

Watts, J., 1996. *Henry VI and the Politics of Kingship* (Cambridge)

—— 2004. 'Pole, William de la, First Duke of Suffolk (1396–1450)', *Oxford Dictionary of National Biography*, online edn 2012 (www.oxforddnb.com/view/article/22461)

Weikel, A., 2004. 'Jerningham, Sir Henry (1509/10–1572)', *Dictionary of National Biography* (Oxford)

White, W., 1844. *History, Gazetteer, and Directory, of Suffolk* (Sheffield)

Whitelock, D., 1930. *Anglo-Saxon Wills* (Cambridge)

Willis, R. and J.W. Clark, 1886. *Architectural History of the University of Cambridge* (Cambridge)

Willoughby, J., 2012. 'Inhabited Sacristies in Medieval England: The Case of St Mary's, Warwick', *Antiquaries Journal*, vol. 92, pp. 331–45

Wilson, C., 2002. 'The Royal Lodgings of Edward III at Windsor Castle: Form, Function, Representation', in L. Keen and E. Scarff (eds), *Windsor. Medieval Archaeology, Art and Architecture of the Thames Valley*, The British Archaeological Association Transactions, vol. XXV (Leeds), pp. 15–94

—— 2003. 'The Functional Design of Henry VII's Chapel: A Reconstruction', in T. Tatton Brown and R. Mortimer (eds), *Westminster Abbey: The Lady Chapel of Henry VII* (Woodbridge), pp. 167–73

Wingfield, J.M., 1925. *Some Records of the Wingfield Family* (London)

Wood, M., 1965. *The English Mediaeval House* (London)

Wroe, A., 2003. *Perkin: A Story of Deception* (London)

Wrottesley, G., 1897. 'Crecy and Calais, AD 1346–47, from the Rolls in the Public Record Office and a MS in the College of Arms', *Collections for a History of Staffordshire*, W. Salt Archaeological Society, vol. XVIII, pt 2 (London)

Index